Computer Programs for
Elementary Decision Analysis

STUDIES IN MANAGERIAL ECONOMICS

Graduate School of Business Administration
Harvard University

Applied Statistical Decision Theory, by Howard Raiffa and Robert Schlaifer (1961)

Tables for Normal Sampling with Unknown Variance: The Student Distribution and Economically Optimal Sampling Plans, by Jerome Bracken and Arthur Schleifer, Jr. (1964)

Strategic Aspects of Competitive Bidding for Corporate Securities, by Charles Christenson (1965)

Computer Programs for Elementary Decision Analysis, by Robert Schlaifer (1971)

COMPUTER PROGRAMS
FOR
ELEMENTARY DECISION ANALYSIS

ROBERT SCHLAIFER

William Ziegler Professor of Business Administration
Harvard University

DIVISION OF RESEARCH
GRADUATE SCHOOL OF BUSINESS ADMINISTRATION
HARVARD UNIVERSITY

Boston 1971

Second Printing
1973

Faculty research at the Harvard Business School is under-
taken with the expectation of publication. In such publication the Faculty member responsible for the research
project is also responsible for statements of fact, opinions,
and conclusions expressed. Neither the Harvard Business
School, its Faculty as a whole, nor the President and
Fellows of Harvard College reach conclusions or make
recommendations as results of Faculty research.

Printed in the United States of America

PREFACE

The Manecon collection of computer programs described and documented in this book was written to facilitate the analysis of problems of decision under uncertainty. The collection is sufficient for analysis of problems of the order of complexity of those presented in the author's *Analysis of Decisions under Uncertainty* (McGraw-Hill, 1969), and the accompanying *Manual of Cases* (also published by McGraw-Hill, 1969). It may also prove useful as the start of a collection aimed at analysis of much more complex problems of the same general type.

Capabilities of the Programs

The most characteristic part of this collection consists of a number of self-contained programs for interactive assessment of judgmental probability distributions and preference (utility) functions. After the user has decided on a few numerical specifications for his distribution (e.g., its quartiles), he can fit a distribution of any of a number of different families to these specifications. He can then immediately test the degree to which the fitted distribution agrees with his judgments overall by computing selected probabilities or fractiles and/or examining graphs of the density or cumulative function of the distribution. If the agreement is good, his assessment problem is solved; if it is not, he can choose another family and/or modify his original specifications, fit a new distribution, examine its implications; and so forth until he has found a distribution whose implications he is willing to accept as a guide to practical action.

The programs for assessment of preference functions work in much the same way. After the user has numerically assessed a few points on his preference curve, he can fit them with a function having general implications of the sort he desires (e.g., risk aversion decreasing as assets increase). He can then immediately test the suitability of the fitted function by computing the certainty equivalents it implies for a variety of gambles. If he is satisfied with these implications, well and good; if not, he can modify his original assessments and repeat the process until he has found a function which he is willing to accept as a valid expression of his general attitudes toward consequences and risk.

Another set of self-contained programs provides solutions for typical Bayesian statistical problems such as computation of posterior probability distributions, evaluation of the net gain to be expected as a result of sampling or experimentation, and determination of optimal sample size. Like the first set of programs, the programs in this second set are written for use on a time-sharing system, but they are easily convertible for use in batch processing and little would be lost if they were so converted. Conversion of the first set is technically just as easy, but much more of the usefulness of the programs would be lost as a result.

The remainder of the collection consists of a set of subroutines and functions intended to facilitate the writing of special programs for analysis of decision problems whose diagrams are too complex to be conveniently analyzed by use of a general-purpose interactive program. These subprograms take care of most of the bothersome details of discretization, interpolation, evaluation of probabilities and preferences, sorting, file operations, tabular and graphic description of probability distributions, and so forth, that may be required in a program written to analyze a problem by backward induction, Monte Carlo simulation, or a mixture of the two. With the aid of these subprograms, a program for analysis of a moderately complex problem in either interactive or batch mode can often be written in a few pages of simple and straightforward Fortran.

Finally, the complete programs and top-level subprograms described above call on a number of supporting subprograms of which the general user of the collection need scarcely be aware. Some of these basic subprograms execute algorithms for mathematical operations such as evaluation of cumulative probabilities under standard probability distributions. Others make the top-level programs and subprograms system-independent by providing free-format input, links to system subroutines for opening and closing files, and so forth.

Description and Documentation

The description and documentation of the Manecon collection in this book is divided into four main parts:

1. Description of the self-contained programs. These descriptions, which occupy Chapters 1–4, define the inputs which the user must supply to the programs and explain the outputs which the programs may deliver. They assume no background beyond that in *Analysis of Decisions under Uncertainty* (referred to as ADU).[1] They are complete in the sense that a person who wishes to run one of these programs should require no other information except a list of the commands required to load and start the program on the particular computer system being used.

2. Descriptions of the general-purpose subprograms. These descriptions occupy Chapters 5–8. The first three chapters are intended more for beginners than for experienced programmers and include not only detailed instructions for use of the subprograms but also a good deal of general advice at a very elementary level on the programming of decision analyses in Fortran IV. Chapter 8 contains summary descriptions of the subprograms which should be self-sufficient for an experienced programmer and at the same time serve as a quick reference for a beginner who has worked through Chapters 5–7.

3. Mathematical notes on the preference (utility) functions and on the methods of discretization and interpolation that are used in the programs. These brief notes occupy Chapters 9 and 10.

4. Technical notes on the programs and subprograms. These notes, which occupy Chapters 11–16, are intended primarily for the person who wants to install the collection

---

[1] In particular, the reader is not assumed to be familiar with the concept of a continuous probability distribution. For this reason, certain parts of Chapter 1 are written in language which is, to say the least, very loose, but a more sophisticated reader should find it easy enough to infer what is meant from what is said.

on a new computer system, augment the capabilities of the collection, or verify or improve the algorithms it employs. They will be of no interest to a person who merely wants to use the collection as installed.

The abbreviation ASDT in the documentation refers to Raiffa and Schlaifer, *Applied Statistical Decision Theory* (Division of Research, Harvard Business School, 1961). PSBD refers to the author's *Probability and Statistics for Business Decisions* (Mc Graw-Hill, 1959).

Availability and Adaptability

The Manecon collection is written in standard Fortran IV. It is currently available in two versions, one for the IBM 360/67 operating under CP/CMS, another operating on the PDP-10 with standard DEC software.[2] Anyone interested in listings or copies on magnetic tape should write to the Director of Computer Services at the Harvard Business School, Boston, Massachusetts 02163.

In writing the collection, all possible care was taken to minimize the difficulty of installing the collection on a new system. No use has been made of nonstandard features of Fortran IV such as multiple entry to subprograms and use of statement numbers as arguments in call lists. Machine-dependent constants are displayed in data statements at the beginning of each program or subprogram, not concealed in numerical form in the interior. For time sharing, completely self-checking free-format input is achieved through a Fortran subroutine easily adapted to any machine and system. File operations are inevitably system-dependent, but the system-dependent aspects are almost entirely concentrated in just four subroutines.

The general structure of the collection has been dictated by the requirement that the collection should be adaptable to systems which allow the user only a very small amount of core. Between 8K and 12K words should suffice on any system.

It is because of this desire to minimize core requirements that the collection consists of a rather large number of single-purpose programs which communicate through files rather than a few programs each capable of analyzing a class of complete decision problems. For example, relatively little core is needed if one program assesses and files the distribution of the payoff of a gamble, another assesses and files the decision maker's preference function, and still a third program reads in the results of two assessments and evaluates the gamble. If the functions of all three programs were combined in one, the amount of core required would be nearly tripled.

Another consequence of the desire to reduce core requirements is seen in the use of selectively loaded supporting files to control the operation of the programs for assessment and filing of probability distributions. These programs are capable of handling a number of completely different families of distributions and would become very large indeed if they were loaded with all the subprograms required to support all of these families. Space requirements are kept small by allowing the loading of supporting files for only one family at a time.

---

[2] There is also an operating but out-of-date version on the CDC 3600 of the Multicomp system.

On systems which provide for overlays or chaining, it would of course be not only possible but quite easy to link several programs, or several options under one program, in such a way that the very existence of distinct programs or supporting files becomes transparent to the user.

Acknowledgments

The author owes much to Arthur Schleifer, Jr., who developed many of the basic algorithms used in the collection, and to John W. Pratt, who gave mathematical assistance at many points. Development of the collection would have been financially impossible without the generous financial support for research in decision analysis provided by the National Science Foundation under contract GS-2994, income from the William Ziegler Professorship of Business Administration, allocations of funds from gifts to the School by The Associates of the Harvard Business School, and the great deal of free computer time provided by the IBM Cambridge Scientific Center as its contribution to joint research by members of its staff and members of the Faculty of the Harvard Business School.

Soldiers Field   Robert Schlaifer
Boston, Massachusetts
May 1971

CONTENTS

Preface v

A. User's Guide to the Self-Contained Programs

1. Assessment and Filing of Probability Distributions: Programs *Cdispri, Disfile* and *Fdispri* 1

    1. Representation of Judgmental Assessments by Continuous Probability Distributions
    2. Description and Assessment of Continuous Distributions: Program *Cdispri*
    3. Grouping and Filing of Distributions: Program *Disfile*
    4. Description of Filed Distributions: Program *Fdispri*

2. Preference Functions Implying Constant or Constant Proportional Risk Aversion: Program *Conaverse* 27

    1. Fitting of Preference Functions with Constant or Constant Proportional Risk Aversion
    2. Evaluation of Gambles under the Fitted Function

3. Preference Functions Implying Decreasing Positive Risk Aversion: Programs *Prefpoint, Piecexfit, Sumexfit,* and *Prefeval* 32

    1. Assessment of Five Points on a Preference Curve: Program *Prefpoint*
    2. Fitting Preference and Bounding Functions Through Five Specified Points
    3. Fitting a Sumex Preference Function to Three Arbitrarily Chosen Fifty-Fifty Gambles
    4. Evaluation of Preferences, Certainty Equivalents, and Bounds Thereon: Program *Prefeval*

4. Posterior and Preposterior Analysis: Programs *Postdis, Betadif, Truchance, Valinfo,* and *Opsama* 54

    1. Posterior Distribution of a Population Fraction or Average: Program *Postdis*
    2. Posterior Distribution of the Difference between Two Population Fractions: Program *Betadif*
    3. Calibration of Chances Quoted by an Expert: Program *Truchance*
    4. Value of Perfect Information and Net Gain of Sampling: Program *Valinfo*
    5. Optimal Sample Size: Program *Opsama*

B. Programmer's Guide to the General Purpose Subprograms

5. Computations Involving Probability Distributions Grouped into Brackets of Equal Probability 81

    1. Input and Storage of EP Distributions
    2. Probabilities, Fractiles, and Mean and Variance
    3. Expectation of a Function of a Single UQ
    4. Distribution of a Function of a Single UQ
    5. Expectation of a Function of Two or More UQ's
    6. Distribution of a Function of Two or More UQ's
    7. Random Sampling of End Positions

6. Computations Involving Probability Distributions Grouped into Brackets of Equal Width 110

    1. Input and Storage of EW Distributions
    2. Probabilities, Fractiles, and Mean and Variance
    3. Expectation of a Function of a Single UQ
    4. Distribution of a Function of a Single UQ
    5. Expectation of a Function of Two or More UQ's
    6. Distribution of a Function of Two or More UQ's

7. Computations Involving Piecex or Sumex Functions; Evaluation and Description of Continuous Probability Distributions 130

    1. Piecex and Sumex Functions
    2. Evaluation of Strictly Continuous Probability Distributions
    3. Printed Description of Continuous Distributions: Subroutine *Prbpri*

8. Summary Description of the General-Purpose Subprograms 141

    1. Grouped Probability Distributions
    2. Piecex and Sumex Functions
    3. Continuous Probability Distributions
    4. Miscellaneous Functions
    5. Sorter
    6. Subprograms for Input from Terminal and Opening and Closing of Files
    7. Index of the General-Purpose Subprograms

C. Mathematics of Preference Functions and Grouped Approximations

9. Mathematics of Preference Functions 155

    1. Local Risk Aversion
    2. Preference Functions with Constant Absolute or Proportional Risk Aversion
    3. Piecex Preference and Bounding Functions
    4. Sumex Preference Functions

10. Mathematics of Grouped Approximations 163

    1. Grouped Approximations with Brackets of Equal Probability
    2. Grouped Approximations with Brackets of Equal Width

D. Technical Notes on the Programs

11. Fitting and Evaluation of Preference Functions 174

    1. Program *Piecexfit*
    2. Evaluation of Piecex Functions
    3. Program *Sumexfit*
    4. Evaluation of Sumex Functions
    5. Auxiliary Functions

12. Programs for Description, Grouping, and Filing of Probability Distributions 193

    1. Programs *Cdispri, Fdispri,* and *Disfile*
    2. Addition of New Families of Continuous Distributions to the Manecon Collection

13. Evaluation of Continuous Probability Distributions 199

    1. Standard Beta Cumulative Function: Subroutine *Dbetcu*
    2. Standard Gamma Cumulative Function: Subroutine *Dgascu*
    3. Unit Normal Cumulative Function: Subroutines *Unrcuq* and *Dunrcu*
    4. Fractiles of Standard Distributions: Functions *Betfrq, Gasfrc,* and *Unrfrc*
    5. Complete Gamma Function: Functions *Algama* and *Dlgama*

14. Fitting of Continuous Probability Distributions to Points on the Cumulative Function 213

    1. Beta Distribution
    2. Gamma-q Distribution
    3. Logstudent Distribution
    4. Arcsinh-normal Distribution
    5. Piecewise Quadratic Distribution

15. Posterior and Preposterior Analysis: Programs *Postdis, Truchance*, and *Valinfo* . . . 228

    1.   Program *Postdis*
    2.   Program *Truchance*
    3.   Program *Valinfo*

16. Optimal Sample Size: Program *Opsama* 233

    1.   Beta and Hyperbinomial Distributions; Reduction of the Hypergeometric to the Binomial Case
    2.   Analysis When the Number of Units Subjected to the Terminal Act is Fixed
    3.   Analysis When the Number of Units Subjected to the Terminal Act Depends on the Sample Size

CHAPTER 1

Assessment and Filing of Probability Distributions: Programs Cdispri, Disfile, and Fdispri

In the present chapter we discuss three Manecon programs that are of use in the assessment of judgmental probability distributions and in the filing of the assessed distributions in a form suitable for input to other Manecon programs and subroutines.

1. Program Cdispri is an aid to assessment of continuous probability distributions.[1] It allows the user to specify a continuous distribution of any of a variety of types and then allows him to examine the implications of his specification by providing various forms of graphic and tabular description of the distribution. The name Cdispri is mnemonic for "continuous distribution printout".

2. After the user has assessed a probability distribution, program Disfile will file the distribution in a form which can be read by other Manecon programs and subroutines. The distribution may be discrete, continuous, or mixed;[2] a continuous distribution or the continuous part of a mixed distribution will be grouped (ADU 7.4.3-7.4.6) according to the user's specifications before it is filed.

3. Program Fdispri provides various forms of printed description of any discrete, grouped, or mixed distribution which has been filed by program Disfile or any other Manecon program or subroutine. The name Fdispri is mnemonic for "filed distribution printout".

---

[1] With rare exceptions, a reader of the present book who is unfamiliar with the concept of a "continuous" probability distribution will not go wrong if he thinks of a continuous distribution as a distribution which (1) assigns nonzero probability to a very large number of values of the uq, and (2) assigns no substantial probability to any one of these values individually. In the rare contexts where the word "continuous" must be interpreted in its strict or mathematical sense, we shall say so.

[2] A mixed distribution is one in which probabilities summing to less than 1 are assigned to certain individual values of a uq and the remaining probability is distributed smoothly ("continuously") over all values of the uq within some interval, possibly infinite.

In the first section of this chapter we shall discuss the various types or "families" of continuous distributions that can be processed by programs <u>Cdispri</u> and <u>Disfile</u>. We shall then be able to show how programs <u>Cdispri</u> and <u>Disfile</u> can be used to assess, group, and file a probability distribution and how program <u>Fdispri</u> can be used to describe a filed distribution.

Contents of Chapter 1

1. Representation of Judgmental Assessments by Continuous Probability Distributions   3

   1. Piecewise Quadratic Distributions; 2. Fitting of Distributions to a Very Small Number of Numerical Specifications; 3. Families Suitable to UQ's whose Values are Between 0 and 1; 4. Families Suitable to UQ's whose Values are Nonnegative; 5. Families Suitable to UQ's whose Values are Unrestricted; 6. Summary.

2. Description and Assessment of Continuous Distributions: Program <u>Cdispri</u>   12

   1. Capabilities; 2. Specification of the Distribution to be Described; 3. Sample Runs; 4. Use of <u>Cdispri</u> in Assessment of a Continuous Distribution.

3. Grouping and Filing of Distributions: Program <u>Disfile</u>   19

   1. Continuous Distributions; 2. Discrete Distributions; 3. Mixed Distributions.

4. Description of Filed Distributions: Program <u>Fdispri</u>   22

1.1. Representation of Judgmental Assessments by Continuous Probability Distributions

1.1.1. Piecewise Quadratic Distributions

1. Definition of a Piecewise Quadratic Distribution. If a decision maker has assessed a probability distribution of an uncertain quantity (uq) by drawing a graph of its complete cumulative function, he can describe this graph to program Cdispri or Disfile by stating the coordinates of a number of points on its cumulative function. Provided that these points meet certain conditions to be discussed in a moment, either program will be able to call on subroutine Pcqfit to construct a mathematical formula for a smooth cumulative function which passes through the specified points, and the program will then base all further calculations on this formula. Because the cumulative function defined by the formula will consist mainly of a number of quadratic segments smoothly joined together, the corresponding probability distribution will be called a "piecewise quadratic" distribution.[3]

2. General Shape of a Piecewise Quadratic Distribution. All cumulative functions constructed by Pcqfit have a general shape of one of the three types illustrated in Figure 1.1A, where the following points are the essential ones to observe:

1. The steepest or modal portion of the graph is a linear segment.
2. Unless the linear segment is the first segment, the graph to the left of the linear segment is convex when viewed from below and is tangent to the line P = 0 at the point where it meets this line.
3. Unless the linear segment is the last segment, the graph to the right of the linear segment is concave when viewed from below and is tangent to the line P = 1 at the point where it meets this line.

The values of the uq at the points where the graph meets the lines P = 0 and P = 1 will be called respectively the 0 fractile and the 1 fractile of the uq.

3. Formal Requirements on the Input Points. The only formal requirements on the points supplied as input to subroutine Pcqfit are the following:

1. The number of points must not be less than 3 or more than 25.
2. The points must include the 0 and 1 fractile.
3. The points must be such that it is possible to fit them with a curve having one of the three shapes described in Figure 1.1A.

---

[3]Subroutine Pcqfit replaces the subroutine Smooth described on pages 268-271 of ADU. As will appear in what follows, there are a number of material differences between Pcqfit and the older subroutine regarding the nature of the distributions that can be processed, the points that must be supplied to make the program function, the additional points that should be supplied to obtain a good fit, and the nature of the function fitted to the inputs.

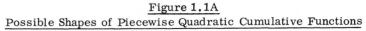

Figure 1.1A
Possible Shapes of Piecewise Quadratic Cumulative Functions

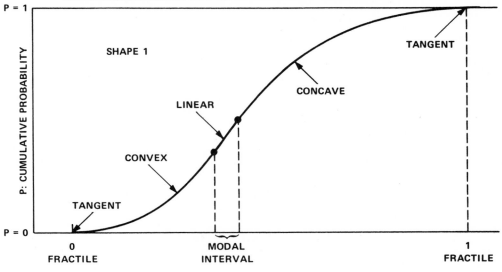

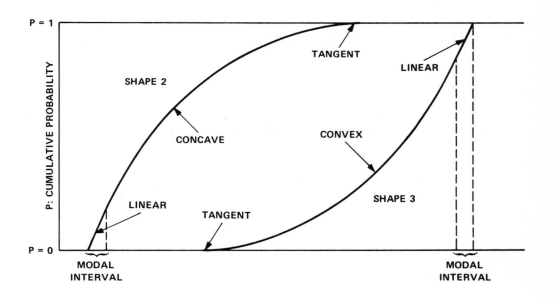

If the input points violate any of these conditions, program Cdispri or Disfile will reject them and print out an explanatory message.

A set of input points will satisfy the third condition if and only if the slopes of line segments joining successive pairs of points either (1) increase monotonically, (2) decrease monotonically, or (3) increase monotonically to a single maximum and then decrease monotonically. Any set of points the user chooses will have this property if they are read with sufficient accuracy from a graph which has one of the three general shapes shown in Figure 1.1A, whether or not the graph actually contains a linear segment. The closer the points are together, the greater the accuracy required.

4. Selection of Points to Ensure a Good Fit. Although subroutine Pcqfit can fit a piecewise quadratic cumulative function to as few as 3 input points, the function it fits to a very small number of points will rarely if ever resemble anything that the user would be willing to accept as describing a "reasonable" probability distribution. To ensure that the function constructed by Pcqfit will agree reasonably well with his original graph, the user should specify ten or a dozen points more or less evenly spaced out along that graph.[4]

In selecting input points, the user should remember that the steepest portion of the cumulative function which Pcqfit will fit to them will be a linear segment. For this reason he should not select the mode of his distribution (the point at which his own graph is steepest) as one of his input points if his graph has the S shape called Shape 1 in Figure 1.1A.[5] Instead, he should select two points marking the ends of a portion of his graph which (1) contains the mode, and (2) is short enough to be practically linear.

1.1.2. *Fitting of Distributions to a Very Small Number of Numerical Specifications*

In the last section we examined the conditions under which a decision maker's judgments about a uq can be represented reasonably well by a mathematical cumulative function of the piecewise quadratic type, and we discussed the numerical specifications he must supply in order to select a suitable particular function of this type. In what follows, we shall examine the conditions under which the decision-maker's judgments can be represented reasonably well by cumulative functions of other mathematical types and discuss the numerical specifications he must supply in order to select a particular function of each of these types. Alternatively, we can say that in the last section we discussed the way in which

---

[4] It cannot be overemphasized that the only legitimate role for Pcqfit is the matching of a distribution which the user has completely defined by constructing a graph of its cumulative function. If the user wants a reasonable distribution fitted to a very small number of numerical specifications — e.g., to specifications of the .25 and .75 fractiles — he should call on Cdispri or Disfile to fit a distribution of one of the types described in Sections 1.1.3-1.1.5 below.

[5] This is one of the important respects in which the requirements of Pcqfit differ from those of the subroutine Smooth described in ADU.

a decision maker can give mathematical expression to his judgments about a uq by selecting a particular member of the piecewise quadratic "family" of distributions, while in what follows we shall discuss the ways in which he can give mathematical expression to his judgments by selecting a member of some other family of distributions.

There are two very important differences between the piecewise quadratic family of distributions and the families we are about to consider.

1. Each of the families we are about to consider is defined by a formula containing only a small, fixed number of parameters (ADU A.3.3), and the number of numerical specifications with which a distribution of any such family can be made to agree is equal to the number of parameters. Accordingly none of these new families is as flexible as the piecewise quadratic family, whose defining formula is built up in such a way that the number of parameters increases with the number of specifications the user chooses to supply.

2. Although the new families are less flexible than the piecewise quadratic, they have the advantage that all of their members are "reasonable" probability distributions. We have already said that this is not true of the piecewise quadratic family, whose members have a reasonable shape only when the points to which they are fitted constrain them to have a reasonable shape.

When a decision maker tries to fit his judgments about a uq with a distribution belonging to one of the families we are about to discuss, he is very likely to find that any distribution that agrees with his intuitive judgments about the central part of the distribution disagrees sharply with his intuitive judgments about the tails of the distribution. Specifically, he is likely to find that any distribution that agrees with his judgments concerning the .25 and .75 fractiles has tails which are substantially longer than he thinks they should be.

If this happens, the decision maker can of course obtain almost exact agreement with all of his intuitive judgments by constructing a graph of his cumulative function and fitting a piecewise quadratic distribution to points read from this graph, but it is by no means certain that this is the right thing to do. A very considerable amount of experimental evidence shows that even people who assess quite reasonable values for the .25 and .75 fractiles of a distribution usually assess values for the .01 fractile which are far too high and values for the .99 fractile which are far too low. It follows that if the decision maker finds that a distribution of inherently reasonable shape which agrees with his .25 and .75 fractiles has tails which at first seem to be too long, he should think seriously about changing his intuitive judgments about the tails before he decides to fit a piecewise quadratic distribution that agrees with these judgments.

In the following description of the families of distributions that can be processed by programs Cdispri and Disfile, we shall consider successively the families suitable to (1) uq's whose values must be between 0 and 1, (2) uq's whose values must not be negative but can have any positive value whatever, including 0, and (3) uq's whose values are unrestricted.

1.1.3.   *Families Suitable to UQ's Whose Values are Between 0 and 1*

Programs Cdispri and Disfile are capable of handling two different families of distributions suitable to a uq whose value must necessarily lie between 0 and

1 — e.g., the fraction of the members of some population who possess some particular attribute. The two families in question are the beta and the bounded lognormal,[6] each of which has two parameters.

    1. <u>Beta Distributions</u>. Despite the fact that the beta family has only two parameters, a beta distribution may have any of a wide variety of shapes. It may be either symmetric or skew; if skew, it may have the long tail on either the left or the right; it may have a mode somewhere between 0 and 1 or it may be J-shaped or U-shaped or uniform.[7]

    Programs <u>Cdispri</u> and <u>Disfile</u> allow the user to specify a particular beta distribution by specifying its parameters, its mean and standard deviation, or its .25 and .75 fractiles. The mean must be between 0 and 1 exclusive; if the mean is m , the standard deviation must be between 0 and $\sqrt{m(1-m)}$ exclusive; the fractiles must be between 0 and 1 exclusive.

    2. <u>Bounded Lognormal Distributions</u>. Bounded lognormal distributions are about as flexible as beta distributions, and a bounded lognormal distribution will in most cases closely resemble a beta distribution fitted to the same assessments. There are two cases, however, in which the two distributions may be quite different. When the beta distribution is nearly uniform, a lognormal distribution with the same .25 and .75 fractiles is bimodal. When substantial probability is assigned to values of the uq very close to 0 or 1, the beta distribution is J-shaped or U-shaped whereas the lognormal distribution has a high, narrow peak very close to 0 or 1 but drops down to the axis before actually reaching 0 or 1.

    The user may specify a particular bounded lognormal distribution by specifying its parameters or its .25 and .75 fractiles. The fractiles must be between 0 and 1 exclusive.

1.1.4. *Families Suitable to UQ's Whose Values are Nonnegative*

    Programs <u>Cdispri</u> and <u>Disfile</u> are capable of handling three different families of distributions suitable to a uq whose value must necessarily be nonnegative — e.g., demand for a product. The simplest and least flexible of the three families is the lognormal, which has only two parameters; the other two are the logstudent and the gamma-q, both of which have three parameters.[8]

    1. <u>Lognormal Distributions</u>. A lognormal distribution is always skew, with the long tail to the right, but the amount of skewness depends on the relation between the distance from the origin to the center of the distribution, as measured by the median, and the spread of the distribution, as measured by the distance

---

[6] For mathematical definitions of beta and bounded lognormal distributions and their parameters, see Sections 8.3.2 and 8.3.5 below.

[7] A distribution is said to be J-shaped if its mass function either decreases monotonically from left to right or increases monotonically from left to right. A distribution is said to be U-shaped if its mass function decreases monotonically to a single minimum and then increases monotonically. Graphs of various beta distributions can be found in PSBD pp. 674-675 or in ASDT pp. 218-219.

[8] For mathematical definitions of lognormal, logstudent, and gamma-q distributions and their parameters, see Sections 8.3.5, 8.3.4, and 8.3.3 below.

from the .25 to the .75 fractile. If the spread is small relative to the distance from the origin to the median, the distribution will be nearly symmetric; as the spread increases, the distribution becomes more and more skew.

Programs Cdispri and Disfile allow the user to specify a particular lognormal distribution by specifying either its parameters, its mean and standard deviation, or its .25 and .75 fractiles. The mean, standard deviation, and fractiles must be greater than 0.

2. Logstudent Distributions. The three-parameter logstudent distribution differs from the two-parameter lognormal in that if the .25 and .75 fractiles of the distribution are fixed, the user can control the length of the tails of the log-student whereas he has no control over the tails of the lognormal. The control over tail length works only in one direction, however. The tails of the logstudent may be longer than the tails of the lognormal by any amount, but they cannot be shorter. If, for example, a logstudent and a lognormal distribution have the same .25 and .75 fractiles, the .875 fractile of the logstudent may be greater than the .875 fractile of the lognormal by any amount but cannot be less; the lognormal is actually the limiting case of the logstudent in the sense that as the .875 fractile of the logstudent approaches the .875 fractile of the lognormal from above, all the fractiles of the logstudent approach the corresponding fractiles of the lognormal.

Programs Cdispri and Disfile allow the user to specify a logstudent distribution by specifying either its three parameters or its .25, .75, and .875 fractiles. The .25 and .75 fractiles must be greater than 0; the .875 fractile must be greater than the .875 fractile of a lognormal distribution with the given .25 and .75 fractiles. The program will reject the inputs and issue an appropriate message if the .875 fractile specified by the user does not meet this condition.

3. Gamma-q Distributions. Like the three-parameter logstudent family, the three-parameter gamma-q family can best be understood by reference to the two-parameter lognormal family. We have just seen that for given .25 and .75 fractiles, the tails of a logstudent distribution can both be longer than the tails of a lognormal by any amount but cannot be shorter. A gamma-q distribution, on the contrary, will have one tail longer and the other tail shorter than the corresponding tails of the lognormal. If the parameter q has a value greater than 0, the gamma-q will have a longer left and shorter right tail than the lognormal; if the parameter q has a value less than 0, the reverse will be true. As the parameter q approaches 0 from either side, the gamma-q distribution approaches the lognormal, which is thus the limiting case of not only the log-student family but also the gamma-q family.

Programs Cdispri and Disfile require that the user specify the numerical value of the parameter q directly; the two additional specifications required to determine the other two parameters of the family may be either the numerical values of those parameters or the .25 and .75 fractiles of the distribution.[9] The fractiles must be greater than 0; the parameter q may in principle have any

---

[9] When q = 1, the other two parameters can also be specified by specifying the mean and standard deviation of the distribution.

positive or negative value other than 0, but if q is very close to 0, the program may be unable to fit the user's .25 and .75 fractiles, in which case it will issue the message "Cannot fit distribution to these inputs",[10] or it may be able to fit them only approximately, in which case it will issue the message "Dgascu did not converge".[11]   In the latter case, the fit may actually be very good, and therefore the user should call on Cdispri to print the .25 and .75 fractiles of the fitted distribution and compare them with his specifications before he concludes that the fit is too bad to be used.   If the fit is in fact too bad to be used, or if no fit can be obtained at all, the user should call on Cdispri or Disfile to fit a lognormal distribution instead of a gamma-q.

  4. Choice of a Distribution.   A user who wishes to find a distribution which will agree as well as possible with his judgments about a uq whose value cannot be negative will often do well to start by fitting a lognormal distribution to his .25 and .75 fractiles and examining its tails with the aid of program Cdispri. Then if he wishes to extend both tails, he can assess his .875 fractile and fit a logstudent distribution; if he wishes to extend one tail and shorten the other, he can fit a gamma-q distribution by holding the values of the .25 and .75 fractiles fixed and using Cdispri to examine the distributions that correspond to various values of the parameter q .   In conducting this search for the "right" value of q , he can start by setting q = +1 if it is the left tail that he wants to extend, −1 if it is the right tail.   Thereafter, doubling or halving the value of q will make an appreciable change in the distribution.

  5. Infinite Means and Variances.   When Cdispri describes any continuous distribution, it treats the distribution as continuous in the strict sense of the word and bases its calculations on formulas derived by use of the calculus. Rather surprisingly, the mean and standard deviation of a logstudent distribution as computed in this way are always infinite, no matter how close the distribution may be to lognormal in most respects; under a gamma-q distribution, the standard deviation is infinite if q has a negative value below a limit which depends on the .25 and .75 fractiles, and the mean is also infinite if q is below another, lower limit.

  It should not be thought, however, that a continuous distribution with infinite mean or standard deviation is of no use to a person who wishes to assess a distribution with finite mean and standard deviation for use in numerical analysis of a decision problem.   Whatever may be the continuous distribution he initially chooses, this distribution will be grouped before it is actually used in analyzing

---

[10] Complete inability to fit a distribution to specified .25 and .75 fractiles is usually if not always due to the fact that the parameters of the distribution which actually agrees with the user's specifications are so large or so small that they would cause overflow or underflow on the particular machine being used.

[11] For given values of the .25 and .75 fractiles, the range of values of q that will result in inaccurate fits depends on the value assigned to the variable NTERMS near the beginning of the subroutine Dgascu which computes cumulative gamma probabilities.   Increasing the value of NTERMS enables Cdispri and Disfile to handle values of q closer to 0.

the problem, and the mean and standard deviation of the grouped distribution will necessarily be finite. The grouped approximation completely disregards the extremely small probabilities in the extreme tails which cause the mean and standard deviation to be infinite when the distribution is treated as continuous in the strict sense of the word.

This same fact implies that even when a continuous distribution with infinite range has a finite mean and standard deviation, the user should ordinarily pay little if any attention to these quantities when he tries to decide whether a grouped approximation to that distribution will agree reasonably well with his judgments about a uq. In examining the original continuous distribution with the aid of Cdispri, he should pay attention to only the part of the continuous distribution which will affect the grouped approximation, namely, the part between the .5/n and the 1-.5/n fractiles if the grouping is into n brackets of equal probability, the part between the .01/n and the 1-.01/n fractiles if the grouping is into n brackets of equal width.[12] Program Cdispri will at the user's request print out the values of the limiting fractiles, but the only way of learning what the mean and standard deviation of the grouped distribution will be is actually to group and file the distribution with the aid of program Distile and then call on program Fdispri to print out the mean and standard deviation of the filed distribution.

1.1.5. *Families Suitable to UQ's Whose Values are Unrestricted*

Programs Cdispri and Disfile are capable of handling two different families of distributions suitable to a uq whose values may be either positive or negative — e.g., the change in price of some commodity or security. The two families in question are the ordinary Gaussian (or "Normal"), which has two parameters, and the arcsinh-normal (pronounced Ark sinch normal), which has four.[13]

1. Gaussian Distributions. The two-parameter Gaussian family is so inflexible that it is of very little use in describing judgmental distributions. All members of the family are symmetric.

Programs Cdispri and Disfile allow the user to specify a Gaussian distribution by specifying either its parameters, its mean and standard deviation, or its .25 and .75 fractiles.

2. Arcsinh-Normal Distributions. Distributions of the four-parameter arcsinh-normal family can be either symmetric or skew, with the long tail to either the left or the right. The only important limitation on the shapes that can be assumed by this family concerns the lengths of the tails. When the distribution is symmetric, the tails must be at least as long as the tails of a Gaussian distribution with the same interquartile range; when the distribution is skew, there is a related but

---

[12] When Disfile groups any distribution into n brackets of equal probability, the first and last bracket medians are the .5/n and 1-.5/n fractiles. When Disfile groups any distribution except a piecewise quadratic distribution into n brackets of equal probability, it truncates the distribution at the .01/n and 1 − .01/n fractiles.

[13] For mathematical definitions of Gaussian and arcsinh-normal distributions and their parameters, see Section 8.3.5.

more complex lower limit on the length of the longer tail.

Programs Cdispri and Disfile allow the user to specify an arcsinh-normal distribution by specifying either its four parameters or the three quartiles (including the median) and the last octile on the longer tail (the .125 fractile if the long tail is to the left, the .875 fractile if the long tail is to the right or the distribution is symmetric). The program rejects the inputs and issues an appropriate message if the specified octile is too close to the adjacent quartile, implying a tail shorter than is possible for an arcsinh-normal distribution.

1.1.6. Summary

Table 1.1A below shows the various families of continuous distributions which can be processed by programs in the Manecon collection and the way or ways in which a particular distribution of any family may be most conveniently specified by the user. A distribution of any family except the piecewise quadratic may also be specified by direct specification of the parameters.

Table 1.1A
Available Families of Distributions
and Permissible Methods of Specifying Individual Members

Family	Range	Method(s) of Specification
Piecewise Quadratic	finite	3 to 25 points on the cumulative function.
Beta	$[0, 1]$	(1) .25 and .75 fractiles; (2) mean and standard deviation.
Bounded lognormal	$[0, 1]$	.25 and .75 fractiles.
Lognormal	$[0, \infty)$	(1) .25 and .75 fractiles; (2) mean and standard deviation.
Logstudent	$[0, \infty)$	.25, .75, and .875 fractiles.
Gamma-q	$[0, \infty)$	parameter q and .25 and .75 fractiles.*
Gaussian	$(-\infty, \infty)$	(1) .25 and .75 fractiles; (2) mean and standard deviation.
Arcsinh-normal	$(-\infty, \infty)$	.25, .5, and .75 fractiles plus one octile**.

---

* Concerning the effect of the parameter q, see paragraph 3 in Section 1.1.4 above.
** The .125 fractile if the long tail of the distribution is to the left, the .875 fractile if it is to the right or the distribution is symmetric.

1.2.   Description and Assessment of Continuous Distributions: Program Cdispri

1.2.1.   Capabilities

Program Cdispri provides at the user's option any or all of the following forms of printed description of a continuous distribution belonging to any of the families listed in Table 1.1A just above:

1. A summary description of the distribution, consisting of its mean, standard deviation, and variance, and its .001, .01, .1, .25, .5, .75, .9, .99, and .999 fractiles.
2. The cumulative probabilities of any specified values of the uq.
3. The values of the uq (fractiles) having any specified cumulative probabilities.
4. A graph of the mass function.[14]
5. A graph of the cumulative function.

If the mean of the distribution is infinite, Cdispri prints an asterisk in place of a numerical value. If the standard deviation and variance are infinite, Cdispri prints an asterisk for the standard deviation and the code 3.000E33 for the variance.[15]

1.2.2.   Specification of the Distribution to be Described

In order to obtain a description of a distribution belonging to any one of the families described in Table 1.1A, the user must load one or more supporting files peculiar to that family at the same time that he loads the file containing the main program Cdispri and any general-purpose supporting files that are required on the particular system being used. The name(s) of the supporting file(s) required for any particular family can be found by listing the first part of the file containing the main program.

Because it is not permissible to load special files for more than one family of distributions on any one run, Cdispri can describe distributions of only one family on any one run. The program can, however, describe any number of different distributions belonging to the same family on one run, since the numerical specifications that select a particular member of the family are supplied by the user in answer to questions asked by the program as it runs.

---

[14] All calculations underlying the description printed out by Cdispri are based on formulas obtained by treating the distribution as continuous in the strict sense of the word. What is called a graph of the mass function here and in the printout of the program is actually a graph of the density function.

[15] Concerning infinite means and variances, see paragraph 5 in Section 1.1.4 above.

1.2.3.   Sample Runs

Figure 1.2A shows a run in which Cdispri fits and describes a piecewise quadratic distribution;[16] Figure 1.2B shows a run in which the program fits and describes a gamma-q distribution. Notice in both examples that after the user specified option 9 to indicate that he had had all the description he wanted of a particular distribution, he could have obtained a description of another distribution of the **same family** by typing yes instead of no when the program asked whether he wanted "another distribution".

Figure 1.2A

Description of a Piecewise Quadratic Distribution

```
HOW MANY POINTS WILL YOU SPECIFY?
>17
VALUES OF UQ IN ASCENDING ORDER
>0 .032 .049 .062 .080 .090 .100 .110 .139 .162 .197 .252 .351
>.530 .596 .710 .840
CUMULATIVE PROBABILITIES IN ASCENDING ORDER
>0 .01 .03 .07 .15 .20 .26 .31 .45 .55 .65 .75 .85 .95 .97 .99 1
LIST PRINTOUT OPTIONS?
>YES

THE FOLLOWING OPTIONS WILL BE AVAILABLE REPEATEDLY
    1   SUMMARY DESCRIPTION OF THE DISTRIBUTION
    2   CUMULATIVE PROBABILITIES OF SPECIFIED VALUES OF THE UQ
    3   VALUES WITH SPECIFIED CUMULATIVE PROBABILITIES (FRACTILES)
    4   GRAPH OF THE MASS FUNCTION
    5   GRAPH OF THE CUMULATIVE FUNCTION
    9   NO FURTHER PRINTED OUTPUT

OPTION?
>1

MEAN      =      0.201
STD DEV   =      0.149
VARIANCE  =      0.222E-01
FRACTILES
 .001    .01    .1    .25    .5    .75    .9    .99    .999
 115     320    692   983   1501  2520  4223  7100   8030
        UQ VALUES JUST ABOVE ARE TO BE MULTIPLIED BY 10E-4
```

(continued)

---

[16] The inputs describe the cumulative function graphed on page 407 of ADU. The actual numerical values are identical to the input data in Figure 10.6 on page 409 of ADU except that no slopes are specified and the point at the mode is replaced by two points on either side of the mode; these exceptions are due to the difference between the subroutines Pcqfit and Smooth that was discussed in Section 1.1.1 above.

Figure 1.2A (continued)

```
OPTION?
>2
ARE VALUES EQUALLY SPACED?
>YES
FIRST VALUE, STEP, LAST VALUE
>0  .2  1

        VALUE     CUM.PROB.
        0.0        0.0
        0.200      0.657
        0.400      0.887
        0.600      0.971
        0.800      0.999
        1.000      1.000

OPTION?
>3
ARE PROBABILITIES EQUALLY SPACED?
>NO
HOW MANY PROBABILITIES?
>2
LIST THEM
>.005  .995

CUM.PROB.      VALUE
   0.005       0.025
   0.995       0.754
```

(continued)

Figure 1.2A (continued)

```
OPTION?
>4

VALUES ON UQ AXIS ARE TO BE MULTIPLIED BY 10E-2
  0*
  -    *
  -           *
  -                              *
  -                                      *
  -                                              *
 10-                                                    *
  -
  -                                        *
  -                              *
  -                    *
 20-                *
  -            *
  -         *
  -      *
 30-      *
  -      *
  -     *
  -    *
  -   *
 40-   *
  -   *
  -  *
  -  *
  -  *
 50- *
  -  *
  - *
  - *
  - *
 60- *
  - *
  - *
  - *
  -*
 70-*
  -*
  -*
  -*
  -*
 80-*
  *
  *
  *
  *
 90*
```

(continued)

Figure 1.2A (continued)

```
OPTION?
>5

VALUES ON UO AXIS ARE TO BE MULTIPLIED BY 10E-2
```

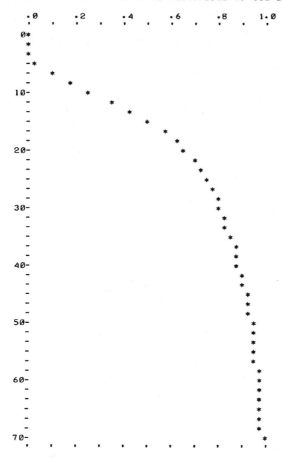

```
OPTION?
>9
ANOTHER DISTRIBUTION?
>NO
```

Figure 1.2B
Description of a Gamma-q Distribution

```
SPECIFY PARAMETER Q OR TYPE 999 FOR INSTRUCTIONS
>999

THE PARAMETER Q, WHICH CAN HAVE ANY POSITIVE OR NEGATIVE VALUE OTHER
THAN 0, CONTROLS THE HEIGHTS OF THE TAILS OF THE DISTRIBUTION. IF Q
IS POSITIVE, THE LEFT TAIL IS HIGHER AND THE RIGHT TAIL IS LOWER THAN
IN A LOGNORMAL DISTRIBUTION. IF Q IS NEGATIVE, THE REVERSE IS TRUE.
THE LARGER THE VALUE OF Q, THE GREATER THE DIFFERENCE. THE ORDINARY
GAMMA DISTRIBUTION HAS Q = 1.

PARAMETER Q
>2
WILL YOU SPECIFY (1)THE PARAMETERS R AND S, OR (2)THE .25 AND .75
FRACTILES?
>2
.25 AND .75 FRACTILES
>1400  2600
MEDIAN IS  1965.905.  WANT TO REASSESS?
>NO
PRINT PARAMETERS?
>YES

R =   1.464
S =   0.183E 04

LIST PRINTOUT OPTIONS?
>NO
OPTION?
>1

MEAN     =   2041.852
STD DEV  =    872.647
VARIANCE =      0.762E 06
FRACTILES
 .001   .01    .1    .25    .5    .75    .9    .99   .999
  190   421   965   1400  1966  2600  3215  4342  5206

OPTION?
>3
ARE PROBABILITIES EQUALLY SPACED?
>NO
HOW MANY PROBABILITIES?
>2
LIST THEM
>.005  .995

CUM.PROB.      VALUE
   0.005      330.645
   0.995     4621.625
```

(continued)

17

Figure 1.2B (continued)

```
OPTION?
>4

VALUES ON UQ AXIS ARE TO BE MULTIPLIED BY 10E 2
    0*
    -*
    - *
    -   *
    -     *
   5-       *
    -         *
    -           *
    -             *
    -               *
  10-                 *
    -                   *
    -                     *
    -                       *
  15-                        *
    -                          *
    -                          *
    -                          *
  20-                         *
    -                        *
    -                       *
    -                     *
  25-                   *
    -                 *
    -               *
    -             *
  30-           *
    -         *
    -       *
    -     *
  35-    *
    -   *
    -  *
    - *
  40- *
    - *
    - *
    - *
  45-*
    -*
    -*
    -*
  50*
    *
    *
    *
  55*

OPTION?
>9
ANOTHER DISTRIBUTION?
>NO
```

1.2.4. *Use of Cdispri in Assessment of a Continuous Distribution*

As we have already suggested, program Cdispri is intended primarily to aid in the actual assessment of judgmental probability distributions.

If the user wishes to fit a distribution of inherently reasonable shape to a very small number of numerical specifications, he must start by using the information in Sections 1.1.3-1.1.5 above to select a family which seems likely to contain a member capable of representing his judgments reasonably well. He can then select a particular member of this family by numerical specifications that express a very few of his judgments (e.g., his .25 and .75 fractiles) and use Cdispri to see if the distribution he has thus specified agrees reasonably well with his other judgments about the uq (e.g., his median, his first and last octiles, etc.). If it does, his assessment problem is solved; if it does not, he can use Cdispri to see whether by making tolerable changes in his original numerical specifications he can find some other member of the same family that "on the average" agrees better with all of his judgments. If ultimately it appears that no member of this family agrees reasonably well with all of his judgments, he can go on to use Cdispri to see whether some other family of distributions contains a more suitable member.

If instead of trying to assess his distribution in the way just described, the user prefers to assess it by drawing a graph of its cumulative function and then fitting a piecewise quadratic distribution to points read from this graph, Cdispri can be used to determine (1) whether the piecewise quadratic cumulative function agrees reasonably well with his original graph, and (2) whether the mass or density function of the fitted distribution has a reasonable shape. This latter test is of considerable importance because hand-drawn cumulative functions tend to imply excessively sharp modes and excessively flat tails.

1.3. Grouping and Filing of Distributions: Program Disfile

1.3.1. *Continuous Distributions*

Program Disfile will group a continuous distribution belonging to any of the families listed in Table 1.1A on page 11 above and write the grouped distribution on a file in a form acceptable as input to other Manecon programs and subprograms. The distribution will be grouped at the user's option into brackets of either equal width (ADU 7.4.3) or equal probability (ADU 7.4.6); the user will be asked to specify the number of brackets and the name for the file on which the distribution is to be written. The number of brackets must not exceed 1000;[17] 100 are more than enough in most applications.

When the file which contains the main program Disfile is loaded, it must be accompanied by a supporting file or files appropriate to the family to which the user's continuous distribution belongs and another supporting file or files appro-

---

[17] The maximum number of brackets is set by the dimension of the vector GDIS and the value assigned to NBRMAX near the start of program Disfile.

priate to the type of grouping (equiprobable or equal-width) he wishes Disfile to perform. The name(s) of the supporting file(s) appropriate to each family of continuous distributions and to either type of grouping will be found at the top of the file containing the main program.

The fact that special supporting files are required for each family of continuous distributions and each type of grouping obviously implies that only one family of distributions and one type of grouping can be handled on any one run of Disfile. The program can, however, process any number of different distributions of the given family on one run, since the numerical specifications that select a particular distribution of a given type are supplied by the user in answer to questions asked by the program as it runs; and if the user does ask the program to process more than one distribution on one run, the program will allow him to specify the number of brackets for each distribution separately.

Two sample runs of Disfile are shown in Figures 1.3A and 1.3B; the distributions which are filed are those described by Cdispri in Figures 1.2A and 1.2B.

Figure 1.3A

Filing of a Piecewise Quadratic Distribution

```
IS DISTRIBUTION PURELY CONTINUOUS?
>YES
HOW MANY POINTS WILL YOU SPECIFY?
>17
VALUES OF UQ IN ASCENDING ORDER
>0 .032 .049 .062 .080 .090 .100 .110 .139 .162 .197 .252 .351
>.530 .596 .710 .840
CUMULATIVE PROBABILITIES IN ASCENDING ORDER
>0 .01 .03 .07 .15 .20 .26 .31 .45 .55 .65 .75 .85 .95 .97 .99 1
NUMBER OF BRACKETS
>100
FILENAME
>ADU409

ANOTHER DISTRIBUTION?
>NO
```

Figure 1.3B

Filing of a Gamma-q Distribution

```
IS DISTRIBUTION PURELY CONTINUOUS?
>YES
SPECIFY PARAMETER Q OR TYPE 999 FOR INSTRUCTIONS
>2
WILL YOU SPECIFY (1)THE PARAMETERS R AND S, OR (2)THE .25 AND .75
FRACTILES?
>2
.25 AND .75 FRACTILES
>1400 2600
NUMBER OF BRACKETS
>100
FILENAME
>GAMMAQ

ANOTHER DISTRIBUTION?
>NO
```

1.3.2.   Discrete Distributions

Program <u>Disfile</u> will accept the user's description of a discrete distribution and write it on a file exactly as described. The user describes the distribution directly from the terminal, by first listing the discrete values of the uq to which he will assign probabilities and then listing the individual (not the cumulative) probabilities of these values. The program checks to see whether the probabilities add to 1 and issues an error message if they do not.

Program <u>Disfile</u> will have adequate support for filing a discrete distribution if it is loaded with any set of supporting files sufficient for grouping and filing a continuous distribution; the type of continuous distribution and the type of grouping do not matter. This means, of course, that both continuous and discrete distributions can be processed on a single run.

A sample run in which <u>Disfile</u> files a discrete distribution is shown in Figure 1.3C.

<u>Figure 1.3C</u>
<u>Filing of a Discrete Distribution</u>

```
IS DISTRIBUTION PURELY CONTINUOUS?
>NO
HOW MANY VALUES OF THE UQ HAVE DISCRETE PROBABILITIES?
>4
LIST THE VALUES
>.01 .05 .15 .25
LIST THEIR PROBABILITIES
>.7 .2 .1 .1
THESE PROBABILITIES ADD TO 1.100.
WANT TO TRY AGAIN?
>YES
HOW MANY VALUES OF THE UQ HAVE DISCRETE PROBABILITIES?
>4
LIST THE VALUES
>.01 .05 .15 .25
LIST THEIR PROBABILITIES
>.7 .1 .1 .1
FILENAME
>PSBD520
```

1.3.3.   Mixed Distributions

In some situations a decision maker may wish to assign individual probabilities which add to less than 1 to one or more discrete values of a uq and then distribute the remaining probability smoothly ("continuously") over some interval of values of the uq, possibly infinite. Program <u>Disfile</u> will group the continuous part of such a "mixed" distribution and then file the complete distribution.

In describing a mixed distribution to program <u>Disfile</u>, the user must first state the unconditional probabilities he assigns to the discrete values of the uq and then specify the <u>conditional</u> continuous distribution that he would assign to the uq if he learned that it had none of these discrete values. In the example illustrated in Figure 1.3D, the user first describes the probabilities that he assignes to $x_1, \ldots , x_4$ on the fork at position A; he then describes the continuous distribution that he assigns to $\tilde{x}$ on the fan at position B . He does not have to state the probability that he assigns to the branch labelled "some other value" on the fork at position A.

Figure 1.3D
Assessment Diagram for a Mixed Distribution

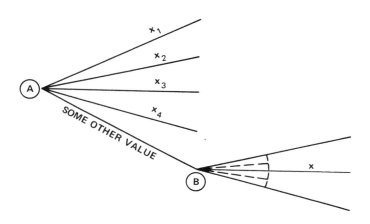

The continuous part of a mixed distribution may be any continous distribution that <u>Disfile</u> could process separately, and the supporting files required for processing the mixed distribution are the same that would be required if only this continuous distribution were to be processed.

Figure 1.3E shows the use of <u>Disfile</u> to file the mixed distribution defined on page 471 of ADU; the continuous part of the distribution is fitted by a piecewise quadratic.

1.4. Description of Filed Distributions: Program Fdispri

Program <u>Fdispri</u> allows the user to obtain printed description of a discrete, grouped, or mixed probability distribution that has been filed by program <u>Disfile</u> or any other Manecon program or subroutine. The printouts it offers are as follows:

1. If the distribution is discrete, a complete listing of the distribution.
2. If the distribution is grouped, the same options that are offered by

Figure 1.3E
Filing of a Mixed Distribution

```
IS DISTRIBUTION PURELY CONTINUOUS?
>NO
HOW MANY VALUES OF THE UQ HAVE DISCRETE PROBABILITIES?
>1
LIST THE VALUES
>0
LIST THEIR PROBABILITIES
>.4
THESE PROBABILITIES ADD TO 0.400.
IS DISTRIBUTION OF REMAINING PROBABILITY CONTINUOUS?
>YES
HOW MANY POINTS WILL YOU SPECIFY?
>12
VALUES OF UQ IN ASCENDING ORDER
>.100 .120 .131 .137 .142 .146 .151 .158 .166 .177 .196 .225
CUMULATIVE PROBABILITIES IN ASCENDING ORDER
>0 .05 .15 .25 .35 .45 .55 .65 .75 .85 .95 1
NUMBER OF BRACKETS
>100
FILENAME
>ADU471

ANOTHER DISTRIBUTION?
>NO
```

program <u>Cdispri</u> (above, Section 1.2.1) and also a complete listing of the cumulative function.

3. If the distribution is mixed, all the above options for the discrete and continuous parts of the distribution separately and also the mean, standard deviation, and variance of the complete mixed distribution.

Figure 1.4A shows the use of <u>Fdispri</u> to describe the distribution filed in Figure 1.3E. Notice that although probability .4 is assigned to the discrete value 0 of the uq, leaving only .6 probability to be distributed by the continuous part of the distribution, the continuous part is described as if it were distributing probability 1. What is really being described is the conditional distribution of the uq given that the uq does not have the value 0; and this is, of course, exactly what the user described to <u>Disfile</u> when he filed the distribution now being described by <u>Fdispri</u>.

Figure 1.4A

Description of a Mixed Distribution by Program Fdispri

```
NAME OF FILE CONTAINING DISTRIBUTION
>ADU471
PRINT SUMMARY STATISTICS OF COMPLETE DISTRIBUTION:
>YES

   MEAN     =    0.091
   STD DEV  =    0.077
   VARIANCE =    0.588E-02

LIST DISCRETE PART OF DISTRIBUTION?
>YES

   VALUE        PROB
   0.0          0.400

DESCRIBE GROUPED PART OF DISTRIBUTION?
>YES
LIST PRINTOUT OPTIONS?
>YES

THE FOLLOWING OPTIONS WILL BE AVAILABLE REPEATEDLY
     1   SUMMARY DESCRIPTION OF THE DISTRIBUTION
     2   CUMULATIVE PROBABILITIES OF SPECIFIED VALUES OF THE UQ
     3   VALUES WITH SPECIFIED CUMULATIVE PROBABILITIES (FRACTILES)
     4   GRAPH OF THE MASS FUNCTION
     5   GRAPH OF THE CUMULATIVE FUNCTION
     6   COMPLETE LISTING OF THE CUMULATIVE FUNCTION
     9   NO FURTHER PRINTED OUTPUT

OPTION?
>1

MEAN     =    0.152
STD DEV  =    0.022
VARIANCE =    0.502E-03
FRACTILES
  .001    .01    .1    .25    .5    .75    .9    .99    .999
  1014   1097   1264  1370   1483  1660  1849  2118   2231
        UQ VALUES JUST ABOVE ARE TO BE MULTIPLIED BY 10E-4
```

(continued)

Figure 1.4A (continued)

```
OPTION?
>5

VALUES ON UQ AXIS ARE TO BE MULTIPLIED BY 10E-3
```

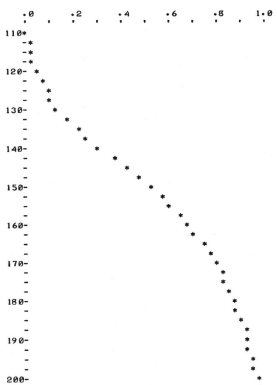

(continued)

Figure 1.4A (continued)

```
OPTION?
>6
```

PRINTED UQ VALUES ARE TO BE MULTIPLIED BY 10E-4
VMIN = 1000   VMAX = 2250

VALUE	PROB	VALUE	PROB	VALUE	PROB	VALUE	PROB	VALUE	PROB
1071	.005	1345	.205	1442	.405	1547	.605	1716	.805
1123	.015	1351	.215	1446	.415	1554	.615	1727	.815
1154	.025	1356	.225	1450	.425	1562	.625	1739	.825
1175	.035	1362	.235	1454	.435	1569	.635	1751	.835
1192	.045	1367	.245	1458	.445	1576	.645	1764	.845
1207	.055	1373	.255	1462	.455	1584	.655	1777	.855
1221	.065	1378	.265	1466	.465	1591	.665	1790	.865
1234	.075	1383	.275	1471	.475	1599	.675	1805	.875
1247	.085	1389	.285	1475	.485	1607	.685	1822	.885
1259	.095	1394	.295	1481	.495	1614	.695	1839	.895
1270	.105	1399	.305	1486	.505	1622	.705	1859	.905
1281	.115	1404	.315	1491	.515	1630	.715	1879	.915
1290	.125	1409	.325	1496	.525	1638	.725	1901	.925
1299	.135	1414	.335	1502	.535	1647	.735	1923	.935
1306	.145	1418	.345	1507	.545	1656	.745	1947	.945
1314	.155	1422	.355	1513	.555	1665	.755	1973	.955
1320	.165	1426	.365	1519	.565	1674	.765	2003	.965
1327	.175	1430	.375	1526	.575	1684	.775	2038	.975
1333	.185	1434	.385	1533	.585	1694	.785	2083	.985
1339	.195	1438	.395	1540	.595	1705	.795	2153	.995

```
OPTION?
>9
ANOTHER DISTRIBUTION?
>NO
```

CHAPTER 2

Preference Functions Implying Constant or Constant Proportional Risk Aversion: Program Conaverse

In this chapter and the next we describe the Manecon programs that can be used to assess preference functions and to evaluate various types of gambles under the assessed functions.

All the preference functions that can be handled by the programs in the Manecon collection express preferences for values of some scalar "criterion", which in many business applications will be a monetary measure of some kind of assets (ADU 2.2); and with only accidental exceptions the functions imply positive risk aversion[1] which either remains constant or decreases as assets increase. In the present chapter we describe the single program <u>Conaverse</u> which handles functions implying either constant risk aversion or constant proportional risk aversion, the latter being a very special type of decreasing absolute risk aversion.[2]   In the next chapter we shall describe the programs which handle functions implying more general and flexible forms of decreasing risk aversion.

Contents of Chapter 2

1. Fitting of Preference Functions with Constant or Constant Proportional Risk
    Aversion   28
2. Evaluation of Gambles under the Fitted Function   28

---

[1] A person is said to have positive risk aversion if he would be willing to pay more than its actuarial or expected value for insurance against loss.

[2] A person is said to have constant (absolute) risk aversion if a change in his assets would have no effect on the amount of money he would be just willing to pay for insurance against a fixed chance of losing a fixed amount of money. He is said to have decreasing (absolute) risk aversion if an increase in his assets would reduce the amount he would be willing to pay for insurance against a fixed chance of losing a fixed amount of money. He is said to have constant proportional risk aversion if a change in his assets would have no effect on the fraction of his assets that he would be just willing to pay for insurance against a fixed chance of losing a fixed fraction of his assets.

2.1. Fitting of Preference Functions with Constant or Constant Proportional Risk Aversion

When a decision maker has either constant or constant proportional risk aversion, his preference function is fully determined by his certainty equivalent for any one gamble.[3] Program <u>Conaverse</u> will fit a function with risk aversion of either type to any two-outcome gamble that the user describes by stating the two possible payoffs, the chance of the greater payoff, and his certainty equivalent. The only restrictions on the gamble described by the user are the following:

1. The certainty equivalent must be greater than the lesser payoff and less than the greater payoff.
2. In the case of constant proportional risk aversion, the lesser payoff must be nonnegative.

The certainty equivalent and hence the fitted preference function may imply positive, zero, or even negative risk aversion. A function with constant positive proportional risk aversion has decreasing positive absolute risk aversion.

After fitting a preference function to the user's specifications, program <u>Conaverse</u> prints out the "local" risk aversion[4] implied by the function, as shown in Figures 2.3A and 2.3B below. In the case of a function with constant risk aversion, the local risk aversion is of course a definite number; in the case of constant proportional risk aversion, the local risk aversion is equal to a constant divided by the decision maker's assets, which <u>Conaverse</u> represents by the letter V.

2.2. Evaluation of Gambles under the Fitted Function

After a preference function has been fitted, program <u>Conaverse</u> will as shown in Figures 2.3A and 2.3B below compute certainty equivalents and risk premiums for gambles of the following types.

1. <u>Finite Gambles Described at the Terminal.</u> Program <u>Conaverse</u> can evaluate any finite gamble the user describes by stating the payoffs and associated probabilities. The payoffs must be nonnegative if the preference function has constant proportional risk aversion.

2. <u>Gambles with Filed Payoff Distributions.</u> Program <u>Conaverse</u> can evaluate any gamble whose payoff has a distribution which has been filed by program <u>Disfile</u> (above, Section 1.3) or by any other Manecon program or subroutine. The user has only to supply the name of the file containing the distribution.

More generally, <u>Conaverse</u> can evaluate any gamble whose payoff is a linear function of a uq whose distribution is on file. The payoff is assumed to be of the

---

[3] For the mathematics of preference functions with constant and constant proportional risk aversion, see Section 9.2 below.

[4] For the definition of local risk aversion, which can be thought of as an appropriate measure of the concavity of a preference curve at a particular point, see Section 9.1 below.

form a + bx̃, where x̃ is the uq whose distribution is on file and a and b are constants. The user supplies the name of the file containing the distribution of x̃ and the values of the constants a and b.

3. Gambles and Continuous Payoff Distributions. If the user wishes to evaluate a gamble with a Gaussian payoff distribution under any preference function with constant risk aversion, he has no need to group and file the distribution before calling on Conaverse to evaluate the gamble. He can describe the distribution directly to program Conaverse by simply stating its mean and standard deviation.

Similarly, there is no need to group and file a lognormal payoff distribution or a gamma-q distribution[5] with parameter q = 1 in order to evaluate a gamble with such a distribution under any preference function with constant proportional risk aversion except the function with risk aversion 1/V. As in the previous case, the user has only to state the mean and standard deviation of the distribution; in the present case, the mean must be greater than 0.

-----

[5] For a brief description of gamma-q distributions, see Section 1.1.4 above.

Figure 2.3A
Constant Risk Aversion

```
LIST OPTIONS?
>YES

THE FOLLOWING OPTIONS WILL BE AVAILABLE REPEATEDLY

FIT PREFERENCE FUNCTION WITH
    1   CONSTANT RISK AVERSION
    2   CONSTANT PROPORTIONAL RISK AVERSION

EVALUATE GAMBLE WHOSE PAYOFF
    3   HAS DISTRIBUTION TO BE DESCRIBED BY USER
    4   HAS DISTRIBUTION WHICH IS ON FILE
    5   IS A LINEAR FUNCTION OF A UQ WHOSE DISTRIBUTION IS ON FILE
    6   HAS CONTINUOUS GAUSSIAN DISTRIBUTION WITH MEAN AND S.D. TO BE
        SPECIFIED BY USER (CONSTANT RISK AVERSION ONLY)
    7   HAS CONTINUOUS GAMMA OR LOGNORMAL DISTRIBUTION WITH MEAN AND
        S.D. TO BE SPECIFIED BY USER (CONSTANT PROPORTIONAL RISK
        AVERSION ONLY)

LAST OPTION
    9   QUIT

OPTION?
>1
DESCRIBE GAMBLE TO WHICH FUNCTION IS TO BE FITTED BY SPECIFYING WORSE
PAYOFF X, CERTAINTY EQUIVALENT Y, BETTER PAYOFF Z, AND CHANCE P(Z) OF
BETTER PAYOFF
>-10  5  50  .5
RISK AVERSION =   0.04062519

OPTION?
>3
HOW MANY PAYOFFS?
>4
LIST THEM
>-5  0  25  50
LIST PROBABILITIES
>.1  .2  .5  .2
CE =     15.635
RP =      6.365

OPTION?
>5
NAME OF FILE CONTAINING DISTRIBUTION OF UQ
>GAMMAQ
SPECIFY CONSTANTS A AND B OR TYPE 9,9 FOR INSTRUCTIONS
>9,9
PROGRAM ASSUMES PAYOFF WILL BE   A + BX   WHERE X IS UQ WHOSE DISTRI-
BUTION IS ON FILE AND A AND B ARE CONSTANTS.   SPECIFY A AND B.
>-10  .01
CE =      8.961
RP =      1.448

OPTION?
>6
MEAN AND STANDARD DEVIATION OF PAYOFF
>20  10
CE =     17.969
RP =      2.031

OPTION?
>7
NOT AVAILABLE UNDER CONSTANT RISK AVERSION.
```

Figure 2.3B
Constant Proportional Risk Aversion

```
OPTION?
>2
X,Y,Z,P(Z)
>-10  5  50 .5
PREFERENCE FUNCTIONS WITH CONSTANT PROPORTIONAL
RISK AVERSION ARE DEFINED ONLY FOR NONNEGATIVE PAYOFFS.

OPTION?
>2
X,Y,Z,P(Z)
>0  20  50 .5
RISK AVERSION =  0.2435292Ø/V

OPTION?
>3
HOW MANY PAYOFFS?
>4
LIST THEM
>10  20  30  40
LIST PROBABILITIES
>.2 .3 .3 .2
CE =    24.445
RP =    0.555

OPTION?
>6
NOT AVAILABLE UNDER CONSTANT PROPORTIONAL RISK AVERSION.

OPTION?
>7
MEAN AND STANDARD DEVIATION OF PAYOFF
>20  10
                CE        RP
GAMMA         19.414    0.586
LOGNORMAL     19.464    0.536

OPTION?
>9
```

CHAPTER 3

Preference Functions Implying Decreasing Positive Risk Aversion: Programs Prefpoint, Piecexfit, Sumexfit, and Prefeval

In the last chapter we considered the very special case of decreasing positive risk aversion that corresponds to constant positive proportional risk aversion. In the present chapter we describe the Manecon programs that can be used to assess more flexible preference functions with decreasing positive risk aversion and to evaluate various types of gambles under these functions.

One of the most satisfactory ways in which a decision maker can arrive at a set of numerical specifications for a preference function with decreasing positive risk aversion is to assess five points on his preference function by a procedure described in ADU 5.2. Before accepting these assessments as final, however, the decision maker may do well to test their consistency with one additional assessment in the way described in ADU 5.2.5. If this test reveals internal inconsistencies among the assessments, program Prefpoint can in some cases help the decision maker to arrive at new assessments which are free of such inconsistencies.

After a decision maker has established five satisfactory points on his preference curve, any one of the three programs Prefpoint, Piecexfit, and Sumexfit can determine whether or not the points are consistent with decreasing positive risk aversion in the sense that it is theoretically possible to construct a function with decreasing positive risk aversion which passes through the points. If the points are not consistent in this sense, any one of the three programs will tell the user how they must be revised in order to become consistent; if they are consistent, then:

1. Program Piecexfit can always fit the points with (a) a "piecex-average" preference function which has decreasing positive risk aversion, and (b) two other functions which can be used to compute bounds on the preferences and certainty equivalents implied by any preference function with decreasing positive risk aversion that passes through the specified points.

2. Program <u>Sumexfit</u> can usually fit the points with a "sumex" preference
    function which has decreasing positive risk aversion and which is
    smoother than the piecex-average function fitted by program <u>Piecexfit</u>.

In some cases the decision maker may prefer to arrive at numerical specifications concerning his preferences by assessing his certainty equivalents for
three 50-50 gambles with arbitrarily chosen payoffs instead of assessing five
points on his preference curve. Specifications of this sort are not acceptable as
input to program <u>Piecexfit</u>, but program <u>Sumexfit</u> will accept them and can
sometimes fit them with a sumex function which has decreasing positive risk
aversion.

Finally, after appropriate functions have been fitted by <u>Piecexfit</u> and/or
<u>Sumexfit</u>, program <u>Prefeval</u> can (1) tabulate preferences and bounds thereon for
any criterion values specified by the user, and (2) compute preferences, certainty
equivalents, and bounds thereon for various types of gambles—in particular,
gambles in which the payoff has either a discrete probability distribution described
at the terminal or a discrete, grouped, or mixed distribution that has been filed by
a Manecon program or subroutine.

Contents of Chapter 3

1. Assessment of Five Points on a Preference Curve: Program <u>Prefpoint</u>   34

    1. Capabilities; 2. Consistency of Five Points with Decreasing Positive
    Risk Aversion; 3. Excessive Risk Aversion for Small Gambles.

2. Fitting Preference and Bounding Functions Through Five Specified Points   41

    1. Capabilities of Program <u>Piecexfit</u>; 2. Capabilities of Program <u>Sumexfit</u>.

3. Fitting a Sumex Preference Function to Three Arbitrarily Chosen Fifty-Fifty
    Gambles   44

    1. Description of the Input Gambles; 2. Capabilities of Program <u>Sumexfit</u>.

4. Evaluation of Preferences, Certainty Equivalents, and Bounds Thereon:
    Program <u>Prefeval</u>   47

    1. Tabulation of the Functions; 2. Evaluation of Gambles; 3. Tightness
    of the Bounds on Preferences and Certainty Equivalents.

3.1. Assessment of Five Points on a Preference Curve: Program Prefpoint

3.1.1.   Capabilities

Perhaps the most satisfactory way of establishing five points on a preference curve with decreasing positive risk aversion is to proceed as follows (cf. ADU 5.2):

1. Select two reference values V_0 and V_1 for which preferences are 0 and 1 by definition, thus establishing the points labelled A and B in Figure 3.1A;
2. Assess certainty equivalents $V_{.5}$, $V_{.25}$, and $V_{.75}$ for the first three gambles in Table 3.1A, thus establishing the points labelled 2, 1, and 3 in Figure 3.1A.

These assessments imply that the decision maker's certainty equivalent for the last gamble in Table 3.1A <u>should</u> be equal to his certainty equivalent $V_{.5}$ for the first gamble; he can now:

3. Test the internal consistency of his intuitive preferences by actually assessing his certainty equivalent $V^*_{.5}$ for the last gamble in Table 3.1A and checking whether or not it is in fact equal to $V_{.5}$.

If $V^*_{.5}$ is not in fact equal to $V_{.5}$, it establishes an extraneous and inconsistent point like the one labelled 2* in Figure 3.1A.

When the decision maker's assessments are internally consistent in the sense that $V^*_{.5} = V_{.5}$, program <u>Prefpoint</u> can test whether they are also consistent with decreasing positive risk aversion; if they are not, <u>Prefpoint</u> will go on to state how they must be revised in order to become consistent.[1]

When the decision maker's assessments are internally inconsistent because $V^*_{.5}$ is not equal to $V_{.5}$, it is usually because $V^*_{.5}$ is <u>less</u> than $V_{.5}$ as shown in Figure 3.1A; and when this is true, the inconsistency is usually due to a phenomenon discussed in ADU 5.4.2, namely excessive risk aversion for narrow relative to broad gambles. If it is, <u>Prefpoint</u> can produce a set of revised assessments from which this phenomenon is eliminated, test whether these revised assessments are consistent with decreasing positive risk aversion, and state how they must be further revised if they are not consistent.

The inputs required by program <u>Prefpoint</u> are the five criterion values V_0, $V_{.25}$, $V_{.5}$, $V_{.75}$, and V_1 which define five points on the user's preference curve and the value $V^*_{.5}$ which the user may or may not have assessed as equal to $V_{.5}$. All six values must be expressed in units such that no value has more than 6 digits to the left or 3 digits to the right of the decimal point.

---

[1] The program can of course be used to test consistency of V_0, $V_{.25}$, $\ldots$, V_1 with decreasing positive risk aversion even if the user has not actually assessed $V^*_{.5}$ or has assessed V_0, $V_{.25}$, $\ldots$, V_1 by some preocedure other than the one described above. The user has only to answer the program's input requests <u>as if</u> he had assessed $V^*_{.5} = V_{.5}$.

Figure 3.1A
Points on a Preference Curve

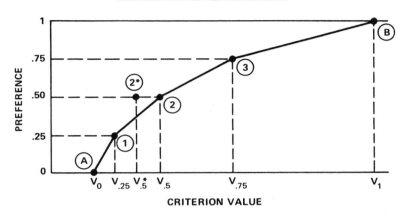

Table 3.1A
Certainty Equivalents for 50–50 Gambles

Payoffs of Gamble	Certainty Equivalent	Point Number	Risk Aversion
	Assessed		
V_0, V_1	$V_{.5}$	2	R_0
V_0, $V_{.5}$	$V_{.25}$	1	R_1
$V_{.5}$, V_1	$V_{.75}$	3	R_3
	Implied		
$V_{.25}$, $V_{.75}$	$V_{.5}$	2	R_2
	Assessed		
	$V^*_{.5}$	2*	R^*_2

3.1.2.   Consistency of Five Points with Decreasing Positive Risk Aversion

In the present section we discuss the output which <u>Prefpoint</u> may deliver when $V^*_{.5}$ is stated by the user to be equal to $V_{.5}$ and <u>Prefpoint</u> is used only to determine whether the five points defined by V_0, $V_{.25}$, ... , V_1 are consistent with decreasing positive risk aversion. The output which <u>Prefpoint</u> may deliver when $V^*_{.5}$ is not equal to $V_{.5}$ will be discussed in Section 3.1.3.

<u>Measures of Risk Aversion</u>. In order to explain the output of <u>Prefpoint</u>, we must first define the "average risk aversion" of a preference curve over an interval.

Let $<v_1, v_2>$ denote a 50-50 gamble which will pay either v_1 or v_2, and suppose that a decision maker has assessed his certainty equivalent for the gamble. If the decision maker had constant risk aversion over the interval $[v_1, v_2]$, then as we saw in Section 2.1 above this one assessment would suffice to determine his preference function and hence the value R of his constant risk aversion; and whether or not the decision maker's risk aversion is in fact constant over $[v_1, v_2]$, we shall say that R as thus calculated is his <u>average</u> risk aversion over the interval $[v_1, v_2]$.

<u>Nonpositive or Nondecreasing Average Risk Aversion</u>. Now consider a set of five specific criterion values V_0, $V_{.25}$, ... , V_1 for which a decision maker has said that his preferences are 0, .25, ... , 1. These assessments imply that his certainty equivalents for the gambles $<V_0, V_{.5}>$, $<V_{.25}, V_{.75}>$, and $<V_{.5}, V_1>$ are respectively $V_{.25}$, $V_{.5}$, and $V_{.75}$; and hence it is possible to calculate his average risk aversion over each of the intervals $[V_0, V_{.5}]$, $[V_{.25}, V_{.75}]$, and $[V_{.5}, V_1]$. These three average risk aversions will be called respectively R_1, R_2, and R_3.

It can be shown that if R_1, R_2, and R_3 do not satisfy the condition $R_1 > R_2 > R_3 > 0$, then it is impossible to construct a preference curve with decreasing positive risk aversion through the five points corresponding to the values V_0, $V_{.25}$, ... , V_1. Accordingly when supplied with these values program <u>Prefpoint</u> makes an initial test of consistency with decreasing positive risk aversion by computing R_1, R_2, and R_3 and testing whether they satisfy the necessary condition. If they do not, either because one or more of them is nonpositive or because they do not decrease from left to right, the program prints out a message of the sort shown in Figure 3.1B.

<u>Average Risk Aversion Decreasing Improperly</u>. Even though the three average risk aversions implied by the user's input points are positive and decreasing, it may still be impossible to construct a function which passes through the points and at the same time has risk aversion which is everywhere positive and decreasing. Such a function can be constructed only if R_2 is not merely less than R_1 but less than a limit which depends in a complicated way on R_3 as well as R_1 and may be smaller than R_1. As a final test of consistency, <u>Prefpoint</u> tests whether R_2 is less than this limit and prints out a message like the one in Figure 3.1C if it is not.

It is difficult to give a nonmathematical explanation of the reason why R_2 has to be less than a limit which may itself be less than R_1, but the following argument may help to reduce the mystery.

Figure 3.1B
Nonpositive or Nondecreasing Average Risk Aversion

```
WANT INSTRUCTIONS?
>YES

PROGRAM WILL TEST CONSISTENCY OF 5 POINTS ON PREFERENCE CURVE WITH
DECREASING POSITIVE RISK AVERSION AND WILL ALSO, IF DESIRED, ATTEMPT
TO RECONCILE AN INCONSISTENT CERTAINTY EQUIVALENT V*(.5) WITH V(.5)
AS ORIGINALLY ASSESSED.  IF YOU HAVE NO SUCH INCONSISTENT CERTAINTY
EQUIVALENT AND MERELY WISH TO TEST CONSISTENCY OF POINTS ON CURVE,
SUPPLY SAME VALUE FOR V*(.5) THAT YOU SUPPLY FOR V(.5).

INPUT VALUES MUST HAVE NO MORE THAN 6 DIGITS TO LEFT OR 3 DIGITS TO
RIGHT OF DECIMAL POINT.

SPECIFY POINTS ON CURVE V(0),V(.25),V(.5),V(.75),V(1)
>0  15  50  80  150
SPECIFY INCONSISTENT CERTAINTY EQUIVALENT V*(.5)
>50

INCONSISTENT WITH DECREASING POSITIVE RISK AVERSION
YOU MUST RAISE V(.25) OR V(.75) OR LOWER V(.5).
    R1 = 0.0360214355
    R2 =-0.0047525051
    R3 = 0.0180107178

ANOTHER RUN?
>YES
POINTS ON CURVE
>0  17.5  50  85  150
V*(.5)
>50

INCONSISTENT WITH DECREASING POSITIVE RISK AVERSION
YOU MUST RAISE V(.25) OR V(.75) OR LOWER V(.5).
    R1 = 0.0255730498
    R2 = 0.0021968086
    R3 = 0.0127865249
```

Figure 3.1C
Improperly Decreasing Average Risk Aversion

```
ANOTHER RUN?
>YES
POINTS ON CURVE
>0  20  50  99  150
V*(.5)
>50
INCONSISTENT WITH DECREASING POSITIVE RISK AVERSION
EVEN THOUGH AVERAGE RISK AVERSIONS ARE POSITIVE AND DECREASING
YOU MUST LOWER V(.25) OR V(.75) OR RAISE V(.5).
    R1 = 0.0164432647
    R2 = 0.0126740504
    R3 = 0.0008002138
```

1. The fact that risk aversion must be everywhere decreasing implies that average risk aversion over the subinterval $[V_{.25}, V_{.5}]$ must not exceed the average risk aversion R_1 over $[V_0, V_{.5}]$.

2. The fact that risk aversion over $[V_{.75}, V_1]$ must not be zero or negative implies that average risk aversion over $[V_{.5}, V_{.75}]$ must not exceed some amount which depends on the average risk aversion R_3 over $[V_{.5}, V_1]$ and may be smaller than R_1.

3. Since the average risk aversion R_2 over $[V_{.25}, V_{.75}]$ is a kind of average of the average risk aversions over $[V_{.25}, V_{.5}]$ and $[V_{.5}, V_{.75}]$, it follows that R_2 must be not only less than R_1 but less than some possibly smaller amount which depends on R_3 as well as R_1.

3.1.3.   *Excessive Risk Aversion for Small Gambles*

Now suppose that a decision maker carries out the complete assessment procedure described by Figure 3.1A and Table 3.1A and finds that his directly assessed certainty equivalent $V^*_{.5}$ for the last gamble in Table 3.1A is less than $V_{.5}$. As we have already suggested, such a result is usually due at least in part to the fact that $V^*_{.5}$ reflects excessive risk aversion for narrow relative to broad gambles.

The last three gambles in Table 3.1A are all narrow relative to the first, and in extreme cases excessive risk aversion for narrow relative to broad gambles can produce a set of points like those in Figure 3.1D below. The decision maker's

Figure 3.1D

Excessive Risk Aversion for Narrow Gambles

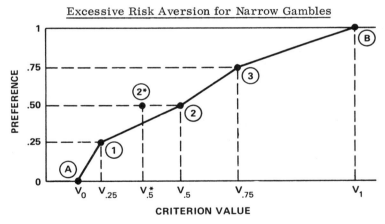

risk premiums for the narrow gambles $< V_0, V_{.5} >$ and $< V_{.5}, V_1 >$ which determine points 1 and 3 are so great relative to his risk premium for the broad gamble $< V_0, V_1 >$ which determines point 2 that the broken line joining points 1, 2, and 3 is convex rather than concave; R_2 is negative and the points are inconsistent with positive risk aversion.[2] In less extreme cases the broken line joining points 1, 2, and 3 will be concave but less concave than the broken line

---

[2] This was the case in the first printout in Figure 3.1B above.

joining points 2, 3, and B; R_2 is positive but less than R_3 and the points are inconsistent with decreasing risk aversion.[3] In either case, point 2* is to the left of point 2 not only because of an excessive risk premium for the narrow gamble < $V_{.25}$, $V_{.75}$ > which directly determines this point but also because the payoffs $V_{.25}$ and $V_{.75}$ are already too far to the left relative to $V_{.5}$.

When a decision maker assesses $V^*_{.5} < V_{.5}$ and thus discovers that his risk premiums for the three narrow gambles in Table 3.1A are excessively large relative to his risk premium for the one broad gamble, he may decide that the inconsistency should be resolved in whole or in part by increasing his risk premium for the broad gamble — i.e., by lowering his certainty equivalent $V_{.5}$. More commonly, however, he will want to resolve the inconsistency simply by reducing his risk premiums for the three narrow gambles; and it may be that he will feel that these premiums should be altered in such a way that the average risk aversions (above, Section 3.1.2) they imply are all reduced in the same proportion. If the decision maker does decide that he would like to reconcile his inconsistencies in this way, program Prefpoint will determine whether it is possible to do so, and if it is, will compute the appropriate revised assessments and then test them for consistency with decreasing positive risk aversion.

When supplied with V_0, $V_{.25}$, ..., V_1 and with $V^*_{.5}$ not equal to $V_{.5}$, Prefpoint first checks whether these values satisfy two conditions which must obviously be satisfied if new assessments consistent with decreasing positive risk aversion are to be derived by simply making a fixed percentage reduction in the average risk aversions R_1, R^*_2, and R_3 defined in Table 3.1A. The conditions in question are:

$$V^*_{.5} < V_{.5}, \qquad R_1 > R^*_2 > R_3 > 0 .$$

If either of these conditions is violated, Prefpoint rejects the problem and prints out an appropriate message, as shown in Figure 3.1E.

If on the contrary the two conditions are satisfied, Prefpoint proceeds to set $V^*_{.5} = V_{.5}$ and compute new values for $V_{.25}$ and $V_{.75}$ such that the average risk aversions R_1, R^*_2, and R_3 are all reduced in the same proportion. It then tests these revised values for consistency with decreasing positive risk aversion[4] and prints out a message like one of the two shown in Figure 3.1F.

In computing revised values for $V_{.25}$ and $V_{.75}$, Prefpoint tries to avoid confusing the user with values having more significant digits than are required. The program first tries to find values consistent with decreasing positive risk aversion which contain no more significant digits than there were in the user's input values. If it succeeds, as it did in the first problem in Figure 3.1F, these are the values which it prints out. If it fails, it tries to find consistent values which contain only one more significant digit and prints them out if it succeeds; if it fails, it repeats the procedure, and so forth until $V_{.25}$ and $V_{.75}$

---

[3] This was the case in the second printout in Figure 3.1B above.

[4] Although the average risk aversions R_1, R_2, and R_3 which are implied by these revised values will necessarily be positive and decreasing, they may be inconsistent with risk aversion which is everywhere positive and decreasing because they decrease "improperly" in the sense of Section 3.1.2 above.

Figure 3.1E
Refusal to Compute Revised Assessments

```
ANOTHER RUN?
>YES
POINTS ON CURVE
>0  15  50  80   150
V*(.5)
>55
PROGRAM HANDLES ONLY CASES WHERE V*(.5) <= V(.5).

ANOTHER RUN?
>YES
POINTS ON CURVE
>0  15  50  80   150
V*(.5)
>30

POINTS ON CURVE INCONSISTENT WITH DECREASING POSITIVE RISK AVERSION
    R1 = 0.0360214355
    R2 =-0.0047525051
    R3 = 0.0180107178
AVERAGE RISK AVERSIONS IMPLIED BY ORIGINAL V(.25), V*(.5), AND V(.75)
ASSESSMENTS ARE NOT DECREASING, AND ADJUSTMENT OF VALUES TO RECONCILE
V*(.5) WITH V(.5) WOULD PRESERVE THIS INCORRECT ORDERING.
    R1 = 0.0360214355
    R2*= 0.0419969616
    R3 = 0.0180107178
```

Figure 3.1F
Computation and Testing of Revised Assessments

```
ANOTHER RUN?
>YES
POINTS ON CURVE
>0  15  50  80   150
V*(.5)
>35

POINTS ON CURVE INCONSISTENT WITH DECREASING POSITIVE RISK AVERSION
    R1 = 0.0360214355
    R2 =-0.0047525051
    R3 = 0.0180107178

ADJUSTMENT OF VALUES TO RECONCILE V*(.5) WITH V(.5) LEADS TO
    V(.25) =     21.
    V*(.5) =     50. (= V(.5))
    V(.75) =     91.

AND THESE ASSESSMENTS ARE CONSISTENT
WITH DECREASING POSITIVE RISK AVERSION.
    R1 = 0.0130238543
    R2 = 0.0099932631
    R3 = 0.0073603816
```

(continued)

Figure 3.1F
(continued)

```
ANOTHER RUN?
>YES
POINTS ON CURVE
>0   20   50   98   150
V*(.5)
>48

ADJUSTMENT OF VALUES TO RECONCILE V*(.5) WITH V(.5) LEADS TO
   V(.25)  =      20.678580
   V*(.5)  =      50.000000 (= V(.5))
   V(.75)  =      98.283067
BUT THESE ASSESSMENTS ARE INCONSISTENT
WITH DECREASING POSITIVE RISK AVERSION
EVEN THOUGH AVERAGE RISK AVERSIONS ARE POSITIVE AND DECREASING
YOU MUST LOWER V(.25) OR V(.75) OR RAISE V(.5).
   R1 = 0.0141119241
   R2 = 0.0131249254
   R3 = 0.0013746326
ON THE OTHER HAND, THE ORIGINAL V(.25), V(.5), V(.75)
ARE CONSISTENT WITH DECREASING POSITIVE RISK AVERSION.
   R1 = 0.0164432647
   R2 = 0.0122765412
   R3 = 0.0016017206

ANOTHER RUN?
>NO
```

have been computed to 6 decimal places. At this point it prints out the revised values whether or not they are consistent with decreasing positive risk aversion, as in the second problem in Figure 3.1F.

3.2. Fitting Preference and Bounding Functions Through Five Specified Points

3.2.1. *Capabilities of Program Piecexfit*

1. Test for Consistency with Decreasing Positive Risk Aversion. When supplied with the five values V_0, $V_{.25}$, ..., V_1 for which the user's preferences are 0, .25, ..., 1, program Piecexfit first determines whether these inputs are logically consistent with decreasing positive risk aversion in the sense that it is theoretically possible to construct a preference function which passes through the five corresponding points and has risk aversion which is everywhere positive but decreasing. The reasons why a given set of inputs may be inconsistent with decreasing positive risk aversion were explained in the discussion of program Prefpoint in Section 3.1.2; the messages printed out by Piecexfit in case of inconsistency are the same as those printed out by Prefpoint.

2. Fitting of Preference and Bounding Functions. Provided only that the inputs are consistent with decreasing positive risk aversion, Piecexfit will always fit the inputs with:

1. A "piecex-average" preference function[5] which passes through the five specified points and has risk aversion which is everywhere positive and decreasing.

This function has an upward jump just to the right of the user's leftmost input point; thereafter, it is continuous and its risk aversion decreases continuously except for downward jumps at two points between $V_{.25}$ and V_1.

2. Two "bounding" functions[6] which delimit the region within which any preference function must lie if it is to pass through the five specified input points and at the same time have risk aversion which is everywhere positive and decreasing.

The exact meaning and "tightness" of the bounds supplied by these functions is discussed in Section 3.4 below.

3. Evaluation of the Accuracy of the Fit. After fitting the preference and bounding functions just described, Piecexfit evaluates the accuracy of the fit. In all examples tried to date, the fit is very good in the sense that all preferences and bounds computed from the fitted functions will be accurate to the full 7 decimal places the program attempts to achieve.[7] If, however, this objective should not be met, Piecexfit will print out an evaluation of the accuracy actually achieved.

4. Output. The output of Piecexfit consists merely of the parameters of the fitted functions. The program will at the user's option print the parameters at the user's terminal and/or write them on a file from which they can be read in by program Prefeval or any other program which needs them to compute preferences, certainty equivalents, and bounds thereon.

Two sample runs of program Piecexfit are shown in Figure 3.2A.

3.2.2. *Capabilities of Program Sumexfit*

1. Test for Consistency with Decreasing Positive Risk Aversion. When supplied with the five values V_0, $V_{.25}$, ..., V_1 for which the user's preferences are 0, .25, ..., 1, program Sumexfit first performs the same test of consistency with decreasing positive risk aversion that is performed by programs Prefpoint and Piecexfit and rejects the problem if the inputs are not consistent; cf. Section 3.1.2. above.

2. Initial Bounds. If the inputs are consistent with decreasing positive risk aversion, Sumexfit next tries to find initial bounds on the parameters of a sumex preference function[8] which will fit the inputs. Bounds have been found in all

---

[5] For the definition of a piecex-average function, see Section 9.3.5 below.

[6] For the definition of the bounding functions, see Section 9.3.4 below.

[7] The accuracy of the fit that Piecexfit attempts to achieve is controlled by the value assigned to the variable TOLRNC near the start of the program.

[8] For the definition of a sumex preference function, see Section 9.4 below.

Figure 3.2A
Two Runs of Program Piecexfit

```
CRITERION VALUES IN ASCENDING ORDER
>-10  -5   5   25   50
PRINT PARAMETERS?
>YES

               FOR V IN                A            B            R
U1  F2  [-1.000D 01 ,  5.910D 00]   6.525D-01   2.500D-01   9.624D-02
    F4  [ 5.910D 00 ,  5.000D 01]   1.000D 00   1.463D 00   9.869D-03
U2  F3  (-1.000D 01 ,  1.737D 01]   8.306D-01   4.744D-01   5.210D-02
    F5  [ 1.737D 01 ,  5.000D 01]   5.000D-01   1.000D-02   ---------

FILE PARAMETERS?
>YES
FILENAME
>MALLPCX

ANOTHER RUN?
>YES
CRITERION VALUES IN ASCENDING ORDER
>0   20   50   95   150
PRINT PARAMETERS?
>NO
FILE PARAMETERS?
>YES
FILENAME
>PRATPCX

ANOTHER RUN?
>NO
```

examples tried to date, but if it should happen that no bounds can be found, Sumexfit will give up the attempt to fit a sumex function and print out "Cannot fit function to these inputs even though they are consistent with decreasing positive risk aversion." The program will not determine whether its inability to find the desired initial bounds is due to inadequacy of the search procedure or to the fact that no sumex function agreeing with the inputs exists.

3. Fitting the Function. If Sumexfit succeeds in finding initial bounds on the region within which it must search for the parameters of a function that will fit the inputs, it attempts to find parameters such that all preferences computed from the fitted function will be accurate to at least 7 decimal places.[9] In all examples tried to date, Sumexfit has succeeded in this attempt, but if it should fail, it will print out a message concerning the accuracy of the fit actually achieved.

4. Risk Aversion of the Fitted Function. The risk aversion of a sumex function is necessarily everywhere decreasing, but it may decrease so far as to become nonpositive; and therefore Sumexfit next proceeds to determine whether the fitted function is (1) risk averse over $(-\infty, \infty)$, or (2) risk averse to the left of some finite criterion value V but risk seeking to the right.[10] If the function is

---

[9] The accuracy of fit which Sumexfit attempts to achieve is controlled by the value assigned to the variable NDEC at the beginning of the program.

[10] Concerning extrapolation of sumex functions to the left of V_0 and to the right of V_1, see paragraph 3 in Section 3.4.1 below.

risk averse over $(-\infty, \infty)$, the program prints "Everywhere risk averse". If the function is risk seeking to the right of some criterion value V but this $V \geq V_1$, the message is "Risk averse over the range of the assessments". If $V < V_1$, the program prints out the actual value of V.

5. Output. The output of Sumexfit, like the output of Piecexfit, consists merely of the parameters of the fitted function; the program will at the user's option print the parameters at the user's terminal and/or write them on a file from which they can be read in by any program which needs them to compute preferences and certainty equivalents under the fitted function.

Two sample runs of program Sumexfit are shown in Figure 3.2B. Notice that the sumex function fitted to the second set of inputs is risk seeking over a part of the interval $[V_0, V_1]$ even though the piecex-average function fitted to these same inputs in Figure 3.2A was everywhere risk averse.

Figure 3.2B

Two Runs of Program Sumexfit

```
WILL YOU SPECIFY POINTS ON CURVE(1) OR DESCRIPTIONS OF GAMBLES(2)?
>1
CRITERION VALUES IN ASCENDING ORDER
>-10  -5  5  25  50
FUNCTION EVERYWHERE RISK AVERSE.
PRINT PARAMETERS?
>YES

  A = 0.1424172955   B = 0.0020396688   C =   56.62142

FILE PARAMETERS?
>YES
FILENAME
>MALLSMX

ANOTHER RUN?
>YES
WILL YOU SPECIFY POINTS ON CURVE(1) OR DESCRIPTIONS OF GAMBLES(2)?
>1
CRITERION VALUES IN ASCENDING ORDER
>0  20  50  95  150
FUNCTION RISK AVERSE BELOW V =   135.462, RISK SEEKING ABOVE.
PRINT PARAMETERS?
>NO
FILE PARAMETERS?
>YES
FILENAME
>PRATSMX

ANOTHER RUN?
>NO
```

3.3. Fitting a Sumex Preference Function to Three Arbitrarily Chosen Fifty-Fifty Gambles

When the user's numerical specifications concerning his preferences are in the form of certainty equivalents for three arbitrarily chosen 50-50 gambles, he can use program Sumexfit to try to fit his specifications with a sumex preference function even though he cannot use <u>Piecexfit</u> to fit them with a piecex–average preference function or with the bounding functions described in Section 3.2.1 above.

3.3.1 Description of the Input Gambles

To describe three arbitrarily chosen 50–50 gambles together with his certainty equivalents for these gambles, the user must state for the i'th gamble (i = 1, 2, 3) the values of

x_i : lesser payoff of the gamble,

y_i : certainty equivalent for the gamble,

z_i : greater payoff of the gamble.

<u>Sumexfit</u> requires that the three gambles be described in order of decreasing average risk aversion;[11] the way in which the user should try to satisfy this requirement depends on whether or not any one of the gambles is strictly nested within another in the sense that (1) the lesser payoff of the first gamble is strictly greater than the lesser payoff of the second, and (2) the greater payoff of the first gamble is strictly less than the greater payoff of the second.

If neither of two input gambles is strictly nested within the other, the gambles should be described to <u>Sumexfit</u> in order of increasing payoffs. For example, a gamble with payoffs < 10, 20 > should be described after a gamble with payoffs < 5, 15 > or < 10, 15 > but before a gamble with payoffs < 15, 25 > or < 15, 20 > . If the user's certainty equivalents for the gambles are consistent with decreasing risk aversion, this ordering guarantees that the average risk aversions of the gambles will be in the decreasing order required by <u>Sumexfit.</u>

If one of two input gambles is strictly nested within the other, there is no simple rule for determining which of the two gambles either has or should have the lesser average risk aversion. In most cases, the only practical course of action is to submit the gambles to <u>Sumexfit</u> in an arbitrary order and let <u>Sumexfit</u> decide whether they are in order of decreasing average risk aversion. If they are, well and good; if not, <u>Sumexfit</u> will print out their average risk aversions and they can then be resubmitted in the proper order.

3.3.2. Capabilities of Program Sumexfit

1. <u>Tests of Consistency.</u> As soon as three input gambles have been described to <u>Sumexfit,</u> the program computes their average risk aversions and rejects the problem if the computed values are not in decreasing order or if any of them is nonpositive. The error messages that may be printed out when a set of inputs is rejected are as follows:

---

[11]For the definition of average risk aversion, see Section 3.1.2 above.

1. If the average risk aversions are not all positive, <u>Sumexfit</u> prints "Inconsistent with decreasing positive risk aversion" and also prints the values of the three average risk aversions in the order in which the gambles were described.

2. If the average risk aversions are all positive but are not in decreasing order, the message printed by <u>Sumexfit</u> depends on the nature of the gambles and the order in which they were described.

a. If the gambles were described in order of increasing payoffs (possible only if none of the gambles is strictly nested within another), then nondecreasing average risk aversions prove that the user's certainty equivalents are inconsistent with decreasing risk aversion. Accordingly <u>Sumexfit</u> prints "Inconsistent with decreasing positive risk aversion" and also prints out the three risk aversions in the order in which the gambles were described, as shown in Figure 3.3A.

Figure 3.3A

<u>Gambles Inconsistent with Decreasing Risk Aversion</u>

```
ANOTHER RUN?
>YES
WILL YOU SPECIFY POINTS ON CURVE(1) OR DESCRIPTIONS OF GAMBLES(2)?
>2
X,Y,Z FOR GAMBLE 1
>0   45   100
X,Y,Z FOR GAMBLE 2
>100   140   200
X,Y,Z FOR GAMBLE 3
>200   248   300
INCONSISTENT WITH DECREASING POSITIVE RISK AVERSION.
    R1 = 0.0040269184
    R2 = 0.0082216323
    R3 = 0.0016017206
```

b. In all other cases, <u>Sumexfit</u> merely prints "Gambles not in order of decreasing risk aversion" and follows with the values of the average risk aversions, as shown in Figure 3.3B.

Figure 3.3B

<u>Gambles Submitted in Incorrect Order</u>

```
ANOTHER RUN?
>YES
WILL YOU SPECIFY POINTS ON CURVE(1) OR DESCRIPTIONS OF GAMBLES(2)?
>2
X,Y,Z FOR GAMBLE 1
>100   145   200
X,Y,Z FOR GAMBLE 2
>0   40   100
X,Y,Z FOR GAMBLE 3
>200   248   300
GAMBLES NOT IN ORDER OF DECREASING RISK AVERSION.
    R1 = 0.0040269184
    R2 = 0.0082216323
    R3 = 0.0016017206

ANOTHER RUN?
>NO
```

2. Initial Bounds. If the average risk aversions of the input gambles are all positive and decreasing, Sumexfit next tries to find initial bounds on the parameters of a sumex function which will fit these inputs. If no such bounds can be found (as can easily happen when the input gambles are nested), Sumexfit gives up the attempt to fit the function and prints out an appropriate message, as follows.

1. In all cases, Sumexfit prints "Cannot fit function to these inputs."

2. If the gambles are nonoverlapping in the sense that $x_2 \geq z_1$ and $x_3 \geq z_2$, then the fact that the average risk aversions were positive and decreasing suffices to prove that the user's certainty equivalents were consistent with decreasing positive risk aversion[12] and Sumexfit adds to the previous message "even though inputs are consistent with decreasing positive risk aversion."

3. Remaining Steps. If Sumexfit succeeds in finding initial bounds on the parameters of a function that will fit the three input gambles, it proceeds from there on in exactly the same way that it proceeds after finding initial bounds on a function that will fit inputs in the form of five points on a preference curve. See Section 3.2.2 above for the messages which may be printed out and the ways in which the output of the program can be delivered.

3.4. Evaluation of Preferences, Certainty Equivalents, and Bounds Thereon: Program Prefeval

After preference and/or bounding functions have been fitted by Piecexfit and/or Sumexfit, program Prefeval can tabulate the fitted functions or use them to compute preferences, certainty equivalents, and bounds thereon for various types of gambles. In the discussion that follows, all illustrations are based on the functions fitted to the first set of inputs in Figures 3.2A and 3.2B above.

3.4.1. Tabulation of the Functions

1. Preferences for Specified Criterion Values. When parameters computed by Piecexfit are supplied to Prefeval, the latter program can print out piecex-average preferences and bounds on preferences for any criterion values specified by the user. When parameters computed by Sumexfit are supplied, Prefeval can print out sumex preferences. If both piecex and sumex parameters are supplied, Prefeval can simultaneously tabulate the two preference functions and the bounds as shown in Figure 3.4A below. Concerning the tightness of the bounds printed out by Prefeval, see Section 3.4.3 below.

2. Criterion Values Corresponding to Specified Sumex Preferences. Program Prefeval can also tabulate the inverse of a sumex preference function — i.e., it can tabulate the criterion values which correspond under a sumex function to any preferences specified by the user. Inverse tabulation is not available for piecex preference or bounding functions.

---

[12]When input gambles overlap in the sense that $x_2 < z_1$ or $x_3 < z_2$, they may be inconsistent with decreasing positive risk aversion even though their average risk aversions are positive and decreasing. See the discussion of "improperly decreasing" average risk aversion in Section 3.1.2 above.

Decreasing Positive Risk Aversion

Figure 3.4A
Tabulation of Preferences by Program Prefeval

```
WANT PIECEX EVALUATIONS?
>YES
NAME OF FILE CONTAINING PIECEX PARAMETERS
>MALLPCX
WANT SUMEX EVALUATIONS?
>YES
NAME OF FILE CONTAINING SUMEX PARAMETERS
>MALLSMX
LIST OPTIONS?
>YES

THE FOLLOWING OPTIONS WILL BE AVAILABLE REPEATEDLY

TABULATION OF
    1   PREFERENCES FOR SPECIFIED CRITERION VALUES
    2   CRITERION VALUES WITH SPECIFIED PREFERENCES (SUMEX ONLY)
EVALUATION OF GAMBLE WHOSE PAYOFF
    3   HAS DISTRIBUTION TO BE DESCRIBED BY USER
    4   HAS DISTRIBUTION WHICH IS ON FILE
    5   IS A LINEAR FUNCTION OF A UQ WHOSE DISTRIBUTION IS ON FILE
    6   HAS CONTINUOUS GAMMA DISTRIBUTION WITH MEAN AND S.D. TO BE
        SPECIFIED BY USER (SUMEX ONLY)
OTHER OPTIONS
    8   CHANGE PREFERENCE FUNCTIONS USED IN EVALUATIONS
    9   QUIT
OPTION?
>1
ARE VALUES EQUALLY SPACED?
>YES
FIRST VALUE, STEP, LAST VALUE
>-10  5  5
         VALUE               PREFERENCE
                    L.BND     PCXAV    SUMEX    U.BND
        -10.000    0.0       0.0      0.0      0.0
         -5.000    0.2500    0.2500   0.2500   0.2500
          0.0      0.3912    0.3978   0.3997   0.4045
          5.000    0.5000    0.5000   0.5000   0.5000
MORE VALUES?
>YES
ARE VALUES EQUALLY SPACED?
>YES
FIRST VALUE, STEP, LAST VALUE
>10  10  50
         10.000    0.5676    0.5757   0.5757   0.5839
         20.000    0.6922    0.6961   0.6962   0.7000
         30.000    0.8000    0.8025   0.8018   0.8051
         40.000    0.9000    0.9037   0.9023   0.9073
         50.000    1.0000    1.0000   1.0000   1.0000
MORE VALUES?
>NO
```

3. Extrapolation of the Functions. As usual, let V_0 denote the least and V_1 the greatest of the criterion values supplied as inputs to Piecexfit and/or Sumexfit.[13]

---

[13]This definition of V_0 and V_1 applies just as well when the user supplies descriptions of three arbitrarily chosen gambles as inputs to Sumexfit as it does when he supplies the criterion values of five points on his preference curve to either Sumexfit or Piecexfit.

Program <u>Prefeval</u> does not regard the various preference and bounding functions fitted by <u>Piecexfit</u> and <u>Sumexfit</u> as defined only for arguments in the interval [V_0, V_1]. It regards all the functions except the piecex-average function as defined for all arguments in $(-\infty, \infty)$, and it regards the piecex-average function as defined for all arguments in [V_0, ∞). Preferences for arguments less than V_0 will of course be less than 0 and preferences for arguments greater than V_1 will be greater than 1; in some cases, <u>Prefeval</u> will print one of the following codes instead of an actual numerical value:

-7.7777: preference undefined
-8.8888: preference less than -8.8887 but finite
-9.9999: preference infinite negative.

An example is shown in Figure 3.4B.

Figure 3.4B
<u>Extrapolation of Preferences beyond the Range of the Assessments</u>

```
OPTION?
>1
ARE VALUES EQUALLY SPACED?
>YES
FIRST VALUE, STEP, LAST VALUE
>-40  10  -10
```

VALUE		PREFERENCE		
	L.BND	PCXAV	SUMEX	U.BND
-40.000	-9.9999	-7.7777	-8.8888	-8.8888
-30.000	-9.9999	-7.7777	-6.4711	-3.8316
-20.000	-9.9999	-7.7777	-1.3224	-1.0590
-10.000	0.0	0.0	0.0	0.0

```
MORE VALUES?
>YES
ARE VALUES EQUALLY SPACED?
>YES
FIRST VALUE, STEP, LAST VALUE
>100  200  1000
```

100.000	1.3480	1.4240	1.4587	1.5000
300.000	1.8177	2.6588	2.8895	3.5000
500.000	1.8829	3.6915	3.8410	5.5000
700.000	1.8920	4.6960	4.4738	7.5000
900.000	1.8933	5.6966	4.8946	9.5000

```
MORE VALUES?
>NO
```

It must be emphasized, however, that preferences based on extrapolation of a preference function outside the interval in which it is well tied down by the user's original numerical specifications are necessarily of very dubious meaning. Only the bounds on preferences are really valid for arguments outside [V_0, V_1], and while these bounds will sometimes show that preferences based on extrapolation to the right of V_1 are well enough defined to be worth serious consideration, they always show as they do in Figure 3.4B that preferences based on extrapolation to the left of V_0 are so poorly defined as to be worthless.

3.4.2.   *Evaluation of Gambles*

1.   Finite Gambles Described at the Terminal. Given a list of the possible payoffs of a gamble and a list of their probabilities, Prefeval will compute and print out the user's preference and certainty equivalent for the gamble under a piecex-average and/or a sumex preference function, and if supplied with piecex parameters will also compute and print out bounds on his preference and certainty equivalent for the gambles. In all cases, the value of the gamble under linear preference is printed out for comparison. An example is shown in Figure 3.4C. For the tightness of the bounds, see Section 3.4.3 below.

Figure 3.4C
Evaluation of a Finite Gamble

```
OPTION?
>3
HOW MANY PAYOFFS?
>4
LIST THEM
>-5   0   25   50
LIST PROBABILITIES
>.1   .2   .5   .2

                     PREF          CE
LOWER BOUND         0.6782        17.824
PCX AVG             0.6796        18.495
SUMEX               0.6799        18.534
UPPER BOUND         0.6809        19.054
LINEAR                            22.000
```

2.   Gambles with Filed Payoff Distributions. If the probability distribution of the payoff of a gamble has been filed by the program Disfile described in Section 1.3 or by any other Manecon program or subroutine, program Prefeval can read the distribution from the file and then provide the same evaluations that it provides for a finite gamble described by the user at the terminal. The user has only to supply the name of the file containing the distribution.

More generally, Prefeval can evaluate any gamble whose payoff is a linear function of a uq whose distribution is on file. The payoff is assumed to be of the form $a + b\tilde{x}$, where $\tilde{x}$ is the uq whose distribution is on file and a and b are constants. The user supplies the name of the file containing the distribution of $\tilde{x}$ and the values of the constants a and b, as shown in Figure 3.4D.

3.   Gambles with Payoffs Outside the Range of the Assessments. Since program Prefeval regards all functions except piecex-average preference functions as being defined for all arguments in $(-\infty, \infty)$ and regards piecex-average preference functions as defined for all arguments in $[V_0, \infty)$, the program can evaluate gambles in which some of the payoffs lie outside the interval $[V_0, V_1]$, responding in some cases with the preference codes defined in Section 3.4.1 above or with the code -7777777.777 for an undefined piecex-average certainty equivalent. An example is shown in Figure 3.4E. The user should, however, remember

Figure 3.4D

Evaluation of a Gamble Whose Payoff is a Linear Function
of a UQ Whose Distribution is on File

```
OPTION?
>5
NAME OF FILE CONTAINING DISTRIBUTION OF UQ
>GAMMAQ
SPECIFY CONSTANTS A AND B OR TYPE 9,9 FOR INSTRUCTIONS
>9,9
PROGRAM ASSUMES PAYOFF WILL BE  A + BX   WHERE X IS UQ WHOSE DISTRI-
BUTION IS ON FILE AND A AND B ARE CONSTANTS.  SPECIFY A AND B.
>-10  .01
```

	PREF	CE
LOWER BOUND	0.5567	8.234
PCX AVG	0.5621	9.032
SUMEX	0.5622	9.025
UPPER BOUND	0.5674	9.988
LINEAR		10.409

Figure 3.4E

Finite Gamble with Payoffs Outside the Range of the Assessments

```
OPTION?
>3
HOW MANY PAYOFFS?
>4
LIST THEM
>-15  0  25  50
LIST PROBABILITIES
>.1  .2  .5  .2
```

	PREF	CE
LOWER BOUND	-9.9999	-15.000
PCX AVG	-7.7777	-7777777.777
SUMEX	0.6096	12.585
UPPER BOUND	0.6155	13.727
LINEAR		21.000

the warning in Section 3.4.1 concerning the meaningfulness of results based on extrapolation of preference functions, particularly extrapolation to the left of V_0.

    4. Gamma Gambles (sumex only). The one case in which extrapolation of a preference function may really be justified is in evaluation of gambles in which the payoff is assumed to have a continuous distribution which assigns no probability to V's less than V_0 and assigns only very small probability to V's greater than V_1. It follows from what has already been said that Prefeval can evaluate a gamble whose payoff has a distribution of this sort which has previously been grouped and filed. In addition, Prefeval can provide a sumex (but not a piecex)

51

evaluation of a gamble whose payoff has a gamma distribution which extends from V_0 to infinity and has a mean and standard deviation specified by the user at the terminal.[14]

The mean of a gamma distribution of this sort must of course be greater than V_0 and the standard deviation must be greater than 0. If the standard deviation S is reasonably small relative to the difference between V_0 and the mean M — if $S < (M - V_0)/3$, say — the shape of the gamma distribution is nearly Gaussian. As S becomes larger with $(M - V_0)$ fixed, the distribution becomes more skewed, with the long tail to the right; when S is equal to or greater than $M - V_0$, the distribution is J-shaped.

Examples of the evaluation of gamma gambles are shown in Figure 3.4F.

Figure 3.4F
Evaluation of Gamma Gambles

```
OPTION?
>6
MEAN AND S.D. OF PAYOFF
>10   5
SUMEX EVALUATION
PREF =      0.5698
CE   =      9.568
RP   =      0.432

OPTION?
>6
MEAN AND S.D. OF PAYOFF
>10   20
SUMEX EVALUATION
PREF =      0.4940
CE   =      4.650
RP   =      5.350

OPTION?
>9
```

3.4.3.   Tightness of the Bounds on Preferences and Certainty Equivalents

1. Bounds on Preferences for Criterion Values. Although neither of the bounding functions constructed by program Piecexfit is itself a preference function with decreasing positive risk aversion, those functions nevertheless bound the region in which any such function must lie, and the bounds they supply are "tight" in the following sense. Given any arbitrarily chosen criterion value V ,

---

[14]The gamma distribution evaluated by program Prefeval has exactly the same shape as the gamma distribution which can be evaluated under constant proportional risk aversion by program Conaverse and which is called a gamma-q distribution with parameter q = 1 in Section 1.1.4; but whereas this latter distribution extends over [0, ∞), the gamma distribution evaluated by Prefeval is shifted laterally so that it extends over [V_0, ∞).

it is possible to construct a preference function with decreasing positive risk aversion which passes through the user's five input points and which also virtually agrees with either the lower or the upper bound on preference for the given V. In other words, a preference function with decreasing positive risk aversion can be constructed through the user's five input points and one additional point if and only if the additional point lies between the two bounding functions.

It is only in very special cases, however, that the bounds on preferences for a number of different criterion values are "jointly tight" in the sense that it is possible to construct a single preference function with decreasing positive risk aversion which passes through the five input points and also virtually agrees with either the lower or the upper bounds on preferences for all the values in question. To describe these special cases, we first agree to say that a criterion value lies within the "generalized interval" I_1 if it lies within any one of the intervals $(-\infty, V_0]$, $[V_{.25}, V_{.5}]$, or $[V_{.75}, V_1]$; and similarly we agree to say that a criterion value lies with the generalized interval I_2 if it lies within any one of the intervals $[V_0, V_{.25}]$, $[V_{.5}, V_{.75}]$, or $[V_1, \infty)$. In other words, we define

$$I_1 = (-\infty, V_0] \cup [V_{.25}, V_{.5}] \cup [V_{.75}, V_1],$$
$$I_2 = [V_0, V_{.25}] \cup [V_{.5}, V_{.75}] \cup [V_1, \infty).$$

We can now say that the bounds on a preference for a number of criterion values are jointly tight if and only if one of the two following conditions is satisfied:

    a. All the criterion values lie within I_1;

    b. All the criterion values lie within I_2.

2. **Bounds on Preference for a Finite Gamble.** Program <u>Prefeval</u> computes a lower bound on preference for a finite gamble by simply taking the expectation of the lower bounds on preferences for the individual payoffs, and similarly for the upper bound. It follows that the bounds on preference for a gamble are tight only if the payoffs or criterion values meet one or the other of the two conditions stated at the end of the last paragraph above.

3. **Bounds on the Certainty Equivalent for a Finite Gamble.** The way in which <u>Prefeval</u> computes bounds on the certainty equivalent for a finite gamble is described in Section 11.2.2 below. The bounds are tight only under one or the other of the two following conditions, where I_1 and I_2 denote the generalized intervals defined in paragraph 1 above.

    a. All payoff V's are in I_1 but the bound on the certainty equivalent is in I_2;

    b. All payoff V's are in I_2 but the bound on the certainty equivalent is in I_1.

CHAPTER 4

Posterior and Preposterior Analysis: Programs Postdis, Betadif, Truchance, Valinfo, and Opsama

In the present chapter we describe the Manecon programs that are of use in analyzing problems involving information that has been or may be obtained from a sample or an experiment.

1. Program Postdis can compute the distribution that should be assigned to the fraction of successes in a population or to the average of the values of the individual members of a population after observing a sample taken from the population by equiprobable sampling.

2. Program Betadif can compute the distribution that should be assigned to the difference between the fractions of successes in two populations after observing samples from the two populations which are large enough to overwhelm the decision maker's prior judgments about the difference.

3. Program Truchance can compute the distribution that should be assigned by a decision maker to the bias or systematic error in chances quoted by an expert when the decision maker knows (1) the chance previously quoted by the expert for each of a number of events, and (2) whether or not each of these events actually occurred. From this distribution of the bias the program can then compute the probability that the decision maker should assign to any still uncertain event for which the expert has quoted the chance of occurrence.

4. Program Valinfo can compute the expected value of perfect information (ADU 14.2.2) concerning any uq in any two-action problem where revenue is linear in the uq. The program will also compute the expected net gain of sampling (ADU 14.1.10) if (1) the uq is a fraction of successes, (2) the sampling is equiprobable, and (3) total revenue will be linear in the uq, the sample size, and the number of successes in the sample.

5. In any problem where Valinfo can compute the expected net gain of specified sample sizes, program Opsama can very rapidly find either the optimal sample size or an approximation thereto.

In this chapter we shall usually talk only about sampling from a finite population, but the reader should remember that anything that is true of equiprobable sampling with replacement from a finite population of successes and failures is equally true of sampling from a Bernoulli process (ADU 11.4).

54

Posterior and Preposterior Analysis

Contents of Chapter 4

1. Posterior Distribution of a Population Fraction or Average: Program Postdis   56

    1. Capabilities; 2. Required Inputs; 3. Output; 4. Equiprobable Posterior Bracket Medians.

2. Posterior Distribution of the Difference between Two Population Fractions: Program Betadif   59

3. Calibration of Chances Quoted by an Expert: Program Truchance   60

    1. Assessment of Probabilities Based on Chances Quoted by Experts;
    2. Ratio of True to Quoted Odds: the Model Assumed by Program Truchance;
    3. Prior Distribution of the True/Quote Ratio; 4. Inputs Required by Truchance; 5. Importance of the Prior Distribution.

4. Value of Perfect Information and Net Gain of Sampling: Program Valinfo   70

    1. Capabilities; 2. Prior Distribution; 3. Revenue Coefficients; 4. Sample Run.

5. Optimal Sample Size: Program Opsama   74

    1. Capabilities; 2. Specification of the Type of Problem and Number of Units Involved; 3. Economics of Sampling and Terminal Action; 4. Nature of the Basic UQ; Sampling Distributions; 5. Prior Distribution of the Basic UQ;
    6. Output of the Program; 7. Running Time.

4.1   Posterior Distribution of a Population Fraction or Average: **Program Postdis**

4.1.1.   Capabilities

Program <u>Postdis</u> can compute the distribution that should be assigned to a uq posterior to sampling in any situation where (1) the uq of interest is either the fraction of successes in a population or the average of the values of the individual members of the population, and (2) a sample has been taken from the population by equiprobable sampling. The program will calculate the posterior distribution on the assumption that the sampling was with replacement, but even if there was no replacement the calculation will yield an excellent approximation provided that the sample size is small relative to the size of the population (ADU 11.5.1). Assuming replacement, the method of calculation is exact in the case when the uq of interest is a population fraction of successes, but when the uq is a population average the calculations are based on "large-sample theory" and consequently are valid only when the sample size is "large" and the decision maker's prior information about the population variance is negligible relative to the information about this variance that is contained in the sample (ADU 12.3.4).

4.1.2.   Required Inputs

The decision maker's prior distribution of the uq of interest must be filed before program <u>Postdis</u> is run; it may be filed by program <u>Disfile</u> (above, Section 1.3) or by any other Manecon program or subroutine, including <u>Postdis</u> itself. The prior distribution may be discrete, grouped, or mixed. Grouping may be either equiprobable or equal-width; the latter usually yields better results. The number of brackets plus the number of uq values with discrete probabilities must not exceed 1025; the detailed printout described in Section 4.1.3 below is available only if this sum does not exceed 585.[1] There is usually no need for more than 100 brackets except in cases where the sample size is so large that the posterior distribution will be very much tighter than the prior distribution.

When <u>Postdis</u> is run, it will first ask the user whether the uq of interest is a fraction (of successes in some population) or an average (of the values of the individual members of some population). If the uq is a fraction of successes, <u>Postdis</u> will next ask for the sample size and number of successes in the sample. If the uq is an average of individual values, <u>Postdis</u> will ask for the sample size and then will allow the user to specify either (1) the values of the individual members of the sample, or (2) the average and the variance of these values.

4.1.3.   Output

The output of program <u>Postdis</u> is of either or both of two types, at the user's option.

---

[1] These limits are respectively 1/4 and 1/7 of the number 4100 which appears as the dimension of S and the value of NDIM at the start of program <u>Postdis</u>.

1. Postdis will print the complete mass function of the posterior distribution together with all the details of its computation in the form of a worksheet like ADU Table 10.6 (page 408) or Table 12.5 (page 490).

2. Postdis will write the posterior distribution on a file which can be read by any Manecon program or subroutine. In particular, program Fdispri can read the file and provide the various forms of description of the posterior distribution that were described in Section 1.4 above.

Two sample runs of Postdis are shown in Figures 4.1A and 4.1B. In Figure 4.1A, the uq is the fraction $\tilde{p}$ of successes in a population and the prior distribution is of the mixed type, with probability .4 assigned to the discrete value $\tilde{p} = 0$ and with the remaining probability distributed smoothly (but not uniformly) over the interval [0, 1] and then grouped into 10 equiprobable brackets. In Figure 4.1B, the uq is the average $\tilde{A}$ of the values of the individual members of

Figure 4.1A
Computation of Posterior Distribution of Population Fraction

```
NAME OF FILE CONTAINING PRIOR DISTRIBUTION
>ROBPRIOR
IS UQ FRACTION(1) OR AVERAGE(2)?
>1
SAMPLE SIZE N AND NUMBER OF SUCCESSES R
>10   0
PRINT DETAILS OF COMPUTATION?
>YES
```

VALUE	PRIOR	COND	JOINT	POST
0.0	.4000	1.0000	.39999992	.7721
0.1200	.0600	0.2785	.01671006	.0323
0.1310	.0600	0.2456	.01473496	.0284
0.1370	.0600	0.2291	.01374865	.0265
0.1420	.0600	0.2162	.01297260	.0250
0.1460	.0600	0.2063	.01238029	.0239
0.1510	.0600	0.1946	.01167426	.0225
0.1580	.0600	0.1791	.01074661	.0207
0.1660	.0600	0.1628	.00976817	.0189
0.1770	.0600	0.1426	.00855364	.0165
0.1960	.0600	0.1129	.00677192	.0131
	1.0000		.51806098	1.0000

```
PRINT SUMMARY STATISTICS?
>YES

MEAN      =    0.034
STD DEV   =    0.063
VARIANCE  =    0.391E-02

UNCONDITIONAL P(R =   0) = .518

FILE POSTERIOR DISTRIBUTION?
>YES
FILED DISTRIBUTION WILL BE REGROUPED INTO BRACKETS OF EQUAL
PROBABILITY WITH SUMMARY STATISTICS

MEAN      =    0.033
STD DEV   =    0.062
VARIANCE  =    0.390E-02

NAME FOR OUTPUT FILE
>ROBPOST
ANOTHER SAMPLE OUTCOME?
>NO
```

a population and the prior distribution is a lognormal distribution grouped into 100 brackets. The prior and posterior distributions of this latter example are described by program <u>Fdispri</u> in Figures 4.1C and 4.1D.

Figure 4.1B

<u>Computation of Posterior Distribution of Population Average</u>

```
ANOTHER PRIOR DISTRIBUTION?
>YES

NAME OF FILE CONTAINING PRIOR DISTRIBUTION
>LNRPRIOR
IS UQ FRACTION(1) OR AVERAGE(2)?
>2
SAMPLE SIZE
>25
WILL YOU SPECIFY INDIVIDUAL SAMPLE VALUES(1)
OR SUMMARY STATISTICS(2)?
>1
LIST THEM
>33 369 84 151 905 610 27 150 201 117 102 33 105 101 63 198 238 38
>108 1 228 1 69 315 225

SAMPLE STATISTICS
    AVERAGE  = 0.178880E 03
    VARIANCE = 0.395136E 05

PRINT DETAILS OF COMPUTATION?
>NO
PRINT SUMMARY STATISTICS?
>NO
FILE POSTERIOR DISTRIBUTION?
>YES
NAME FOR OUTPUT FILE
>LNRPOST
ANOTHER SAMPLE OUTCOME?
>NO
ANOTHER PRIOR DISTRIBUTION?
>NO
```

Figure 4.1C

<u>Prior Distribution of Population Average</u>

```
NAME OF FILE CONTAINING DISTRIBUTION
>LNRPRIOR
LIST PRINTOUT OPTIONS?
>NO
OPTION?
>1

MEAN     =    101.186
STD DEV  =     50.999
VARIANCE =      0.260E 04
FRACTILES
 .001    .01    .1    .25    .5    .75    .9    .99   .999
  198    287   484   650   901  1250  1678  2861  4183
       UQ VALUES JUST ABOVE ARE TO BE MULTIPLIED BY 10E-1

OPTION?
>9
```

Figure 4.1D
Posterior Distribution of Population Average

```
ANOTHER DISTRIBUTION?
>YES

NAME OF FILE CONTAINING DISTRIBUTION
>LNRPOST
OPTION?
>1

MEAN      =    148.679
STD DEV   =     37.139
VARIANCE  =      0.138E 04
FRACTILES
 .001    .01    .1    .25    .5    .75    .9    .99    .999
  269    669   1013  1227  1476  1733  1971  2435   4062
        UQ VALUES JUST ABOVE ARE TO BE MULTIPLIED BY 10E-1

OPTION?
>9
ANOTHER DISTRIBUTION?
>NO
```

4.1.4. *Equiprobable Posterior Bracket Medians*

When the prior distribution supplied to Postdis involves grouping into brackets of equal probability, Postdis first computes a set of unequal posterior probabilities for the prior bracket medians, as shown in Figure 4.1A above. If, however, Postdis is then asked to file the posterior distribution, it does not file the prior bracket medians and their unequal posterior probabilities. Instead, it uses these values and probabilities to compute a continuous approximation to the true posterior distribution of the uq and then computes and files a set of bracket medians which are equiprobable under this continuous approximation.

The bracket medians filed in the example of Figure 4.1A above are shown in Figure 4.1E below, which was produced by program Fdispri. Observe that the continuous distribution filed by Postdis and described by Fdispri has a cumulative function which rises from 0 to 1 even though the total posterior probability distributed by this distribution is only .2279, the other .7721 having been assigned to the discrete value $\widetilde{p} = 0$. As explained in Section 1.3.3 above, the continuous or grouped part of a mixed distribution is described by the conditional distribution that should be assigned to the uq given that the uq does not have any of the discrete values to which individual probabilities are assigned.

4.2. Posterior Distribution of the Difference Between Two Population Fractions: Program Betadif

Let $\widetilde{p}_1$ be the fraction of members of population 1 who possess some particular attribute; let $\widetilde{p}_2$ be the fraction of members of population 2 who possess this attribute; and suppose that a decision maker wishes to assess the distribution he should assign to the difference $\widetilde{d} = \widetilde{p}_1 - \widetilde{p}_2$ posterior to drawing and inspecting a

Figure 4.1E
Equiprobable Posterior Bracket Medians

```
NAME OF FILE CONTAINING DISTRIBUTION
>ROBPOST
PRINT SUMMARY STATISTICS OF COMPLETE DISTRIBUTION?
>NO
LIST DISCRETE PART OF DISTRIBUTION?
>NO
DESCRIBE GROUPED PART OF DISTRIBUTION?
>YES
LIST PRINTOUT OPTIONS?
>NO
OPTION?
>6

           PRINTED UQ VALUES ARE TO BE MULTIPLIED BY 10E-4
                VMIN = 1000              VMAX = 2250
 VALUE  PROB   VALUE  PROB   VALUE  PROB   VALUE  PROB   VALUE  PROB
  1141  .050    1333  .250    1425  .450    1512  .650    1690  .850
  1265  .150    1381  .350    1462  .550    1587  .750    1898  .950

OPTION?
>9
ANOTHER DISTRIBUTION?
>NO
```

sample from each of the two populations. Under conditions which are usually satisfied when the two samples are reasonably large, the distribution of $\tilde{d}$ can be computed by program Betadif; the conditions are stated explicitly in ADU 15.1.3.

If we let n_1 and n_2 denote the sizes of the samples from the two populations and let r_1 and r_2 denote the numbers of successes in the two samples, the inputs required by Betadif are the four quantities or parameters

$$B_1 = r_1 + 1 \ , \qquad\qquad C_1 = n_1 + 2 \ ,$$
$$B_2 = r_2 + 1 \ , \qquad\qquad C_2 = n_2 + 2 \ .$$

After computing the posterior distribution of $\tilde{d} = \tilde{p}_1 - \tilde{p}_2$, Betadif offers the various forms of tabular and graphic description of the distribution that are offered by program Fdispri; cf. Section 1.4 above.

A sample run of program Betadif is shown as Figure 4.2A, where the inputs are those of ADU Figure 15.3 (page 608).

4.3. Calibration of Chances Quoted by an Expert: Program Truchance

4.3.1. *Assessment of Probabilities Based on Chances Quoted by Experts*

Under conditions to be specified later, program Truchance can be used by a decision maker to assess his probability for the truth of the proposition that a

Figure 4.2A
Distribution of the Difference between the Fractions
of Successes in Two Populations

```
PARAMETERS B1, C1, B2, C2
>5   12   4   17

P(P1 < P2) = .144

WANT FURTHER DESCRIPTION OF THE DISTRIBUTION OF D = P1-P2 ?
>YES
LIST PRINTOUT OPTIONS?
>NO
OPTION?
>1

MEAN       =       0.181
STD DEV    =       0.169
VARIANCE   =       0.287E-01
FRACTILES
  .001     .01    .1     .25    .5    .75    .9    .99    .999
 -3322   -2102  -368   657   1813  2977  4008  5656   6693
         UQ VALUES JUST ABOVE ARE TO BE MULTIPLIED BY 10E-4

OPTION?
>9
ANOTHER RUN?
>NO
```

certain event will occur (or has occurred) in a situation of the sort discussed in ADU 6.3.10-6.3.11 — namely, a situation where:

1. The decision maker's only substantial information bearing on the truth of the proposition is the statement of an expert that there is some specific chance q that the proposition is true; and
2. The decision maker has recorded (a) the chances previously quoted by this same expert for the truth of a number of similar propositions, and (b) the truth or falsity of each of these propositions as demonstrated subsequently.

Since by hypothesis the decision maker has no substantial information bearing directly on the chance that the event in which he is interested will occur, his assessment problem is really one of properly taking account of all the available information bearing on the bias that may be present in the chances quoted by his expert. Because this evidence consists not only of the expert's historical record but also of whatever "subjective" evidence the decision maker may have concerning the expert outside of this record, the decision maker may conclude that he can best take account of all the relevant evidence by proceeding as follows.

1. The decision maker selects some simple "model" of the relation between the true chance (cf. ADU 6.3.9) of any event and the chance that the expert would quote for that event.

For example, the decision maker might select a model which asserts that the true chance of any fairly unlikely but seriously unpleasant event is only some fixed but unknown fraction $\tilde{F}$ of the chance the expert quotes or would quote for that event.

2. Using all the "subjective" evidence that is available to him outside of the historical record, the decision maker assesses his "prior" distribution of the parameter(s) of the model.

In the one-parameter model suggested above by way of example, the decision maker would assess his distribution of the uncertain ratio $\tilde{F}$ of the true chance of any event to the chance quoted by the expert.

3. Straightforward arithmetic is used to compute the revised or "posterior" distribution which the decision maker is logically obliged to assign to the parameter(s) in order to take account of both the subjective evidence expressed by the prior distribution and the objective data in the historical record.

The logic underlying these computations will be identical to the logic underlying the computations of posterior distributions that are discussed in ADU Chapters 10 and 12.

4. The posterior distribution of the parameter(s) having been found, straightforward arithmetic is again used to compute the probability that the decision maker is now logically obliged to assign to any still uncertain event for which his expert has quoted the chance of occurrence.

This probability is simply the expectation of the uncertain true chance of the event (cf. ADU 11.4.5). Under the model we have been using as an example, where the true chance is $\tilde{F}$ times the chance quoted by the expert, the expected true chance would be the quoted chance multiplied by the mean of the posterior distribution of $\tilde{F}$.

4.3.2. *Ratio of True to Quoted Odds: the Model Assumed by Program Truchance*

If a decision maker feels certain that the true chance of any event of a certain sort cannot be greater than the chance which a particular expert would quote for that event, a model which asserts that the true chance is some fixed fraction $\tilde{F}$ of the quoted chance may express his beliefs quite well. If, however, he believes that the true chance may possibly be greater than the quoted chance, so that $\tilde{F}$ may be greater than 1, then this model may fail because it may imply that the true chance of some event can be greater than 1.

To eliminate the possibility of failures of this kind, the model assumed in program Truchance is expressed in terms of the "odds" in favor of an event rather than the chance of an event. If the chance that an event will occur is 3/5, so that the chance that it will not occur is 2/5, then by definition the odds in favor of the event are 3 to 2 in ordinary English or 3/2 in mathematical language. In general, if the chance of an event is c , the odds in favor of the event are $o = c/(1 - c)$. Observe that whereas the chance of an event must lie between 0 and 1, the odds in favor of an event may be anywhere between 0 and infinity.

Program Truchance can be used to solve an assessment problem of the kind defined in Section 4.3.1 above when the decision maker feels that the true odds in favor of any event of a particular kind are (practically speaking) a fixed though unknown fraction of the odds which a particular expert would quote for that same event. To say the same thing in other words, let the subscripts t and q respectively denote true and quoted chances or odds, and define the "true/quote ratio" or "T/Q ratio" for any event to be

$$R = \frac{o_t}{o_q} = \frac{c_t/(1 - c_t)}{c_q/(1 - c_q)} \ .$$

The model used in program Truchance assumes that the T/Q ratio R is some fixed though unknown number, the same for all events in the historical record as it is for the event for which the decision maker now wishes to assess his probability.[2] When supplied with the prior distribution of $\widetilde{R}$ and the data in the historical record, Truchance will calculate the posterior distribution of $\widetilde{R}$ which is correct on the basis of this model and will then use this distribution to calculate the probability that the decision maker should assign to any still uncertain event for which his expert has quoted the chance of occurrence.

4.3.3. *Prior Distribution of the True/Quote Ratio*

To be acceptable to program Truchance, the decision maker's prior distribution of the T/Q ratio $\widetilde{R}$ must be purely continuous[3] — it must not assign individual probabilities to any discrete values of $\widetilde{R}$.

If the prior distribution of $\widetilde{R}$ is uniform — i.e., if it assigns equal probabilities to all values of $\widetilde{R}$ in some finite interval — the user can supply the distribution to Truchance directly, by merely stating the least and greatest possible values of $\widetilde{R}$. If the prior is not uniform, then before running Truchance the user must call on program Disfile (above, Section 1.3.1) to group the distribution into brackets of equal width (not equal probability) and write it on a file from which it can be read by Truchance. The continuous distribution which is grouped and filed by Disfile may be either (1) a piecewise quadratic

---

[2] A more sophisticated model would assert that the ratio R is composed of two parts, a fixed element or "bias" that is the same on each occasion on which the expert quotes a chance, and a "random" element which is generated by some random process and varies from one occasion to the next. Such a model was not used in program Truchance because it obliges the user not only to assess a prior distribution of the fixed element but also to assess a prior distribution of the parameters of the process which generates the random element.

[3] For the meaning of "continuous", see the note at the beginning of Chapter 1.

distribution fitted to points on the user's graph of the cumulative function, or (2) a member of any of the families discussed in Sections 1.1.3 and 1.1.4 — namely, the beta, bounded lognormal, lognormal, logstudent, and gamma-q families. It may be grouped into as many as 1000 brackets,[4] but 100 brackets will be adequate in almost all cases.

4.3.4. Inputs Required by Truchance

The first question asked by program <u>Truchance</u> is whether the user's prior distribution of the T/Q ratio $\tilde{R}$ is uniform or on file. If it is uniform, the program next asks for the minumum and maximum values of the ratio; if it is on file, the program asks for the name of the file.

The next questions asked by <u>Truchance</u> concern the historical record of chances quoted for previous events and occurrences or nonoccurrences of those events. To make clear the meanings of these questions, we shall apply them to the example defined by Table 4.3A. The decision maker wishes to assess his probability for event X on the basis of a statement by an expert that the chance of this event is .10. The expert has previously quoted chances for 10 similar events A to J, and for 9 of these 10 events it is now known either that the event in fact occurred or that the event failed to occur; it is still uncertain whether the event H will or will not occur.

Table 4.3A
<u>Record of Events and Chances Quoted by an Expert</u>

Event	Quoted Chance	Subsequent Fact
<u>Past Occasions</u>		
A	.05	failed to occur
B	.10	failed to occur
C	.10	failed to occur
D	.20	failed to occur
E	.05	failed to occur
F	.05	occurred
G	.01	failed to occur
H	.02	as yet unresolved
I	.10	failed to occur
J	.10	failed to occur
<u>Present Occasion</u>		
X	.10	as yet unresolved

---

[4] The limit is set by the dimension assigned to TQMASS, TQCUM, and SAMLIK and by the value assigned to NDIM at the start of program <u>Truchance</u>.

The questions which <u>Truchance</u> asks about the historical record and the answers which should be given in the example we are discussing are shown in Figure 4.3A, where two points deserve special attention.

1. Because it is not yet known whether event H will occur, that event provides no information about the expert's bias in quoting chances and must therefore be excluded from the historical record. With this event excluded, the <u>different</u> chances the expert has quoted in the past are .01, .05, .10, and .20; and accordingly the user answers 4 when the program asks how many different chances have been quoted prior to now.

2. The event X for which the decision maker now wishes to assess his probability similarly provides no information about the expert's bias, and therefore it is not counted among the number of times that the expert has quoted a chance of .10.

Figure 4.3A

Calibration of Quoted Chances

```
IS PRIOR DISTRIBUTION OF T/Q RATIO ON FILE(1) OR UNIFORM(2)?
>2
MINIMUM AND MAXIMUM VALUES OF RATIO
>.1  2.0
ARE OBSERVATIONAL DATA ON FILE?
>NO
NUMBER OF DIFFERENT CHANCES QUOTED PRIOR TO NOW
>4
LIST THEM
>.01  .05  .10  .20
NUMBER OF TIMES CHANCE WAS QUOTED AS .010 AND NUMBER OF TIMES EVENT
ACTUALLY OCCURRED THEREAFTER
>1  0
SAME FOR QUOTE OF .050
>3  1
SAME FOR QUOTE OF .100
>4  0
SAME FOR QUOTE OF .200
>1  0
FILE THESE DATA?
>YES
FILENAME
>TQDATA
DESCRIBE POSTERIOR DISTRIBUTION OF T/Q RATIO?
>NO
COMPUTE PROBABILITY OF UNCERTAIN EVENT?
>YES
QUOTED CHANCE THEREOF
>.1
PROBABILITY = .112

ANOTHER EVENT?
>YES
QUOTED CHANCE THEREOF
>.02
PROBABILITY = .023

ANOTHER EVENT?
>NO
ANOTHER RUN?
>NO
```

4.3.5. *Importance of the Prior Distribution*

When there is a great deal of frequency evidence on the value of a uq, it often happens that the mass or density function of the decision maker's prior distribution of the uq is "nearly uniform relative to the sample likelihood function" (ADU 11.2.7); and when this is true, the posterior distribution that would result from the decision maker's true prior distribution is almost identical to the posterior distribution that would result from a strictly uniform prior distribution. The decision maker is then justified in adopting a posterior distribution computed from a uniform prior, thus sparing himself the trouble of actually assessing his true prior.

Because it is so convenient to assume that use of a uniform prior is legitimate, the assumption is likely to be made without checking its validity. The assumption is very likely to be false, however, in problems of the kind now under discussion. Whenever the frequency data bear on events all of which have a very small chance of occurring, it takes a very great number of observations to constitute any substantial amount of evidence. If there are only 10 or 20 observations in the record, they may well constitute so little evidence that the sample likelihood function is actually less tight than the mass or density function of the decision maker's true prior distribution; and if this is so, then the posterior that results from a uniform prior will be nothing like the posterior that would result from the decision maker's true prior.

The best way of testing whether it is necessary to assess and use a true prior distribution is to look at a graph of the likelihood function over the relevant range of values of the T/Q ratio. If, for example, the decision maker feels that there is really no chance whatever that the T/Q ratio is less than .1 or greater than 2, he can obtain a graph of the likelihood function over the interval [.1, 2] by making a preliminary run of Truchance in which he pretends that his prior distribution is uniform over [.1, 2] and asks the program to print out a graph of the corresponding posterior mass function, which is identical to the likelihood function over [.1, 2] except for a vertical scale factor that does not appear in the printout (cf. ADU 11.1.1). If after inspecting this graph, the decision maker feels that any prior distribution he could reasonably assess would be nearly uniform relative to the likelihood function over the relevant range, then he can accept this tentative posterior distribution as definitive and avoid the trouble of assessing his true prior distribution. If, on the contrary, he feels that his true prior would be as tight as or tighter than the likelihood function, then he must actually assess his true prior and make a new run of Truchance to obtain his true posterior.

A graph of the sort just described is shown for our example in Figure 4.3B, and and from the graph it is clear that the decision maker of our example would almost certainly be obliged to assess and use his true prior. The likelihood function is so nearly uniform that instead of being much less tight than the likelihood function, almost any reasonable prior distribution would actually be tighter than the likelihood function. Instead of being overwhelmed by the frequency evidence, the prior evidence could easily overwhelm the frequency evidence. Figure 4.3C shows a lognormal prior distribution that a decision maker might reasonably have assessed if he believed that his expert tended to be somewhat pessimistic; Figure 4.3D shows the posterior distribution that results from combining this prior with the data that underlie Figure 4.3B; and the posterior distribution is obviously almost identical to the prior.

Figure 4.3B
Graph of Likelihood Function

```
IS PRIOR DISTRIBUTION OF T/Q RATIO ON FILE(1) OR UNIFORM(2)?
>2
MINIMUM AND MAXIMUM VALUES OF RATIO
>.1  2.0
ARE OBSERVATIONAL DATA ON FILE?
>YES
FILENAME
>TQDATA
DESCRIBE POSTERIOR DISTRIBUTION OF T/Q RATIO?
>YES
LIST PRINTOUT OPTIONS?
>NO
OPTION?
>4

VALUES ON UQ AXIS ARE TO BE MULTIPLIED BY 10E-1
   0*
    *
    -      *
    -     *
   2-    *
    -     *
    -      *
    -      *
   4-      *
    -      *
    -       *
    -       *
   6-       *
    -        *
    -        *
    -         *
   8-         *
    -         *
    -          *
    -          *
  10-          *
    -          *
    -          *
    -           *
  12-           *
    -           *
    -           *
    -           *
  14-           *
    -           *
    -           *
    -           *
  16-           *
    -           *
    -          *
    -          *
  18-          *
    -          *
    -          *
    -          *
  20-          *

OPTION?
>9

COMPUTE PROBABILITY OF UNCERTAIN EVENT?
>NO
ANOTHER RUN?
>NO
```

Figure 4.3C
Lognormal Prior Distribution of the T/Q Ratio
as Described by Program Fdispri
(Mean = .75, Standard Deviation = .20)

```
NAME OF FILE CONTAINING DISTRIBUTION
>TQPRIOR
LIST PRINTOUT OPTIONS?
>NO
OPTION?
>4

VALUES ON UO AXIS ARE TO BE MULTIPLIED BY 10E-1
    3*
     -*
     -   *
    4-      *
     -         *
     -             *
    5-                *
     -                   *
     -                      *
    6-                         *
     -                           *
     -                            *
    7-                             *
     -                             *
     -                            *
    8-                          *
     -                       *
     -                    *
    9-                 *
     -              *
     -           *
   10-         *
     -       *
     -      *
   11-    *
     -     *
     -   *
   12- *
     -  *
     -  *
   13- *
     -  *
     -*
   14-*
     -*
     -*
   15*
     *
     *
   16*
     *
     *
   17*
```

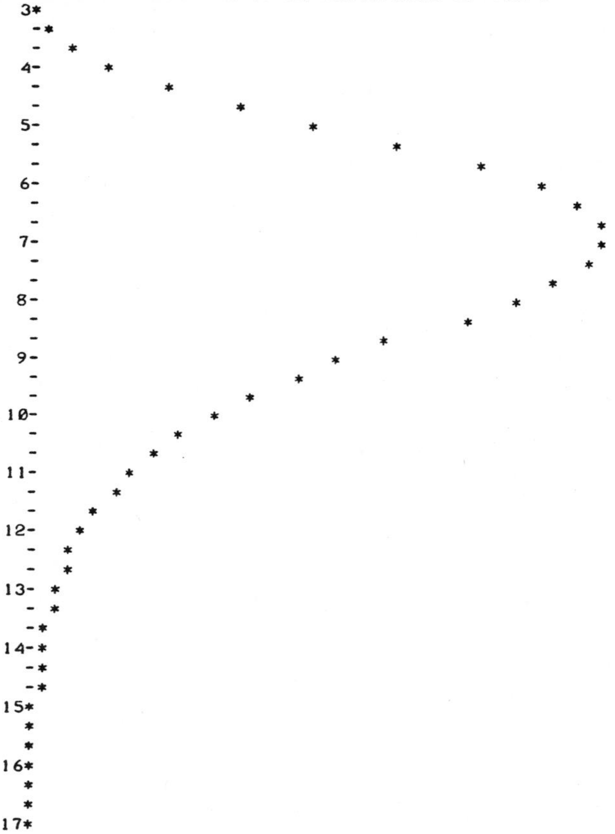

Figure 4.3D
Posterior Distribution of the T/Q Ratio
Computed from the Prior Distribution of Figure 4.3C

```
IS PRIOR DISTRIBUTION OF T/Q RATIO ON FILE(1) OR UNIFORM(2)?
>1
FILENAME
>TQPRIOR
ARE OBSERVATIONAL DATA ON FILE?
>YES
FILENAME
>TQDATA
DESCRIBE POSTERIOR DISTRIBUTION OF T/Q RATIO?
>YES
LIST PRINTOUT OPTIONS?
>NO
OPTION?
>4

VALUES ON UQ AXIS ARE TO BE MULTIPLIED BY 10E-1
    3*
    -*
    - *
    4-    *
    -       *
    -         *
    5-          *
    -             *
    -               *
    6-                *
    -                  *
    -                    *
    7-                     *
    -                      *
    -                     *
    8-                   *
    -                  *
    -                *
    9-              *
    -            *
    -          *
   10-        *
    -       *
    -      *
   11-    *
    -    *
    -   *
   12-   *
    -    *
    -  *
   13- *
    -  *
    -  *
  14-*
    -*
    -*
   15-*
    *
    *
   16*
    *
    *
   17*
```

(continued)

Figure 4.3D
(continued)

```
OPTION?
>9

COMPUTE PROBABILITY OF UNCERTAIN EVENT?
>YES
QUOTED CHANCE THEREOF
>.1
PROBABILITY = .078

ANOTHER EVENT?
>YES
QUOTED CHANCE THEREOF
>.02
PROBABILITY = .015
```

4.4. Value of Perfect Information and Net Gain of Sampling: Program Valinfo

4.4.1.   Capabilities

Program Valinfo will compute the expected value of perfect information or EVPI (ADU Section 14.2.2) in a broad class of problems of choice between two acts, and it will compute the expected net gain of sampling or ENGS (ADU Section 14.1.10) in most of these problems when the uq on which consequences depend is the fraction of successes that would be generated by some process or that is contained in some population.

To be more specific about the problems that can be analyzed by Valinfo, we first define

$\tilde{v}$: The "basic" uq on which the revenue that will result from either of the two possible acts depends;

and when $\tilde{v}$ represents the fraction of successes that is contained in a population or would be generated by a Bernoulli process we further define:

n: size of a proposed sample,

$\tilde{r}$: the uncertain number of successes in the sample.

We can now say that:

1. Valinfo can compute EVPI in any two-action problem in which the revenue that would result from either act is linear in the basic uq $\tilde{v}$.
2. Valinfo can compute ENGS in any two-action problem in which (1) the basic uq $\tilde{v}$ is an uncertain fraction of successes, and (2) the total revenue that will result from sampling and then taking either act is linear in $\tilde{v}$, n, and $\tilde{r}$.

The computation of ENGS assumes that the sampling distribution of $\tilde{r}$ is binomial and hence is exact when the sample is to be drawn from a Bernoulli process (ADU 11.4.1) or drawn by equiprobable sampling with replacement from a finite

population. When the sample is to be drawn from a finite population by equiprobable
sampling without replacement, the computation yields an excellent approximation
provided that the size of the sample is small relative to the size of the population
(ADU 11.5.1).

4.4.2. Prior Distribution

The prior distribution of the uq $\tilde{v}$ may be any discrete, grouped, or mixed
distribution which has been filed by program Disfile or any other Manecon program
or subroutine. Grouping may be either equiprobable or equal-width; the latter
usually yields better results. The number of brackets may be as great as 1000,[5]
but 100 brackets are adequate in almost all cases. The number of uq values with
discrete probabilities may be as great as 25.[6]

4.4.3. Revenue Coefficients

When program Valinfo is run, it will ask the user to describe the economics
of the problem to be analyzed by supplying certain coefficients from which it can
compute the revenue (not the cost) that will result from either act given any set
of events that may occur in the problem. When only EVPI is to be computed, the
user must supply the four coefficients A_f, A_v, B_f, and B_v which are implicitly
defined by the revenue formulas at the end positions of Figure 4.4A. (Figure
4.4A is a diagram for computing the EVASROPI or expected value of action subsequent to receipt of perfect information; the EVPI is equal to the EVASROPI less

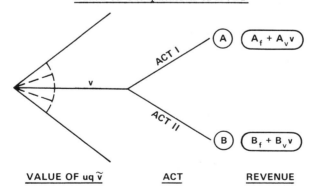

Figure 4.4A
Diagram for Computation of EVASROPI
Prior to Computation of EVPI

---

[5] The limit on the number of brackets is set by the dimension assigned to GDIS,
ALGP, and ALGQ and by the value assigned to NBMX at the start of program
Valinfo.
[6] The limit on the number of discrete values is set by the dimension assigned to
DVAL and DPRB and by the value assigned to NDMX at the start of program Valinfo.

the expected revenue of the optimal terminal act without sampling.[7]) It is assumed that the revenue from act I will consist of a certain fixed amount A_f plus a "variable" amount $A_v v$ which is proportional to the value v of the uq $\tilde{v}$, and similarly for act II. Each of the four coefficients may be positive, zero, or negative.

When ENGS is to be computed, the user must supply not only the same four revenue coefficients that are required for computation of EVPI but also eight additional coefficients implicitly defined by the revenue formulas at end positions C and D in Figure 4.4B. It is assumed that if act I is chosen after a sample has been taken, the total revenue will consist of a fixed amount C_f plus an amount $C_v v$ proportional to v plus an amount $C_n n$ proportional to the sample size n plus an amount $C_r r$ proportional to the number r of successes in the sample; and similarly for act II. Again, each of the coefficients may be positive, zero, or negative.

Figure 4.4B

Diagram for Computation of Expected Revenue with Optimal Sampling

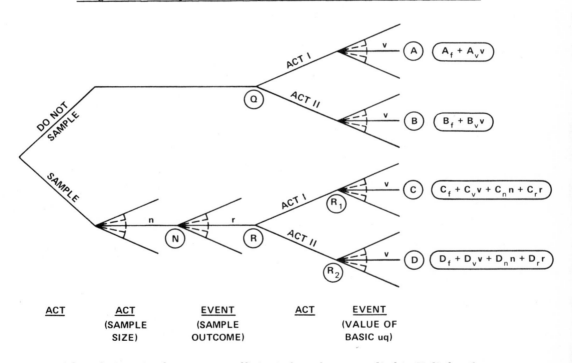

After the required revenue coefficients have been supplied to <u>Valinfo</u>, the program will at the user's option write them on a file from which they can be read by <u>Valinfo</u> if the user decides to make a new run of the program after the current run is terminated.

---

[7] Cf. ADU 14.2, where essentially the same calculations are carried out in terms of cost rather than revenue.

4.4.4. Sample Run

A sample run of <u>Valinfo</u> is shown in Figure 4.4C, where the values of the revenue coefficients are taken from Figure 14.1 on page 572 of ADU with signs reversed so as to give revenue rather than cost:

Revenue without sampling:

$$\text{act I: } -205 + \quad 0 \times p$$

$$\text{II: } \quad 0 - 800 \times p$$

Revenue including sampling:

$$\text{act I: } -205 + \quad 0 \times p + 0 \times n + 0 \times r$$

$$\text{II: } - \quad 5 + 800 \times p - 1 \times n + 4 \times r$$

Another run is shown in Figure 4.4D, where the revenue coefficients are read from the file written on the previous run.

<u>Figure 4.4C</u>
<u>Computation of EVPI and ENGS;</u>
<u>Revenue Coefficients Supplied from the Terminal</u>

```
COMPUTE EVPI?
>YES
COMPUTE ENGS?
 (AVAILABLE ONLY IF SAMPLING IS BINOMIAL)
>YES
HAVE REVENUE COEFFICIENTS BEEN FILED?
>NO
SPECIFY COEFFICIENTS AT
POSITION A (AF,AV)
>-205  0
POSITION B (BF,BV)
>0  -800
POSITION C (CF,CV,CN,CR)
>-205  0  0  0
POSITION D (DF,DV,DN,DR)
>-5  -800  -1  4
FILE COEFFICIENTS?
>YES
FILENAME
>ADU572
NAME OF FILE CONTAINING PRIOR DISTRIBUTION
>ADU409

NO-SAMPLE V =     -160.79
EVASROPI    =     -128.64
EVPI        =       32.15

HOW MANY SAMPLE SIZES?
>5
LIST THEM
>1  2  3  4  5
N =    1   ENGS =     4.01
N =    2   ENGS =     4.49
N =    3   ENGS =     8.79
N =    4   ENGS =    11.52
N =    5   ENGS =    12.12
```

(continued)

<u>Figure 4.4C (continued)</u>

```
MORE SAMPLE SIZES?
>YES
HOW MANY?
>5
LIST THEM
>10   15   20   25   30
N =   10    ENGS =      15.42
N =   15    ENGS =      16.16
N =   20    ENGS =      15.54
N =   25    ENGS =      14.71
N =   30    ENGS =      13.58

MORE SAMPLE SIZES?
>NO
ANOTHER PROBLEM?
>NO
```

<u>Figure 4.4D</u>
Computation of ENGS;
<u>Revenue Coefficients Read from a File</u>

```
COMPUTE EVPI?
>NO
COMPUTE ENGS?
 (AVAILABLE ONLY IF SAMPLING IS BINOMIAL)
>YES
HAVE REVENUE COEFFICIENTS BEEN FILED?
>YES
FILENAME
>ADU572
NAME OF FILE CONTAINING PRIOR DISTRIBUTION
>ADU409
HOW MANY SAMPLE SIZES?
>9
LIST THEM
>11   12   13   14   15   16   17   18   19
N =   11    ENGS =      15.89
N =   12    ENGS =      15.90
N =   13    ENGS =      15.69
N =   14    ENGS =      16.08
N =   15    ENGS =      16.16
N =   16    ENGS =      15.96
N =   17    ENGS =      15.84
N =   18    ENGS =      15.92
N =   19    ENGS =      15.82

MORE SAMPLE SIZES?
>NO
ANOTHER PROBLEM?
>NO
```

4.5. Optimal Sample Size: Program Opsama

4.5.1. *Capabilities*

Program <u>Opsama</u> can find an optimal or near–optimal sample size very rapidly and economically in almost any problem for which the program <u>Valinfo</u> discussed in the previous section can compute the ENGS of specified sample sizes. In terms of applications rather than decision diagrams, program <u>Opsama</u> can be used in any decision problem where:

1. The decision maker must ultimately choose one or the other of just two possible terminal acts.
2. The profit or cost of at least one of these acts will depend on the unknown number of successes that are contained in some population or that will be generated by some process.
3. Whether or not any sample units from this population or process have already been drawn and observed, at most one (additional) sample can now be drawn before choosing a terminal act.
4. The profits or costs of sampling and of both terminal acts are linear in all relevant variables.
5. If the sample is drawn from a finite population, the sampling will be equiprobable <u>without</u> replacement (ADU 11.5.1); if it is drawn from a process, the process can be regarded as a Bernoulli process (ADU 11.4.1).

Problems having these characteristics typically arise when a decision must be made whether or not to:

1. Produce a certain number of pieces by a certain process when there is uncertainty about the process fraction defective. The problem may specify either the total number of pieces to be produced or the number of pieces to be produced in addition to the sample pieces, if any.
2. Reject (screen) a lot of manufactured pieces when there is uncertainty about either the fraction of pieces in the lot that are defective or the process fraction defective of the process that produced the lot.
3. Administer a certain treatment to all members of a certain population when there is uncertainty about either the fraction of all members that are in need of treatment or the chance that any particular member is in need of treatment.
4. Administer a certain treatment (offer a certain product) to all members of a certain population when there is uncertainty about either the fraction of all members who will respond favorably or the chance that any particular member will respond favorably.

Program <u>Opsama</u> can find a strictly optimal sample size only if the user's uncertainties about the fraction of successes or the chance of a success can be expressed by a prior distribution of an appropriate mathematical type, to be discussed in Section 4.5.5 below. As will be explained in that section, however, the prior distribution will ordinarily be of virtually the required type if any substantial number of sample units have already been drawn and observed; and even when the prior distribution is not of the required type, a nearly optimal sample size can usually be obtained by substituting for the true prior distribution a distribution of the required type that has the same mean and standard deviation.

4.5.2. *Specification of the Type of Problem and Number of Units Involved*

1. <u>Finite Population or Infinite Process</u>. In all problems which can be analyzed by program <u>Opsama</u>, the user of the program is thought of as wanting to decide how many "sample units" to inspect before choosing between two "terminal acts" which will affect a number of "terminal units".

In some problems — e.g., a problem of deciding whether or not to readjust a machine before making a production run — the decision maker can produce any number of sample units he pleases before producing a predetermined number of terminal units. Such problems will be said to involve an "infinite process".

In other problems — e.g., a problem of deciding whether or not to offer a product to a certain group of potential purchasers — the total number of units available for use as sample and/or terminal units is predetermined and out of the decision maker's control. Such problems will be said to involve a "finite population".

    2. <u>Number of Terminal Units to be Generated by an Infinite Process</u>. If the user's problem involves an infinite process, meaning that any units taken as a sample will be produced <u>in addition</u> to a fixed number of terminal units, <u>Opsama</u> will ask the user to state how many terminal units will be affected by his terminal act.

    3. <u>Population Size and Number of Terminal Units in Problems Involving</u> <u>a Finite Population</u>. If the user's problem involves a finite population, meaning that the <u>total</u> number of units available for use as sample and/or terminal units is fixed, <u>Opsama</u> will ask the user to specify this total number of units in the population[8] and to state whether or not the terminal act will affect the units used as a sample, if any.[9]

4.5.3. *Economics of Sampling and Terminal Action*

Two conditions concerning the economics of sampling and terminal action must be met if a problem is to be analyzed by program <u>Opsama</u>. In stating these conditions, we shall use the word "now" to denote the time at which the analysis is made; "past" and "future" are defined relative to "now".

    1. <u>Terminal Economics.</u> The <u>revenue</u> (positive or negative) that will result from choice of terminal act a_i ($i = 1, 2$) must be expressible in the form

$$V_t(a_i, n_t, r_t) = \begin{cases} 0 & \text{if } n_t = 0 \\ F_i + A_i n_t + B_i r_t & \text{if } n_t > 0 \end{cases} \quad i = 1, 2,$$

where F_i, A_i, and B_i are constants each of which may be positive, zero, or negative, n_t is the number of units not already inspected in the past that will be sub-

---

[8] If any units have <u>already</u> been drawn from the population as a "pilot sample", these units should be excluded in computing the number of units <u>now</u> in the population.
[9] In most situations, sample units drawn from a finite population are not later subjected to the chosen terminal act. This is the case, for example, when sample units drawn from a population are "treated" in the course of sampling inspection, will not be treated again if the chosen terminal act is to treat the remainder of the population, and will not be "detreated" if the chosen terminal act is not to treat the remainder of the population. In some situations, however, sample units are later subjected to the chosen terminal act, exactly like units not included in the sample. This is the case, for example, when sampling inspection consists in merely asking each member of the sample whether he would buy a product if it were offered for sale, and the terminal act will result in either actually offering or not offering the product for sale to all members of the population, those who were included as well as those who were not included in the sample.

jected to the chosen terminal act, and r_t is the number of successes among these n_t units.[10]

2. Sampling Economics. The <u>revenue</u> (positive or negative) that will result from future sampling prior to choice of a terminal act must be expressible in the form

$$V_s(n_s, r_s) = \begin{cases} 0 & \text{if } n_s = 0 , \\ F_s + A_s n_s + B_s r_s & \text{if } n_s > 0 , \end{cases}$$

where F_s, A_s, and B_s are constants, n_s is the number of sample units inspected in the future, and r_s is the number of successes among these n_s units. The coefficients F_s and A_s will usually be negative, representing respectively the fixed cost associated with taking a sample of any size and the incremental cost per unit in the sample; the coefficient B_s may be either negative (e.g., if the defectives in a sample are reworked at a cost regardless of the choice of terminal act), zero, or positive (e.g., if a sample mailing of a catalog results in orders from customers that give rise to a profit regardless of the choice of terminal act).

4.5.4. *Nature of the Basic UQ; Sampling Distributions*

When the problem analyzed by <u>Opsama</u> involves an infinite process which will generate some as yet undetermined total number of sample and terminal units, the program assumes that each unit generated by the process has the same fixed though unknown chance p of being a success, regardless of the pattern of successes or failures among units previously generated by the process. In this case the sampling distribution of $\tilde{r}_s$ given p is binomial.

When the problem analyzed by <u>Opsama</u> involves a finite population of fixed size N , the program allows the user to formulate the problem in either of two ways. (1) The user may formulate the problem in terms of the fraction $\tilde{f}$ of successes among the members actually in the population, in which case the sampling distribution of $\tilde{r}_s$ given f is hypergeometric. (2) Alternatively, the user may regard each member of the population as independently having the same fixed chance p of being a success and may formulate the problem in terms of this chance, in which case the sampling distribution of $\tilde{r}_s$ given p is binomial.

4.5.5. *Prior Distribution of the Basic UQ*

1. Assumptions Concerning the Type of Prior Distribution. The computational methods used in program <u>Opsama</u> are based on the assumption that:

1. If the problem is expressed in terms of an unknown chance $\tilde{p}$, so that sampling is binomial, the prior distribution assigned to $\tilde{p}$ will be a beta distribution.

---

[10]If sample units already inspected in the past will be subjected to the chosen terminal act, the revenue that will result from subjecting them to terminal act a_i must be included in the fixed revenue F_i, since these units and the successes among them are not counted in n_t and r_t.

2. If the problem is expressed in terms of an unknown fraction $\tilde{f}$, so that sampling is hypergeometric, the prior distribution assigned to $\tilde{f}$ will be a hyperbinomial distribution.[11]

The user may specify a particular distribution of either type by specifying either the values of two parameters or the mean and standard deviation.

2. Specification of Parameters. If a number of sample units have already been drawn and observed in the past, and if the user feels that any other information he may have about the value of $\tilde{p}$ or $\tilde{f}$ is negligible by comparison with the information contained in these sample observations, then it can usually be shown that (1) the user's prior distribution of $\tilde{p}$ or $\tilde{f}$ should logically be of the type assumed by Opsama, and (2) that the parameters B and C of this distribution should logically have nearly if not exactly the values

C = number of units already observed + 2,
B = number of successes among these units + 1.

The specific conditions under which this proposition is true for a beta distribution of $\tilde{p}$ are stated in ADU 11.2.7, and exactly the same conditions apply to a hyperbinomial distribution of $\tilde{f}$.

3. Specification of Mean and Standard Deviation. When the conditions of the previous section do not obtain, the user's prior distribution of $\tilde{p}$ or $\tilde{f}$ may or may not be of the form required for exact analysis by program Opsama. If, however, his objective is simply to obtain a near-optimal sample size for practical use, he will rarely go far wrong if he pays no attention to the exact form of prior distribution that will be assumed by the program and specifies merely that this distribution shall have a mean and standard deviation equal to the mean and standard deviation of his true prior distribution of $\tilde{p}$ or $\tilde{f}$. Many numerical examples indicate that a sample size which is optimal under one prior distribution will be nearly optimal — i.e., will have nearly the greatest achievable net gain — under another prior distribution having the same mean and standard deviation, even though the shapes of the two distributions are substantially different.[12] The only important exception discovered to date is the case where the true prior distribution assigns a really substantial probability mass to $\tilde{p}$ or $\tilde{f} = 0$ or 1.

---

[11] For mathematical definitions of beta and hyperbinomial distributions and their parameters, see Section 16.1.1.

[12] Observe that it is not asserted that if distributions A and B have the same mean and standard deviation, the sample size which is optimal under A will differ very little from the sample size which is optimal under B; the optimal sample sizes as such may differ substantially. Nor is it asserted that the net gain of any sample size as computed under one distribution will be nearly equal to the net gain of that same sample size as computed under another distribution; these figures also may differ substantially. What is asserted is that the net gain under B of the sample size which is optimal under A will be very nearly equal to the net gain under B of the sample size which is optimal under B.

4.5.6.   *Output of the Program*

Given the input data required to define a problem meeting the conditions discussed above, program <u>Opsama</u> first identifies the optimal sample size and prints it out together with (1) the proper critical number[13] for a sample of that size, and (2) information about the revenue and ENGS to be expected with a sample of that size. The program then offers to print out the proper critical number and ENGS for any sample sizes specified by the user.

A sample run of program <u>Opsama</u> is shown in Figure 4.5A, where the inputs are those of ADU Figure 14.11 (page 585).

4.5.7.   *Running Time*

<u>Opsama</u> finds the optimal sample size by successively computing expected total revenue with sample sizes $n = 1, 2, 3, \ldots$ up to some n which it can prove to be greater than the optimal n. The computation proceeds very rapidly, however, because the successive sample sizes are evaluated recursively. On the CDC-3600, for example, 1000 successive sample sizes are evaluated in a little less than .8 seconds of CPU time.

---

[13]The critical number is the number c which appears in a decision rule of the form "select act I if the number of successes in the sample exceeds c, otherwise select act II."

Figure 4.5A
Sample Run of Program Opsama

```
FINITE POPULATION(1) OR INFINITE PROCESS(2)?
>1
SIZE OF POPULATION
>200
DESCRIBED BY FRACTION OF SUCCESSES(1) OR CHANCE OF SUCCESS(2)?
>1
WILL YOU SPECIFY PARAMETERS(1) OR MOMENTS(2) OF PRIOR?
>2
MEAN AND STANDARD DEVIATION
>.2010  .1491
WILL TERMINAL ACT AFFECT SAMPLE UNITS?
>NO
REVENUE (FIXED, PER UNIT, PER SUCCESS) FROM
SAMPLING
>-5  -1  0
TERMINAL ACT 1
>0  -1  0
TERMINAL ACT 2
>0  0  -4

OPTIMAL SAMPLE SIZE IS   13.
SELECT ACT 1 IF SUCCESSES EXCEED      3.
W/O SAMPLING, ACT 2 IS OPTIMAL.

SAMPLE-STAGE REVENUE =    -18.00
TERMINAL-STAGE   "   =   -127.08
TOTAL REVENUE        =   -145.08
REVENUE W/O SAMPLING =   -160.80
NET GAIN OF SAMPLING =     15.72

PRINT ENGS OF SELECTED SAMPLE SIZES?
>YES
FIRST SIZE, STEP, LAST SIZE
>1  5  31

     N      C     ENGS
     1      0      4.11
     6      1     12.75
    11      3     14.91
    16      4     15.71
    21      5     15.28
    26      6     14.31
    31      8     13.13
MORE SAMPLE SIZES?
>YES
FIRST SIZE, STEP, LAST SIZE
>11  1  15

     N      C     ENGS
    11      3     14.91
    12      3     15.52
    13      3     15.72
    14      3     15.60
    15      4     15.45
MORE SAMPLE SIZES?
>NO

ANOTHER RUN?
>NO
```

CHAPTER 5

Computations Involving Probability Distributions Grouped into Brackets of Equal Probability

The present chapter and the next three have two main purposes. They describe the various Manecon subprograms that are intended to facilitate numerical analysis of decision problems, and in addition they contain advice to beginners on Fortran programming of the computations most frequently required in such analysis. The present chapter deals with computations involving distributions grouped into brackets of equal probability (ADU 7.4.4-7.4.6), or EP distributions for short. Chapter 6 deals with computations involving distributions grouped into brackets of equal width (ADU 7.4.3), or EW distributions for short. Chapter 7 deals with computations involving mathematically continuous probability distributions and piecex and sumex preference functions. Chapter 8 contains brief summary descriptions of the subprograms whose use is discussed in the preceding chapters and some other subprograms not intended for use by beginners.

Many of the problems that even a beginning programmer will want to analyze will require reading of probability distributions or preference parameters from files and may require writing of computed distributions on files. As will appear in what follows, there are Manecon subprograms which permit the programmer to carry out these operations very easily, and if these are the only file operations in his program, he will have no need to know about opening and closing of files and "unit" or "data-set" numbers. If the programmer does open other files on his own, he must take care that the data-set number that will automatically be used by a Manecon file-reading or writing subroutine is not already in use when the subroutine is called.[1]

Computation based on grouping into brackets of equal probability is discussed before computation based on grouping into brackets of equal width simply because the former is easier for beginners. Which method of grouping is actually better in any particular application will usually depend on several factors of which the following are perhaps the most important.

---

[1]All Manecon subroutines use the same data-set number; what this number is on a particular system can be learned from the listing of any one of the subroutines that read or write files.

1. Computation of the expectation of a function of one or more uq's is always much faster when based on EP grouping but often more accurate when based on EW grouping.

2. Convolution based on EW grouping is both the most accurate and the fastest way of computing the distributions of many functions of two or more uq's.

3. EP grouping greatly facilitates calculations based on random sampling (the "Monte Carlo" method of computation).

The methods of computation and interpolation used by the subprograms discussed in the present chapter are described in Section 10.1 below.

Contents of Chapter 5

1. Input and Storage of EP Distributions   84

   1. Description of EP distributions; 2. Input of EP distributions.

2. Probabilities, Fractiles, and Mean and Variance   85

   1. Cumulative Probabilities and Fractiles; 2. Probabilities of Individual
   Values of a UQ; 3. Mean and Variance.

3. Expectation of a Function of a Single UQ   87

   1. Method of Computation; 2. Separately Defined Functions; 3. Expected
   Preference.

4. Distribution of a Function of a Single UQ   89

   1. Partially Constant Functions; 2. Computation by use of Subroutine Epfdis;
   3. Shortcuts for Monotone Functions; 4. Filing of Distributions; 5. Printed
   Description of Distributions.

5. Expectation of a Function of Two or More UQ's   95

   1. Computation by Evaluation of All End Positions; 2. Shortcut Evaluation
   of Expectations of Sums and Products; 3. Evaluation via Computation of
   Intermediate Distributions; 4. Reduction of the Number of End Positions.

6. Distribution of a Function of Two or More UQ's   100

   1. Functions of Two UQ's; 2. Functions of More than Two UQ's; 3. Printed
   Description of Computed Distributions.

7. Random Sampling of End Positions   103

   1. Justification for Random Sampling; 2. Equiprobable Sampling with
   Replacement; 3. Computation of the Expectation of a Function; 4. Computation of the Distribution of a Function; 5. Measurement of the Risk of Error;
   6. Control of the Risk of Error in a Computed Expectation; 7. Control of
   the Risk of Error in a Computed Distribution.

5.1. Input and Storage of EP Distributions

5.1.1. Description of EP Distributions

If an EP distribution is to be processed by any of the subprograms in the Manecon collection, the programmer must provide for storing the description of the distribution in the form of the following numbers or values:

1. The least and greatest possible values of the uq, or two values which are to be treated as if they were the least and greatest possible values;
2. A set of (equiprobable) bracket medians of the distribution of the uq;
3. The number of bracket medians in this set.

The bracket medians must be stored in positions 1, 2, 3, ... of an array or "vector". The number of bracket medians must be stored as an integer, all other values as real (floating-point) numbers.

For example, the EP distribution of a uq $\tilde{x}$ might be described by storing

```
XMIN = 0.
XMAX = 1000.
XBRMD(1) = 31.7
XBRMD(2) = 55.3
XBRMD(3) = 74.6
.....
XBRMD(64) = 963.1
NXBRAK = 64
```

Notice the implicit typing of the various variables as real or integer, and recall that if 64 bracket medians are to be stored in the vector XBRMD the program must contain a dimension statement which assigns at least 64 storage locations to XBRMD.

The reader should note the mnemonic scheme used in describing the EP distribution of $\tilde{x}$ in the example above. In later examples, the same mnemonics will be used with other letters in place of X to describe the distributions of uq's other than $\tilde{x}$.

5.1.2. Input of EP Distributions

A programmer will ordinarily have no need to concern himself with the actual computation of the various values which define an EP distribution of a "basic" uq—i. e., one whose distribution is directly supplied by the user of his program. He can simply call the Manecon subroutine Gdread to read in the distribution from a file on which the user has caused it to be written by the program Disfile described in Section 1.3 above or by some other Manecon program or subroutine.

For example, suppose that a programmer wishes to read in an EP distribution of a uq which he will think of as $\tilde{x}$ although the user thinks of it as "demand", and suppose that he believes that the distribution filed by the user will have no more than 100 bracket medians. He can get the distribution from the file by writing

```
DIMENSION XBRMD(100)
NXBRMX = 100
.....
.....
WRITE(n,31)
31 FORMAT(52H TYPE NAME OF FILE CONTAINING DISTRIBUTION OF DEMAND)
CALL GDREAD(1, NXBRMX, XMIN, XMAX, XBRMD, NXBRAK, IERROR)
```

The following points require attention.

1. When Gdread is called, it prints a ready signal at the terminal and then waits for the user to supply the name of the file to be read. If the programmer wants an explanatory message like the one in statement 31 above to be printed out before the ready signal is printed, he must make provision for the message in his own main program.

2. The letter n in the WRITE statement is to be replaced by the integer that represents output to the terminal on the particular system being used.

3. The first two arguments in the call list of Gdread contain input to the subroutine; the remainder will contain the output.

4. The integer 1 which appears as the first argument informs Gdread that the distribution to be read should have EP grouping.

5. The input NXBRMX is the number of locations that the programmer has made available for storage of bracket medians; the output NXBRAK is the number of bracket medians that Gdread actually finds in the file and stores in the first NXBRAK positions of the vector XBRMD.

6. The output IERROR is a trouble indicator. Subroutine Gdread will assign the value 0 to IERROR if it succeeds in reading an EP distribution from the file specified by the user. Otherwise, it will print out a message explaining why it failed and will assign a value greater than 0 to IERROR.

Following his call to Gdread, the programmer should include provision for handling cases where Gdread fails to read the distribution and so indicates by returning a value of IERROR greater than zero. Since the failure to read the distribution may be due merely to a typing error or a noisy telephone line, he may want to give the user a second chance to specify the file name; he can do so by simply arranging to call Gdread a second time.

5.2. Probabilities, Fractiles, and Mean and Variance

5.2.1. Cumulative Probabilities and Fractiles

Cumulative probabilities under an EP distribution stored in core can be obtained by use of the Manecon function Epcum. For example, the probability that $\tilde{x}$ is less than or equal to 117.5 under the distribution described in Section 5.1.1 above can be obtained and stored under the name PROB by writing

PROB = EPCUM(117.5, XMIN, XMAX, XBRMD, NXBRAK)

Fractiles can be obtained by use of the Manecon function Epfrc. For example, the .25 fractile of the distribution of $\tilde{x}$ can be obtained and stored under the name QUAR1 by writing

QUAR1 = EPFRC(.25, XMIN, XMAX, XBRMD, NXBRAK)

5.2.2. *Probabilities of Individual Values of a UQ*

In order to obtain the probability that a uq is exactly equal to any one of its possible values, the programmer must first obtain and store the total number of possible values from the least to the greatest possible value inclusive. He can then obtain the desired probability by use of the Manecon function Epden. For example, suppose that the total number of possible values of $\tilde{x}$ from XMIN to XMAX inclusive has been stored as a real number under the name XNPVAL, and suppose that 117.5 is one of these possible values. Then the probability that $\tilde{x}$ has the value 117.5 can be obtained and stored under the name XMASS by writing

DENS = EPDEN(117.5, XMIN, XMAX, XBRMD, NXBRAK)
XMASS = DENS*(XMAX – XMIN)/XNPVAL

The value delivered directly by the function Epden is the value of the density function which $\tilde{x}$ possesses when its distribution is thought of as continuous in the strict sense of that word.

5.2.3. *Mean and Variance*

The mean of an EP distribution (the expectation of the uq) can be obtained by use of the Manecon function Epmean. For example, the expectation of $\tilde{x}$ can be obtained and stored under the name XMEAN by writing

XMEAN = EPMEAN(XBRMD, NXBRAK)

Both the mean and the variance can be obtained by calling the Manecon subroutine Epmomt. For example, the mean and variance of $\tilde{x}$ can be obtained and stored under the names XMEAN and XVAR respectively by writing

CALL EPMOMT(XBRMD, NXBRAK, XMEAN, XVAR)

Observe that XBRMD and NXBRAK contain input to the subroutine, XMEAN and XVAR contain the output.

5.3. Expectation of a Function of a Single UQ

5.3.1. Method of Computation

If $\tilde{w}$ is a function of a uq $\tilde{x}$ which has a truly discrete distribution, the expectation of $\tilde{w}$ can be computed by multiplying the value of $\tilde{w}$ corresponding to each possible value of $\tilde{x}$ by the probability of that value of $\tilde{x}$ and adding the products (ADU 7.3.4). When the distribution of $\tilde{x}$ is not truly discrete but is represented by an EP approximation, the expectation of the function $\tilde{w}$ can be computed by treating the equiprobable bracket medians of $\tilde{x}$ as if they were the only possible values of $\tilde{x}$, each one having probability equal to 1 divided by the number of bracket medians (ADU 7.4.5). The fact that the probabilities are all the same implies, however, that it is not really necessary to multiply each individual value of $\tilde{w}$ by the probability of the corresponding value of $\tilde{x}$. The expectation of $\tilde{w}$ can be obtained more easily by simply adding the values of $\tilde{w}$ and then multiplying their sum by the probability of any one value of $\tilde{x}$. Whether this shortcut is used or not, the least and greatest possible values of $\tilde{x}$ do not enter the computation.

For example, suppose that the programmer wishes to compute the expectation of the function

$$\text{contribution} = \begin{cases} -a - bq + c\tilde{x} & \text{if } \tilde{x} \le q, \\ -a - bq + cq & \text{if } \tilde{x} > q, \end{cases}$$

and suppose that he has already stored in core not only the distribution of $\tilde{x}$ but also the values of the coefficients a, b, c, and q. He can compute the desired expectation and store it under the name EXPCON by writing

```
      SUM = 0.
      DO 29 I = 1, NXBRAK
      X = XBRMD(I)
      IF (X .GT. Q)  GOTO 26
      CON = -A - B*Q + C*X
      GOTO 27
   26 CON = -A + (C-B)*Q
   27 SUM = SUM + CON
   29 CONTINUE

      EXPCON = SUM/FLOAT(NXBRAK)
```

We leave it to the reader to devise a more efficient program in which the constants -A -B*Q and -A+(C-B)*Q are computed once and for all before the beginning of the DO loop instead of being recomputed on each iteration of the loop.

5.3.2.   *Separately Defined Functions*

In the example above, the function whose expectation was being computed was in effect defined within the DO loop that computed the successive function values CON. The programmer may, however, prefer to define the function separately, as either a "subprogram function" or an "arithmetic-statement function".

To define the function of our example by a separate subprogram, the programmer could write as follows:

```
    FUNCTION CON(X, Q, A, B, C)
    IF (X .GT.  Q)  GOTO 10
    CON = -A - B*Q + C*X
    RETURN
 10 CON = -A + (C-B)*Q
    RETURN
    END
```

Given this definition of the function, the expectation of the function could be computed in the main program by storing the values of the parameters Q, A, B, and C and then writing

```
    SUM = 0.
    DO 29 I = 1, NXBRAK
    X = XBRMD(I)
    SUM = SUM + CON(X, Q, A, B, C)
 29 CONTINUE

    EXPCON = SUM/FLOAT(NXBRAK)
```

Alternatively, the function could have been defined as an arithmetic-statement function within the main program itself by writing

```
    CON (X) = -A - B*Q + C*AMIN1 (X, Q)
```

immediately before the first executable statement in the program. Because this definition is an integral part of the main program, the parameters q, a, b, and c do not have to be passed to the function through its call list; and to agree with the fact that x is the only argument in the call list of this definition of the function, the statement just before statement 29 in the main program just above must be altered to read

```
    SUM = SUM + CON (X)
```

5.3.3. *Expected Preference*

If the criterion value that will result from a gamble is a function of some uq, then the decision maker's preference for the resulting value is a function of this uq. It follows that his (expected) preference for the gamble as a whole is simply the expectation of the preference function and can be computed in the same way that the expectation of any function is computed (cf. ADU 7.3.4).

To illustrate, suppose that in the situation of the example just discussed the programmer has defined a function PREFCN(V) which returns the decision maker's preference for any criterion value V , and suppose that the criterion value will be equal to the contribution as calculated by the arithmetic-statement function CON plus a "base value" which the programmer has stored under the name VBASE. Then the decision maker's (expected) preference for the gamble which gives rise to the uncertain contribution can be computed and stored under the name EXPREF by writing

```
    SUM = 0.
    DO 29 I = 1, NXBRAK
    X = XBRMD(I)
    V = VBASE + CON(X)
    SUM = SUM + PREFCN(V)
 29 CONTINUE

    EXPREF = SUM/FLOAT(NXBRAK)
```

If the programmer has also defined a function CEFCN(Q) which returns the criterion value or certainty equivalent corresponding to any preference or expected preference Q , he can compute the decision maker's certainty equivalent for the gamble under consideration and store it under the name CE by the one additional statement

```
    CE = CEFCN(EXPREF)
```

Piecex and Sumex Preference Functions. The Manecon collection includes subprograms which make it easy for the programmer (1) to read in the parameters of piecex or sumex preference functions that have been computed and filed by program Piecexfit or Sumexfit, and (2) to evaluate preferences and certainty equivalents under the functions defined by these parameters. These subprograms are described in Section 7.1 below.

5.4. Distribution of a Function of a Single UQ

5.4.1. *Partially Constant Functions*

In what follows we shall discuss methods for computing distributions of functions of uq's with EP distributions, but our discussion will be restricted to functions whose distributions can also be represented by EP distributions, and this means that there is one type of function that will not be covered. If a function $\widetilde{w}$ of a uq $\widetilde{x}$ is "partially constant" in the sense that $\widetilde{w}$ has exactly the same value for a substantial number of different values of $\widetilde{x}$,[2] then even though the distribution of $\widetilde{x}$ is continuous and can therefore be represented by a set of equiprobable bracket medians, the distribution of $\widetilde{w}$ will not be continuous and therefore cannot be represented by a set of equiprobable bracket medians. For example, if $\widetilde{w} = 127$ for all values of $\widetilde{x}$ greater than 432, and if the total probability of these values of $\widetilde{x}$ is .57, then the single function value $\widetilde{w} = 127$ has probability .57 and it is only the remaining .43 probability that is spread out smoothly over the remaining values of $\widetilde{w}$ and can be described by an EP distribution.[3]

5.4.2.   *Computation by use of Subroutine Epfdis*

Suppose that $\widetilde{w}$ is a function of a uq $\widetilde{x}$ which has an EP distribution. Provided only that $\widetilde{w}$ is not partially constant in the sense just defined, an EP distribution of $\widetilde{w}$ can be very easily computed by (1) computing the least and greatest possible values of $\widetilde{w}$, (2) computing the value of $\widetilde{w}$ corresponding to each bracket-median value of $\widetilde{x}$, (3) sorting these computed values into increasing order, and finally (4) interpolating among the sorted values to obtain the required bracket medians of $\widetilde{w}$. The Manecon subroutine Epfdis will carry out the last two steps in this procedure; the programmer has to take care of only the first two.

Specifically, a programmer who wishes to derive the distribution of a function $\widetilde{w}$ of a uq $\widetilde{x}$ by use of subroutine Epfdis can proceed as follows:

1. Dimension a vector in which to store the bracket medians of the function $\widetilde{w}$;
2. Dimension a scratch or working-space vector with a number of positions at least equal to twice the number of bracket medians in the EP distribution of the underlying uq $\widetilde{x}$;
3. Compute and store the least and greatest possible values of $\widetilde{w}$;
4. Compute the value of $\widetilde{w}$ that corresponds to each bracket-median value of $\widetilde{x}$ and store these values in positions 1, 2, 3, ... of the scratch vector;

---

[2] The contribution function defined in Section 5.3.1 above is such a function for many values of the parameter q .

[3] In the language of Section 1.3.3 above, a partially constant function has a "mixed" distribution and in general both the discrete and the continuous parts of this distribution must be duly represented in describing the distribution and in executing computations based on the distribution. If, however, the programmer uses EW rather than EP grouping, it is often possible to obtain reasonably accurate results by simply treating a partially constant function as if it were not partially constant; cf. Section 6.4.1 below.

5. Store in an integer variable the number of values of $\tilde{w}$ that are stored in the scratch vector, and store in another integer variable the number of bracket medians of $\tilde{w}$ that Epfdis should compute;

6. Call Epfdis.

The only part of the procedure that may be at all tricky is the computation of the least and greatest possible values of the function $\tilde{w}$.

As a first example, suppose that the programmer wishes to compute a 50-bracket EP distribution of the function $\tilde{w} = 1/\tilde{x}$; suppose that he knows that the EP distribution of $\tilde{x}$ filed by the user of his program will have no more than 100 bracket medians; and suppose that he knows that the least possible value of $\tilde{x}$ under this distribution will be greater than 0. He can accomplish his purpose by writing:

```
DIMENSION SCRTCH(200), WBRMD(50)
. . . . .
. . . . .
WMIN = 1./XMAX
WMAX = 1./XMIN

DO 55 I = 1, NXBRAK
SCRTCH(I) = 1./XBRMD(I)
55 CONTINUE

NWVAL = NXBRAK
NWBRAK = 50
CALL EPFDIS (WMIN, WMAX, SCRTCH, NWVAL, NWBRAK, WBRMD)
```

The following points should be observed.

1. The vector SCRTCH is dimensioned large enough to provide not only 100 locations for storage of the function values corresponding to the bracket medians of $\tilde{x}$ but also another 100 locations for use by Epfdis in sorting these values.

2. Because any increase in $\tilde{x}$ produces a decrease in $\tilde{w} = 1/\tilde{x}$ when all possible values of $\tilde{x}$ are positive, the greatest possible value of $\tilde{x}$ gives rise to the least possible value of $\tilde{w}$, and similarly at the other end of the range.

3. All arguments except the last in the call list of Epfdis are inputs, the last is output.

4. NWVAL tells Epfdis how many values of $\tilde{w}$ are being supplied in the vector SCRTCH; NWBRAK tells Epfdis how many bracket medians of $\tilde{w}$ to compute.

5. The NWBRAK bracket medians computed by Epfdis will be delivered in the first NWBRAK positions of the vector WBRMD.

6. After Epfdis has done its work, the working-space vector SCRTCH is free for any new use to which the programmer wishes to put it.

As a trickier example which can be omitted on a first reading, make the same assumptions as in the previous example except that the function $\tilde{w}$ whose distribution is defined by $\tilde{w} = (\tilde{x}-c)^2$, where c is some constant whose value will be supplied from the terminal by the user of the program. The distribution of $\widetilde{w}$ can be calculated as follows.

```
DIMENSION SCRTCH(200), WBRMD(50)
...
...
WMIN = 0.
IF (XMIN .GT. C)  WMIN = (XMIN - C)**2
IF (XMAX .LT. C)  WMIN = (C - XMAX)**2
WMAX = AMAX1 ((XMAX - C), (C - XMIN))
WMAX = WMAX**2

DO 65 I = 1, NXBRAK
SCRTCH(I) = (X - C)**2
65 CONTINUE

NWVAL = NXBRAK
NWBRAK = 50
CALL EPFDIS(WMIN, WMAX, SCRTCH, NWVAL, NWBRAK, WBRMD)
```

5.4.3. *Shortcuts for Monotone Functions* [4]

When a function $\widetilde{w}$ of a uq $\widetilde{x}$ is strictly monotone over the range (ADU 7.5.3) of $\widetilde{x}$, in the sense that either (a) $\widetilde{w}$ always increases when x increases, or else (b) $\widetilde{w}$ always decreases when $\widetilde{x}$ increases, the distribution of $\widetilde{w}$ can be computed more rapidly by use of the function <u>Epfrc</u> than by use of subroutine <u>Epfdis</u>. The method of computation exploits the fact that the probability that $\widetilde{w}$ is less than or equal to any particular value w is simply the total probability of all values of $\widetilde{x}$ that give rise to values of $\widetilde{w}$ less than or equal to w. In executing the computation, the programmer must remember that the i'th bracket median of any n-bracket distribution is the (i-.5)/n fractile of the distribution, not the i/n fractile.

    1. Increasing Functions. As a first example, suppose that a programmer wishes to derive a 50-bracket EP distribution of $\widetilde{w} = \widetilde{x}^3$. Because $\widetilde{w}$ increases as $\widetilde{x}$ increases, the smallest possible value of $\widetilde{w}$ is the cube of the smallest possible value of $\widetilde{x}$, the .1 fractile of the distribution of $\widetilde{w}$ is the cube of the .1 fractile of the distribution of $\widetilde{x}$, and so forth; and it follows that the programmer can obtain the required distribution as follows.

```
WMIN = XMIN**3
WMAX = XMAX**3
NWBRAK = 50
```

---

[4] This section is not required in anything that follows and may be omitted on a first reading.

```
40 DO 49 I = 1, NWBRAK
   P = (FLOAT(I) - .5)/FLOAT(NWBRAK)
   XFRCTL = EPFRC(P, XMIN, XMAX, XBRMD, NXBRAK)
   WBRMD(I) = XFRCTL**3
49 CONTINUE
```

The program would be more efficient, however, if statements 40–49 were rewritten to compute the successive P's by addition rather than division, as follows:

```
40 PINC = 1./FLOAT(NWBRAK)
   P = -.5*PINC
   DO 49 I = 1, NWBRAK
   P = P + PINC
   XFRCTL = EPFRC(P, XMIN, XMAX, XBRMD, NXBRAK)
   WBRMD(I) = XFRCTL**3
49 CONTINUE
```

If the programmer wanted exactly the same number of bracket medians of the function $\widetilde{w}$ that he actually has of $\widetilde{x}$, he would not even have to use the function <u>Epfrc</u>. Statements 40–49 in the two programs just above could be replaced by

```
40 DO 49 I = 1, NXBRAK
   XFRCTL = XBRMD(I)
   WBRMD(I) = XFRCTL**3
49 CONTINUE
```

2. <u>Decreasing Functions.</u> Suppose next, as we did in Section 5.4.2 above, that a programmer wishes to compute a 50-bracket EP distribution of the function $\widetilde{w} = 1/\widetilde{x}$, and suppose as we did there that the programmer knows that all possible values of $\widetilde{x}$ are greater than 0, so that over the range of $\widetilde{x}$ the function $\widetilde{w}$ always decreases as $\widetilde{x}$ increases. In this case, the smallest possible value of $\widetilde{w}$ will correspond to the largest rather than the smallest value of $\widetilde{x}$, the .1 fractile of $\widetilde{w}$ will correspond to the .9 fractile of $\widetilde{x}$, and so forth, and the distribution of $\widetilde{w}$ can be computed as follows:

```
   WMIN = 1./XMAX
   WMAX = 1./XMIN
   NWBRAK = 50
   PINC = 1./FLOAT(NWBRAK)

50 P = -.5*PINC
   DO 59 I = 1, NWBRAK
   P = P + PINC
   XFRCTL = EPFRC(1.-P, XMIN, XMAX, XBRMD, NXBRAK)
   WBRMD(I) = 1./XFRCTL
59 CONTINUE
```

If the programmer wanted exactly the same number of bracket medians of $\tilde{w}$ that he actually has of $\tilde{x}$, statements 50–59 could be replaced by

```
50 DO 59 I = 1, NXBRAK
   XFRCTL = XBRMD(NXBRAK + 1 - I)
   WBRMD(I) = 1./XFRCTL
59 CONTINUE
```

5.4.4. *Filing of Distributions*

After computing an EP distribution of a function, the programmer may wish to write the distribution on a file from which it can later be read in by another program. He can do so by use of the Manecon subroutine Epfile, which will write out the distribution in a form suitable for input not only to subroutine Gdread but also to various Manecon main programs which accept or require filed distributions as input, e.g., Fdispri, Postdis, Valinfo, and Prefeval. [5]

For example, suppose that the programmer wishes to write a file containing the distribution of some function $\tilde{w}$ which he has computed and stored in core. He can accomplish his purpose by writing simply:

```
   WRITE(n, 71)
71 FORMAT(51H SPECIFY NAME FOR FILE TO CONTAIN DISTRIBUTION OF W)
   CALL EPFILE(WMIN, WMAX, WBRMD, NWBRAK)
```

Epfile will call on the user at the terminal to supply a name for the file, but the only signal that Epfile will give the user is a ready signal. An explanatory message like the one in statement 71 above must be provided by the main program.

5.4.5. *Printed Description of Distributions*

By use of the Manecon subroutine Epprin, the programmer can allow the user to obtain any of the various forms of tabular or graphic description of an EP distribution that are offered by program Fdispri and are described in Section 1.4 above. The subroutine is called by a statement of the form

```
   CALL EPPRIN(WMIN, WMAX, WBRMD, NWBRAK)
```

---

[5] To satisfy the requirements of some of these latter programs, subroutine Epfile not only files the distribution itself but also computes and files the mean and variance of the distribution.

5.5. Expectation of a Function of Two or More UQ's

5.5.1. *Computation by Evaluation of All End Positions*

The expectation of a function of two or more uq's with EP distributions can in principle always be obtained by multiplying the value of the function at each end position of the joint probability diagram of the uq's by the probability of the end position and adding the products (ADU 9.4.6), or more quickly by simply adding the function values and multiplying their sum by the probability of any one end position. This probability is of course equal to 1 divided by the product of the numbers of bracket medians in the distributions of the individual uq's. [6]

1. Two Independent UQ's. When there are only two jointly distributed uq's, the method of computation described above is not only correct in principle but almost always feasible in practice. For example, suppose that a programmer wishes to compute the expectation of the function $\tilde{w} = \max\{\tilde{x}, \tilde{y}\}$ where $\tilde{x}$ and $\tilde{y}$ are independent. He can compute the expectation and store it under the name EXPW by writing

```
      SUM = 0.
   31 DO 39 I = 1, NXBRAK
      X = XBRMD(I)
      DO 38 J = 1, NYBRAK
   35 Y = YBRMD(J)

      W = AMAX1(X, Y)
      SUM = SUM + W
   38 CONTINUE
   39 CONTINUE

      EXPW = SUM/FLOAT(NXBRAK*NYBRAK)
```

If the distributions of $\tilde{x}$ and $\tilde{y}$ are grouped into 100 bracket medians, this computation will involve evaluation of the function at $100^2 = 10,000$ end positions and the cost of calculation will be reasonable on a moderately fast machine.

2. Two Interdependent UQ's. If the uq's $\tilde{x}$ and $\tilde{y}$ of the last example were interdependent rather than independent as we assumed above, computation of the expectation of the function $\tilde{w} = \max\{\tilde{x}, \tilde{y}\}$ would require use of a different conditional distribution of one of the two uq's for each bracket-median value of the other, but while this creates a serious problem for the person who has to assess

---

[6] We assume throughout that if two or more jointly distributed uq's have EP distributions, the end positions of their joint probability diagram will be equiprobable. This implies that if any uq has several different (conditional) distributions, all these distributions must be grouped into the same number of brackets, but it does not imply that distributions of two different uq's must be grouped into the same number of brackets.

the required distributions, it creates no particular problem for the programmer who wishes to use them. If the user could assess and file a different conditional distribution of $\tilde{y}$, say, for each bracket-median value of $\tilde{x}$, it might be impossible to store all of these distributions in core simultaneously, but it would be easy to arrange the computations in such a way that only one conditional distribution had to be present in core at any one time.

In fact, however, the user will virtually never be able to make a separate, direct assessment of a different conditional distribution of one uq for every bracket-median value of the other. If he cannot reformulate his problem in terms of substitute uq's which are independent, he will directly assess and file at most two or three conditional distributions and give rules for computing all other conditional distributions from these (ADU 9.7).

For example, suppose that the user files two conditional distributions of $\tilde{y}$, one of which applies if $\tilde{x}$ has its smallest possible value while the other applies if $\tilde{x}$ has its greatest possible value, and suppose that he says that any fractile of his conditional distribution for any other value of $\tilde{x}$ may be calculated by linear interpolation between the corresponding fractiles of these two distributions. If the programmer stores the two distributions of $\tilde{y}$ under names beginning with Y1 and Y2 respectively, he can compute the expectation of $\tilde{w} = \max\{\tilde{x}, \tilde{y}\}$ by a program like the last one above except that statements 31-35 are replaced by the following:

```
31 DO 39 I = 1, NXBRAK
    X = XBRMD(I)
    FACTOR = (X - XMIN)/(XMAX - XMIN)
    DO 38 J = 1, NYBRAK
35 Y = FACTOR*Y2BRMD(J) + (1.-FACTOR)*Y1BRMD(J)
```

3. More than Two UQ's. As already stated, the expectation of a function of more than two uq's with EP distributions can in principle be computed in exactly the same way that the expectation of a function of just two uq's is computed, by adding the values of the function at all end positions of the joint probability diagram and dividing by the number of end positions. For example, suppose that $\tilde{x}$, $\tilde{y}$, and $\tilde{z}$ are mutually independent. The expectation of $\tilde{w} = \max\{\tilde{x}, \tilde{y}, \tilde{z}\}$ can in principle be found by writing:

```
    SUM = 0.
    DO 99 I = 1, NXBRAK
    DO 98 J = 1, NYBRAK
    DO 97 K = 1, NZBRAK
    W = AMAX1(XBRMD(I), YBRMD(J), ZBRMD(K))
    SUM = SUM + W
97 CONTINUE
98 CONTINUE
99 CONTINUE
    EXPW = SUM/FLOAT(NXBRAK*NYBRAK*NZBRAK)
```

Before writing such a program, however, the programmer must make sure that the cost of computation will not be excessive because of the number of end positions at which the function has to be evaluated. If three uq's have 100 bracket medians each, there are $100^3 = 1$ million end positions; if five uq's have 50 bracket medians each, there are $50^5 \doteq .3$ billion end positions; and so forth.

5.5.2. Shortcut Evaluation of Expectations of Sums and Products

In many problems, exactly the same result that could be obtained by evaluating all end positions can be obtained far more cheaply by making use of one or both of the following propositions:

1. The expectation of the sum or any other <u>linear</u> function of a number of uq's can be found by substituting the (unconditional) expectation of each individual uq in the definition of the function.

2. The expectation of the <u>product</u> of a number of <u>mutually independent</u> uq's is equal to the product of their (unconditional) expectations.

Observe that although the second proposition is restricted to mutually independent uq's, the first applies to all uq's without restriction.

As an example of the use of the first proposition, suppose that a programmer wishes to compute the expectation of the function $\tilde{w} = a\tilde{x} + b\tilde{y}$ where a and b are constants. He can call the function <u>Epmean</u> (Section 5.2.3 above) to compute separately the mean $\bar{x}$ of $\tilde{x}$ and the mean $\bar{y}$ of $\tilde{y}$, after which he can compute $\bar{w} = a\bar{x} + b\bar{y}$.

As an example of the use of the second proposition, suppose that a programmer wishes to compute the expectation of the function $\tilde{w} = \tilde{x}\tilde{y}\tilde{z}$ where $\tilde{x}$, $\tilde{y}$, and $\tilde{z}$ are mutually independent. He can call <u>Epmean</u> to compute the individual expectations of $\tilde{x}$, $\tilde{y}$, and $\tilde{z}$, and he can then multiply these three expectations together to obtain the expectation of $\tilde{w}$.

As an example of the use of both propositions together, suppose that a programmer wishes to compute the expectation of the function $\tilde{w} = \tilde{x} + \tilde{y}\tilde{z}$ where $\tilde{y}$ and $\tilde{z}$ are unconditionally independent. If he defines a new uq $\tilde{v} = \tilde{y}\tilde{z}$, he can compute its expectation by use of the second proposition, and he can then compute the expectation of $\tilde{w} = \tilde{x} + \tilde{v}$ by use of the first proposition. The end result is simply $\bar{w} = \bar{x} + \overline{yz}$.

As another example of the use of an "intermediate function", suppose that a programmer wishes to compute the expectation of the function $\tilde{w} = \tilde{x}\tilde{y}/\tilde{z}$ where $\tilde{x}$, $\tilde{y}$, and $\tilde{z}$ are mutually independent. If he defines a new uq $\tilde{s} = 1/\tilde{z}$, he can easily compute the expectation of $\tilde{s}$ in the way described in Section 5.3.1 above, and then after calling <u>Epmean</u> for the expectations of $\tilde{x}$ and $\tilde{y}$ he can compute the expectation of $\tilde{w}$ by simply multiplying together the expectations of $\tilde{x}$, $\tilde{y}$, and $\tilde{s}$. Because $\tilde{z}$ is independent of $\tilde{x}$ and $\tilde{y}$, $1/\tilde{z} = \tilde{s}$ is independent of $\tilde{x}$ and $\tilde{y}$.

As a final example, suppose that a programmer wishes to compute the distribution of $\tilde{w} = \tilde{x} \log(\tilde{y} + \tilde{z})$ where $\tilde{x}$ is independent of $\tilde{y}$ and $\tilde{z}$, and suppose that the distributions of $\tilde{x}$, $\tilde{y}$, and $\tilde{z}$ are grouped into 100 brackets each. If he defines a new function of just two uq's by writing $\tilde{v} = \log(\tilde{y} + \tilde{z})$, he can evaluate its expectation by calculating its value at the 10,000 end positions of the diagram of the distribution of the two uq's $\tilde{y}$ and $\tilde{z}$, and then after calling <u>Epmean</u> for the expectation of $\tilde{x}$ he can obtain the expectation of $\tilde{w}$ by multiplying together the expectations of $\tilde{x}$ and $\tilde{v}$. He does not have to evaluate the function $\tilde{w}$ at the $10^3 = 1$ million end positions of the diagram of $\tilde{x}$, $\tilde{y}$, and $\tilde{z}$.

5.5.3. Evaluation via Computation of Intermediate Distributions

When the expectation of a function of three or more mutually independent uq's cannot be computed by computing the expectations of individual uq's or of intermediate functions of one or two uq's, it can sometimes be conveniently computed by first computing the complete distribution of some intermediate function of some or all of the uq's.

For example, suppose that a programmer wishes to compute the expectation of the function $\tilde{w} = \log(\tilde{x} + \tilde{y} + \tilde{z})$, and suppose that the distributions of $\tilde{x}$, $\tilde{y}$, and $\tilde{z}$ are grouped into 50 brackets each. If he can first compute the distribution of the intermediate function

$$\tilde{v} = \tilde{x} + \tilde{y} + \tilde{z} \ ,$$

it will then be easy to compute the expectation of $\tilde{w} = \log(\tilde{v})$; and it is shown in Section 5.6.2 below how if $\tilde{x}$, $\tilde{y}$, and $\tilde{z}$ are mutually independent he can compute the distribution of $\tilde{v}$ quite accurately by evaluating only $(3-1) \times 50^2 = 5000$ end positions of two intermediate probability diagrams even though there are $50^3 = 125,000$ end positions on the diagram of $\tilde{x}$, $\tilde{y}$, and $\tilde{z}$.

5.5.4. Reduction of the Number of End Positions

When the expectation of a function of three or more uq's cannot be evaluated by any of the shortcuts just described, either because of the nature of the function or because the uq's are not mutually independent, it may be necessary to make do with an estimate of the expectation based on evaluation of the function at only a sample of all the end positions on the joint probability diagram. This does not imply, however, that the sample must necessarily be a "random" sample. Random sampling is not the only possible kind of sampling, and in many situations it is not the best kind.

The alternative to random sampling is "systematic" or "deterministic" sampling, under which the programmer deliberately selects each end position in the sample instead of leaving the selection to chance; and it is now time to emphasize that even if we work with <u>all</u> the end positions of a probability diagram based on EP distributions of the individual uq's, we are in fact working with only a systematic sample of all the end positions on a really complete diagram of the true joint distribution of the uq's. The distribution of any uq in a really complete probability distribution would have to be represented by a fork with one branch for every possible value of the uq, and the number of end positions in such a diagram would usually be astronomical. The end positions of a diagram based on EP approximations to the distributions of the individual uq's constitute a sample which includes only those end positions on the complete diagram that correspond to the bracket-median values of the indivudual uq's.

When we use a systematic sample based on bracket medians to compute the expectation of a function of one or two uq's, we do so because such a sample is more likely than a random sample to be accurately representative of most aspects of the complete population and hence is likely to yield more accurate values for the expectations of most functions. It is only in very exceptional cases that the random error in an expectation calculated from a random sample is likely to be less than the systematic error or bias in an expectation calculated from a bracket-median sample of the same size.

As the number of uq's on which a function depends increases, there is usually an increasing chance that the random error due to a random sample will be less than the bias due to a bracket-median sample, but even so a programmer should not resort to random sampling simply because representation of the distribution of each uq by some arbitrary number of bracket medians results in a sample of end positions which is too large to evaluate. Unless the nature of the function with which he is dealing is such that an expectation calculated from a bracket-median sample would clearly be seriously biased, he should first ask whether representation of the distribution of each individual uq by a smaller but still reasonably large number of bracket medians will reduce the sample of end positions to a reasonable size.

Suppose then that the programmer does decide that the cost of computation will be nothing to worry about if each individual distribution is grouped into enough but only enough brackets to eliminate any serious doubt about the accuracy of the computed expectation. If the user has grouped his distributions into a greater number of brackets than the programmer wants, the programmer can easily regroup them into the desired number of brackets by use of the function Epfrc. If n is the required number of new bracket medians, the i'th new bracket median is the $(i - .5)/n$ fractile of the distribution defined by the old bracket medians.

For example, suppose that the programmer wants to work with a distribution of $\tilde{x}$ having just 10 bracket medians but believes that the user may file up to 1000 bracket medians. He can accomplish his purpose by writing:

```
      DIMENSION XBRMD(10), USERBM(1000)
      . . . . .
      . . . . .
      WRITE(n, 11)
   11 FORMAT(42H NAME OF FILE CONTAINING DISTRIBUTION OF X)
      CALL GDREAD(1, 1000, XMIN, XMAX, USERBM, NUSERB, IERROR)

      NXBRAK = 10
      PINC = 1./FLOAT(NXBRAK)

      P = -.5*PINC
      DO 19 I = 1, NXBRAK
      P = P + PINC
      XBRMD(I) = EPFRC(P, XMIN, XMAX, USERBM, NUSERB)
   19 CONTINUE
```

The following points should be observed.

1.   The number of bracket medians filed by the user is read and stored as NUSERB; the bracket medians themselves are read into the vector USERBM.

2.   The vector USERBM is free for another use as soon as the 10 bracket medians of $\tilde{x}$ that are wanted by the programmer have been computed and stored in the vector XBRMD.   In particular, the programmer could now read into USERBM the bracket medians of the user's distribution of some other uq; there is no need to reserve space in core for simultaneous storage of the bracket medians of the user's distributions of all the uq's involved in the problem.

5.6.   Distribution of a Function of Two or More UQ's

5.6.1.   *Functions of Two UQ's*

Provided that a function of two uq's is not partially constant in the sense that it has exactly the same value at a substantial fraction of the end positions of the joint probability diagram (cf. Section 5.4.1 above), its distribution can be found by using Epfdis in exactly the same way that Epfdis is used to obtain the distribution of a function of a single uq.   Essentially, the programmer first computes the least and greatest possible values of the function and the value of the function at every end position of the joint probability diagram of the underlying uq's.   He then calls Epfdis to sort these values into order of increasing size and compute a specified number of bracket median values by interpolation among the sorted values.

Independent uq's.   For example, suppose that a programmer wishes to derive a 40-bracket EP distribution of the function $\tilde{w} = \tilde{x}\tilde{y}$ where $\tilde{x}$ and $\tilde{y}$ are independent and necessarily positive; and suppose that the programmer knows that the distributions of $\tilde{x}$ and $\tilde{y}$ will be grouped by the user into not more than 50 brackets each.   He can accomplish his purpose by writing

```
     DIMENSION WBRMD(40), SCRTCH(5000)
     . . . . .
     . . . . .
     WMIN = XMIN*YMIN
     WMAX = XMAX*YMAX

     K = 0
  31 DO 39 I = 1, NXBRAK
     X = XBRMD(I)
     DO 38 J = 1, NYBRAK
  35 Y = YBRMD(J)

     K = K + 1
     SCRTCH(K) = X*Y
  38 CONTINUE
  39 CONTINUE
```

NWVAL = NXBRAK*NYBRAK
NWBRAK = 40
CALL EPFDIS (WMIN, WMAX, SCRTCH, NWVAL, NWBRAK, WBRMD)

The points which deserve notice are the same as in our earlier discussion of
Epfdis in Section 5.4.2:

1. The vector SCRTCH is dimensioned large enough to include not only the
$50 \times 50 = 2500$ positions which may be required to store the function values at
the end positions of the joint probability diagram but also another 2500 positions
for use by Epfdis in sorting these values.

2. All arguments except the last in the call list of Epfdis are inputs; the
last is output.

3. NWVAL tells Epfdis how many values of w are being supplied in the
vector SCRTCH; NWBRAK tells Epfdis how many bracket medians of $\tilde{w}$ to
compute.

4. The NWBRAK bracket medians computed by Epfdis will be delivered in
the first NWBRAK positions of the vector WBRMD.

5. After Epfdis has done its work, the working-space vector SCRTCH is
free for any new use to which the programmer wishes to put it.

Interdependent UQ's. If the uq's $\tilde{x}$ and $\tilde{y}$ were interdependent rather than
independent as assumed above, computation of the distribution of the function $\tilde{w}$
would require use of the appropriate conditional distribution of one of the two
underlying uq's in conjunction with each bracket-median value of the other. The
problem of assessing all these conditional distributions has already been pointed
out in paragraph 2 of Section 5.5.1, and if the assessment problem is solved in
the manner suggested there by way of example, the distribution of the function
can be obtained by a program identical to the last one above except that statements 31-35 must be altered in the same way that they were altered in paragraph 2 of Section 5.5.1.

5.6.2. *Functions of More than Two UQ's*

The distribution of a function of more than two uq's can in principle be
derived by use of Epfdis in exactly the same way that the distribution of a function
of just two uq's is derived. The programmer supplies Epfdis with the least and
greatest possible values of the function and the value of the function at every
end position of the joint probability diagram; Epfdis does the rest. In practice,
however, the amount of core required to store and sort the computed function
values will make this method infeasible for more than a very few uq's. Three
uq's with 20 bracket medians each require $2 \times 20^3 = 16,000$ locations; four uq's
with only 10 bracket medians each require $2 \times 10^4 = 20,000$ locations; five uq's
with 10 bracket medians each require 200,000 locations; and so forth.

There is no universally applicable, convenient way out of this difficulty,
but when n jointly distributed uq's are mutually independent it is very often
possible to compute the distribution of a function of these uq's in such a way that
(1) the amount of core required is no greater than the amount required in the

case of just two uq's, and (2) the amount of computation required increases linearly rather than geometrically with n . More specifically, the distribution of a function of n mutually independent uq's can often be computed by computing n – 1 distributions of functions of just two independent uq's.

For example, suppose that $\tilde{x}$, $\tilde{y}$, and $\tilde{z}$ are mutually independent; suppose that each of their distributions is described by 50 bracket medians; and suppose that a programmer wishes to compute the distribution of the function $\tilde{w} = \tilde{x}\tilde{y}\tilde{z}$. If he starts by defining a new function of just two uq's by writing $\tilde{v} = \tilde{x}\tilde{y}$, he can with the aid of subroutine Epfdis compute a distribution of $\tilde{v}$ with 50 bracket medians just as if the uq $\tilde{z}$ did not exist. Then redefining $\tilde{w}$ as a function of just two uq's by writing $\tilde{w} = \tilde{v}\tilde{z}$, he can with the aid of Epfdis obtain the distribution of $\tilde{w}$ and store it in the same locations used to store the distribution of the "intermediate" uq $\tilde{v}$. Because the computations carried out by Epfdis involve only two rather than three uq's at a time, the working space required for either computation is only $2 \times 50^2 = 5000$ core locations rather than $2 \times 50^3 = 250,000$; and the same working space used for the first computation can be reused for the second.

We remind the reader, however, that the "pairwise" method of computation that we have just described is applicable only when the jointly distributed uq's are mutually independent; and we now further observe that there are functions whose distributions cannot be computed in this way even though the jointly distributed uq's are mutually independent. For example, consider the function $\tilde{w} = \tilde{x}\tilde{y} + \tilde{y}\tilde{z} + \tilde{z}\tilde{x}$. It would be easy enough to compute the unconditional distributions of $\tilde{a} = \tilde{x}\tilde{y}$, $\tilde{b} = \tilde{y}\tilde{z}$, and $\tilde{c} = \tilde{z}\tilde{x}$, but the distribution of $\tilde{w} = \tilde{a} + \tilde{b} + \tilde{c}$ cannot be computed from these unconditional distributions because the fact that both $\tilde{a}$ and $\tilde{b}$ are functions of $\tilde{y}$ means that $\tilde{a}$ and $\tilde{b}$ are not independent, and similarly for $\tilde{b}$ and $\tilde{c}$ and for $\tilde{c}$ and $\tilde{a}$.

When the distribution of a function of several uq's cannot be computed by the method described in the present section, it will usually be necessary to resort to random sampling of end positions. A suitable procedure will be described in Section 5.7 below.

5.6.3. *Printed Description of Computed Distributions*

In Sections 5.4.4 and 5.4.5 we showed how subroutine Epfile can be used to file an EP distribution of a function and how subroutine Epprin can be used to provide printed description of such a distribution; and it obviously makes absolutely no difference in principle whether the function in question is a function of one or of many uq's.

On a small machine, however, there may be insufficient core to allow use of Epprin to describe a function of two or more uq's that has been computed by use of Epfdis, since Epprin requires a substantial amount of program space and Epfdis requires a substantial amount of scratch space when used to compute the distribution of two or more uq's. When the programmer is in fact unable to use Epprin for lack of space, he should write the computed distribution on a file. The user will then be able to obtain printed description of the distribution by use of program <u>Fdispri</u>, which will read the distribution from the file and provide the same printout options that are provided by <u>Epprin</u>.

5.7. Random Sampling of End Positions

5.7.1. Justification for Random Sampling

As we said in Section 5.5.4, all the methods that we have described above for computing either the expectation or the complete distribution of a function of several uq's are actually based on only a sample of the end positions of a really complete joint probability diagram, even though the sample in question is not a random sample but a systematic sample obtained by taking the end positions that correspond to the bracket medians of EP distributions of the individual uq's. We argued in Section 5.5.4 that a bracket-median sample of this kind is in general very likely to give more accurate results than a random sample of the same size, but we have not yet paid any real attention to the problem of deciding on the sample size. We recognized that the cost of computation could easily be excessive if the sample size were determined by grouping the distribution of each individual uq into an arbitrary number of brackets, but we considered only the case where the programmer could decide on reasonable numbers of brackets such that he had no need to worry about either the cost of computation or the risk of serious error in the results.

Such an easy solution of the sample-size problem is often possible in problems involving only a few jointly distributed uq's, but in many problems there are so many jointly distributed uq's that a decision on sample size involves a very serious problem of tradeoff between the cost of computation and the risk of error in the computed expectation. If, for example, there are 30 uq's, then even if each of their distributions were represented by only 2 bracket medians their joint probability diagram would have $2^{30} \doteq 1$ billion end positions. The cost of computing the expectation of a function by the method of Section 5.5.1 might well be considered prohibitive, and it would be flatly impossible to compute the complete distribution of a function by the method of Section 5.6.1. The number of end positions could be reduced by letting the distributions of some of the individual uq's be represented by only a single bracket median (i.e., the median of the entire distribution); but no matter how the programmer finally decided to select a bracket-median sample, he would not feel at all sure that his sample represented anything like a proper balance between cost of computation and risk of serious error in the results.

It is in such situations that random sampling of the end positions of the complete probability diagram is usually preferable to systematic sampling. Even here, the reason is not that the random sample will yield a more accurate result than a systematic sample of the same size; it is quite likely to yield a <u>less</u> accurate result. The reason is rather that whereas it is usually impossible to say anything useful about the possible error in an expectation or distribution computed from a systematic sample, the risk of error in a result computed from a random sample can be very precisely described and therefore the user can arrive at a reasonable sample size by increasing the number of end positions in his sample until a point is reached where the remaining risk of error seems too small to justify any further increase in the sample size.

5.7.2. *Equiprobable Sampling with Replacement*

The simplest form of random sampling that permits rational error control is equiprobable sampling with replacement from the end positions of a probability diagram in which each distribution of an individual uq is represented by a reasonably large set of equiprobable bracket medians,[7] and this is the only form of random sampling that will be considered in what follows. After explaining how to draw such a sample and how to use it to compute the expectation or the complete distribution of a function, we shall show how to measure the risk of error in the computed result and allow the user to continue sampling if the risk of error seems excessive.

When a sample of end positions is to be drawn by equiprobable sampling with replacement from the end positions of a probability diagram based on EP distributions of the individual uq's, the easiest way of drawing each successive end position in the sample is to use random numbers to select a path through the probability diagram. One random number is used to draw a bracket-median value from the distribution of the first uq in the diagram, a second random number is used to draw a value from the appropriate distribution of the next uq in the diagram, and so forth until an end position is reached (ADU 13.2). Ordinarily, these bracket-median values are calculated directly from the continuous distributions originally assessed by the user, without first computing and storing all of the bracket medians required to define each EP distribution (ADU 13.2.3). In some circumstances, however, it is preferable or even necessary to compute and store the bracket medians in advance,[8] and it is this latter case that is considered here.

When n bracket medians of a distribution are stored in a vector in core, one of these bracket medians can be drawn equiprobably by simply calling the Manecon function Nrandf to return a random integer between 1 and n inclusive and taking the corresponding element of the vector. If, for example, the vector XBRMD contains NXBRAK bracket medians of $\tilde{x}$, the programmer can generate a random integer I and then use it to select a random bracket median X by writing

---

[7] More precisely, the distributions of the individual uq's must be such as to guarantee that any calculation based on <u>all</u> the end positions of their joint probability diagram would result in a completely negligible error.

[8] Computation and storage of all the bracket medians in advance is more efficient when many different uq's have the same probability distribution. It may be necessary on small computers where there is insufficient core to load all the subprograms required to compute bracket medians directly from a number of different continuous distributions.

```
I = NRANDF(NXBRAK)
X = XBRMD(I)
```

Alternatively, he could write simply

```
X = XBRMD(NRANDF(NXBRAK))
```

Using random integers obtained in this way, it is easy to draw an end position by drawing a bracket median from the appropriate (unconditional or conditional) distribution of each successive uq in the probability diagram. For example, suppose that $\tilde{x}$, $\tilde{y}$, and $\tilde{z}$ are mutually independent. An end position of their joint probability diagram can be drawn by writing

```
X = XBRMD(NRANDF(NXBRAK))
Y = YBRMD(NRANDF(NYBRAK))
Z = ZBRMD(NRANDF(NZBRAK))
```

The values X, Y, and Z generated by this procedure are the values of the uq's $\tilde{x}$, $\tilde{y}$, and $\tilde{z}$ at a particular end position and determine the value of any function of $\tilde{x}$, $\tilde{y}$, and $\tilde{z}$ at that end position. A sample of 500 end positions could be drawn by simply repeating this procedure 500 times.

5.7.3. *Computation of the Expectation of a Function*

Either the expectation or the complete distribution of a function of a number of uq's is computed from a random sample of end positions in exactly the same way that it would be computed if the sample included every end position of the probability diagram. If only the expectation of the function is desired, the appropriate method of computation is the one described in Section 5.5.1 above, which amounts simply to averaging the values of the function at the various end positions in the sample. To economize on core, the programmer should calculate the value of the function at each sample end position as soon as the end position has been drawn and add this value into a running sum; there is no need to store the individual end-position values of either the function or the underlying uq's.

For example, suppose that a programmer wishes to compute the expectation of $\tilde{w} = \max\{\tilde{x}, \tilde{y}, \tilde{z}\}$ where $\tilde{x}$, $\tilde{y}$, and $\tilde{z}$ are mutually independent, and suppose that he wishes to base his computation on a random sample of 1000 end positions. He can do so as follows:

```
SUM = 0.
DO 39 KOUNT = 1,1000
X = XBRMD(NRANDF(NXBRAK))
Y = YBRMD(NRANDF(NYBRAK))
Z = ZBRMD(NRANDF(NZBRAK))
```

```
        W = AMAX1(X, Y, Z)
        SUM = SUM + W
   39 CONTINUE

        EXPW = SUM/1000.
```

5.7.4.   Computation of the Distribution of a Function

If the complete distribution of a function is desired, the appropriate method of computation is the one based on the use of Epfdis which is described in Section 5.6.1 above. The individual end-position values of the function have to be stored but not the values of the underlying uq's.

For example, a 100-bracket distribution of the function $\tilde{w} = \tilde{x}\tilde{y}\tilde{z}$ where $\tilde{x}$, $\tilde{y}$, and $\tilde{z}$ are mutually independent and necessarily positive can be computed in the following way from a sample of 1000 end positions.

```
   DIMENSION SCRTCH(2000), WBRMD(100)
        . . . . .
        . . . . .
   WMIN = XMIN*YMIN*ZMIN
   WMAX = XMAX*YMAX*ZMAX
   NWBRAK = 100
   NWVAL = 1000

30 DO 39 K = 1, NWVAL
        X = XBRMD(NRANDF(NXBRAK))
        Y = YBRMD(NRANDF(NYBRAK))
        Z = ZBRMD(NRANDF(NZBRAK))
        W = X*Y*Z
        SCRTCH(K) = W
   39 CONTINUE

   CALL EPFDIS(WMIN, WMAX, SCRTCH, NWVAL, NWBRAK, WBRMD)
```

5.7.5.   Measurement of the Risk of Error

As we pointed out earlier, the chief if not the only real advantage of random over systematic sampling lies in the fact that it permits rational tradeoffs between the cost of sampling and the risk of error in results based on sampling. In the remainder of this chapter we shall show how a programmer can evaluate the risk of error in an expectation or cumulative probability computed from a random sample of any given size and allow the user to enlarge the sample if the risk seems excessive.

Let n denote the number of end positions in a sample drawn by equiprobable sampling with replacement, and let p and e respectively denote any cumulative probability and any expectation computed from the sample in the way described above. Then by an extension of the reasoning in ADU Section 13.1.6 it can be shown that:

1. Unless the quantity p(1 - p)n is less than 25, say, the user's probability distribution of the error in the computed cumulative probability p should be almost exactly Gaussian with mean 0 and standard deviation S = $\sqrt{p(1 - p)/n}$;

2. Unless n itself is less than 100, say, the user's probability distribution of the error in the computed expectation e should be almost exactly Gaussian with mean 0 and standard deviation S = $\sqrt{v/n}$, where v is the variance of the individual values of the function at the end positions in the sample.

Furthermore, the fact that the user's distribution of an error is Gaussian with mean 0 and standard deviation S can be shown to imply that:

1. The square root of the expected square of the error is S ;
2. The expected absolute magnitude or "size" of the error is .80 S ;
3. The chances that the magnitude of the error will exceed certain multiples of S are as follows: [9]

Magnitude of Error	Chance of Exceeding
.67S	.5
1.64S	.1
2.58S	.01
3.29S	.001

5.7.6. *Control of the Risk of Error in a Computed Expectation*

As a first example of the use of these results to permit rational error control, consider again the problem of computing the expectation of $\tilde{w} = \max\{\tilde{x}, \tilde{y}, \tilde{z}\}$ where $\tilde{x}$, $\tilde{y}$, and $\tilde{z}$ are mutually independent, and suppose again that the programmer wants to base an original estimate of this expectation on a sample of only 1000 end positions; but now suppose that after printing out this estimate the programmer wants to consider the error it may contain, print out a bound on the error which has only 1 chance in 100 of being exceeded, and allow the user to enlarge the sample size if this bound seems excessively large. Making use of the fact that the variance of a set of numbers is equal to the average of their squares minus the square of their average, he can accomplish his objective as follows:

---

[9]The error magnitude .67S is sometimes called the "probable error", and when an error figure is attached to an estimate by a $\pm$ sign (e.g., 12.7 $\pm$ .2) it is usually the probable error which follows the sign.

```
     SUMVAL = 0.
     SUMSQR = 0.
     NVALUS = 0.

10 DO 20 KOUNT = 1,1000
     X = XBRMD(NRANDF(NXBRAK))
     Y = YBRMD(NRANDF(NYBRAK))
     Z = ZBRMD(NRANDF(NZBRAK))
     VALUE = AMAX1(X, Y, Z)
     SUMVAL = SUMVAL + VALUE
     SUMSQR = SUMSQR + VALUE**2
20 CONTINUE

     NVALUS = NVALUS + 1000
     AVGVAL = SUMVAL/FLOAT(NVALUS)
     AVGSQR = SUMSQR/FLOAT(NVALUS)
     VARVAL = AVGSQR - AVGVAL**2

     ESTEXP = AVGVAL
     S = SQRT(VARVAL/FLOAT(NVALUS))
     BOUND = 2.58*S
     WRITE(n, 30) ESTEXP, BOUND
30 FORMAT(24H ESTIMATED EXPECTATION = , G14.7/14H
     ERROR BOUND =,G14.7/
  $     32H SHOULD ANOTHER SAMPLE BE TAKEN?)
     IF (IANSWR(0) .EQ. 1) GOTO 10
```

The following points should be observed:

1. The DO loop in statements 10–20 computes the sum of the 1000 individual function values under the name SUMVAL and computes the sum of the squares of these values under the name SUMSQR.

2. These sums are divided by the number of values NVALUS to find the average value AVGVAL and the average square AVGSQR, after which the variance of the individual values can be computed as VARVAL.

3. The estimate ESTEXP of the expectation of the function is simply the average of the function values in the sample.

4. The parameter S of the Gaussian distribution of the error in the estimate of the expectation is $\sqrt{v/n}$ where v = VARVAL and n = NVALUS.

5. The Manecon function *Ianswr* which is called in the last statement of the program prints a ready signal at the terminal and waits for the user to type his answer to the question previously printed out by the main program. If the user types YES or 1, the function returns the value 1; if he types NO or 0(zero), it returns 0. The function may be called with any argument whatever.

6. If the user of the program decides that the error bound is too large and answers yes to the question whether another sample should be taken, the program will loop back to statement 10, add 1000 more function values to SUMVAL, add their squares to SUMSQR, change NVALUS to 2000, and compute

a new estimated expectation and error bound from the pooled sample of 2000 end-position values in exactly the same way that it computed the original estimate and bound from the original sample of 1000 values; then finally it will ask the user whether he is now satisfied or wants to add still another 1000 end positions to the sample.

5.7.7. *Control of the Risk of Error in a Computed Distribution*

Now suppose that the programmer wants to compute the complete distribution of the function $\tilde{w} = \tilde{x}\tilde{y}\tilde{z}$ where $\tilde{x}$, $\tilde{y}$, and $\tilde{z}$ are mutually independent and wants to do so in such a way that the user can control the risk of error. The results in Section 5.7.5 above do not permit direct measurement of the risk of "over-all" error in the complete distribution of $\tilde{w}$ but they do permit measurement of the risk or error in any particular cumulative probability. If the programmer feels that he can give the user sufficient information by printing out (1) a bound on the error in a probability which is computed as .5, and (2) a bound on the error in a probability which is computed as .01, he can accomplish his purpose by exhibiting the error bounds corresponding to various sample sizes and allowing the user to select a sample size before he actually computes the distribution of $\tilde{w}$. This kind of control of errors in cumulative probabilities is actually simpler than control of errors in expectations because the Gaussian parameter S can be computed from the formula $\sqrt{p(1-p)/n}$ before any end positions are actually drawn as a sample, whereas the formula $\sqrt{v/n}$ cannot be evaluated until a sample of end positions has actually been drawn and the variance v of the function values at these end positions has been computed.

CHAPTER 6

Computations Involving Probability Distributions Grouped into Brackets of Equal Width

The present chapter contains the same kind of information concerning computations involving EW distributions that Chapter 5 contained concerning computations involving EP distributions. Although the present chapter is logically self-contained except for explicit references to Chapter 5, it neither repeats nor cross-references many of the general remarks on the Manecon collection and Fortran programming which are found in Chapter 5, and therefore a beginner should not try to read this chapter before he has carefully studied Chapter 5.

The methods of computation and interpolation used by the subprograms discussed in the present chapter are described in Section 10.2 below.

Contents of Chapter 6

1. Input and Storage of EW Distributions — 111
   1. Description of an EW Distribution; 2. Input of Basic EW Distributions; 3. Cumulative Bracket Probabilities; 4. Alternate Storage of Individual and Cumulative Probabilities.
2. Probabilities, Fractiles, and Mean and Variance — 113
   1. Cumulative Probabilities and Fractiles; 2. Probabilities of Individual Values of a UQ; 3. Mean and Variance.
3. Expectation of a Function of a Single UQ — 114
4. Distribution of a Function of a Single UQ — 115
   1. Partially Constant Functions; 2. Computation by Evaluation of Cumulative Probabilities; 3. Computation by Assignment of Individual Probabilities; 4. Description and Filing of a Distribution.
5. Expectation of a Function of Two or More UQ's — 119
   1. Computation by Evaluation of All End Positions; 2. Shortcut Evaluation of Expectations; 3. Reduction of the Number of End Positions.
6. Distribution of a Function of Two or More UQ's — 123
   1. General Functions of Two UQ's; 2. Sums and Differences of Two Independent UQ's; 3. Reduction of Other Functions to Sums or Differences; 4. Functions of More than Two UQ's; Computation by Repeated Reduction.

6.1.   Input and Storage of EW Distributions

6.1.1.   Description of an EW Distribution

If an EW distribution is to be processed by any of the subprograms in the Manecon collection, the programmer must provide for storing the description of the distribution in the form of the following numbers or values:

1. The least and greatest possible values of the uq, or two values which are to be treated as if they were the least and greatest possible values;
2. The probability of each of the brackets into which all values of the uq between the least and greatest possible values have been grouped;
3. The number of brackets.

The probabilities of the brackets must be stored in positions 1, 2, 3, ... of an array or "vector". The number of brackets must be stored as an integer; all other values as real numbers.

For example, the EW distribution of a uq $\tilde{x}$ might be described by storing

```
XMIN = 0.
XMAX = 1000.
XMASS(1) = .0001
XMASS(2) = .0002
XMASS(3) = .0004
.....
XMASS(64) = .0001
NXBRAK = 64
```

6.1.2.   Input of Basic EW Distributions

The Manecon subroutine <u>Gdread</u> can read into core any EW distribution which has been written on a file by any Manecon program or subroutine. The general procedure for using this subroutine was described in Section 5.1.2; when the distribution to be read is EW rather than EP, the call is of the form

CALL GDREAD(2, NXBRMX, XMIN, XMAX, XMASS, NXBRAK, IERROR)

where the integer 2 indicates that the distribution should have EW grouping and XMASS is the vector in which <u>Gdread</u> is to store the individual bracket probabilities it will read from the file.

6.1.3.   Cumulative Bracket Probabilities

For many purposes it is necessary to have available a vector containing the cumulative rather than the individual probabilities of the brackets of an EW distribution. If the programmer has stored NXBRAK individual probabilities in a vector XMASS, he can call the Manecon subroutine <u>Accum</u> to compute the corresponding cumulative probabilities and store them in a vector XCUM by writing

CALL ACCUM(XMASS, NXBRAK, XCUM)

For reasons which will appear later, the inverse of this computation may also be required—a programmer will sometimes have need for a vector containing individual bracket probabilities when all that he has available is a vector containing cumulative probabilities. If he has stored NXBRAK cumulative probabilities in a vector XCUM, he can call the Manecon subroutine <u>Decum</u> to compute the corresponding individual probabilities and store them in a vector XMASS by writing

CALL DECUM(XCUM, NXBRAK, XMASS)

6.1.4. *Alternate Storage of Individual and Cumulative Probabilities* [1]

In some situations the available core will not suffice to store both individual and cumulative probabilities simultaneously, and since either set of probabilities can be very quickly computed from the other there is no real need to do so.

If the programmer has stored NXBRAK individual probabilities in a vector called XMASS and then at some point in his program needs cumulative probabilities, he can call <u>Accum</u> to compute them and <u>substitute</u> them for the individual probabilities in XMASS by writing

CALL ACCUM(XMASS, NXBRAK, XMASS)

Then if at a later point in his program he needs the individual probabilities again, he can call the Manecon subroutine <u>Decum</u> to compute them and substitute them for the cumulative probabilities now in XMASS by writing

CALL DECUM(XMASS, NXBRAK, XMASS)

For the sake of clarity, however, we shall assume in what follows that a vector with a name like XMASS always contains individual probabilities and that cumulative probabilities are always stored in a vector with a name like XCUM. In an actual program, this same aid to clarity can be obtained with no loss of core by dimensioning both XMASS and XCUM and then writing the statement

EQUIVALENCE(XMASS, XCUM)

---

[1] This section is not required in anything that follows and may be omitted on a first reading.

which causes the two vectors to share the same locations in core; there is in effect a single vector which can be called by either of two names. Then when the programmer wants to switch from individual to cumulative probabilities he can write

CALL ACCUM(XMASS, NXBRAK, XCUM)

and thereafter refer to the vector as XCUM. When he wants to switch back to individual probabilities he can write

CALL DECUM(XCUM, NXBRAK, XMASS)

and thereafter refer to the vector as XMASS.

6.2. Probabilities, Fractiles, and Mean and Variance

6.2.1. *Cumulative Probabilities and Fractiles*

If the programmer has available in core the cumulative probabilities of all the brackets in an EW distribution, the function Ewcum will deliver the cumulative probability of any value of the uq and the function Ewfrc will deliver the value of the uq (fractile) corresponding to any cumulative probability. For example, the probability that $\tilde{x}$ is less than or equal to 117.5 can be obtained and stored under the name PROB by writing

PROB = EWCUM(117.5, XMIN, XMAX, XCUM, NXBRAK)

or the .25 fractile of the distribution can be obtained and stored under the name QUAR1 by writing

QUAR1 = EWFRC(.25, XMIN, XMAX, XCUM, NXBRAK)

6.2.2. *Probabilities of Individual Values of a UQ*

In order to obtain the probability that a uq is exactly equal to any one of its possible values, the programmer must first obtain and store the total number of possible values from the least to the greatest possible value inclusive. He can then obtain the desired probability in either of two ways.

1. If the programmer has available the cumulative probabilities of the brackets, he can obtain the probability of an individual value by use of the function Ewden. For example, suppose that the total number of possible values of $\tilde{x}$ from XMIN to XMAX inclusive has been stored as a real number under the name XNPVAL, and suppose that 117.5 is one of these possible values. Then the probability that $\tilde{x}$ has the value 117.5 can be obtained and stored under the name PROB by writing

DENS = EWDEN(117.5, XMIN, XMAX, XCUM, NXBRAK)
PROB = DENS*(XMAX - XMIN)/XNPVAL

The value delivered directly by the function <u>Ewden</u> is the value of the density function which $\tilde{x}$ possesses when its distribution is thought of as continuous in the strict sense of the word.

2. If the programmer has available the <u>individual</u> probabilities of the brackets, he can obtain this same probability that $\tilde{x} = 117.5$ exactly by writing

IX = (X - XMIN)/(XMAX - XMIN)*FLOAT(NXBRAK) + 1.
PROB = XMASS(IX)/XNPVAL*FLOAT(NXBRAK)

6.2.3. *Mean and Variance*

If the programmer has available the <u>individual</u> probabilities of the brackets of an EW distribution, he can obtain the mean of the distribution by use of the Manecon function <u>Ewmean</u>. For example, the expectation of $\tilde{x}$ can be obtained and stored under the name XMEAN by writing

XMEAN = EWMEAN(XMIN, XMAX, XMASS, NXBRAK)

Both the mean and the variance can be obtained by calling the Manecon sub-routine <u>Ewmomt</u>. For example, the mean and variance of $\tilde{x}$ can be obtained and stored under the names XMEAN and XVAR respectively by writing

CALL EWMOMT(XMIN, XMAX, XMASS, NXBRAK, XMEAN, XVAR)

Observe that the first four entries in the call list contain input to the subroutine while the last two contain the output.

6.3. Expectation of a Function of a Single UQ

If $\tilde{w}$ is a function of a discrete uq $\tilde{x}$, the expectation of $\tilde{z}$ can be computed by multiplying the value of $\tilde{z}$ corresponding to each possible value of $\tilde{x}$ by the probability of that value of $\tilde{x}$ and adding the products (ADU 7.3.4). When $\tilde{x}$ is really continuous but its distribution is represented by an EW approximation, the expectation of the function $\tilde{w}$ can be computed by treating the midpoints of the brackets of $\tilde{x}$ as if they were the only possible values of $\tilde{x}$, each one having probability equal to the entire probability of its bracket (ADU 7.4.3). The least and greatest possible values of $\tilde{x}$ do not enter the computation.

For example, suppose that a programmer wishes to compute the expectation of the function

$$\text{contribution} = \begin{cases} -a - bq + cx & \text{if } x \le q, \\ -a + (c - b)q & \text{if } x > q; \end{cases}$$

suppose that he has already stored in core the values of the coefficients a , b , c , and q ; and suppose that he has available the <u>individual</u> probabilities of the brackets of $\tilde{x}$. He can compute the desired expectation and store it under the name EXPCON by writing

```
      EXPCON = 0.
      XINC = (XMAX - XMIN)/FLOAT(NXBRAK)
      C1 = -A -B*Q
      C2 = -A +(C - B)*Q

      X = XMIN - .5*XINC
      DO 29 I = 1, NXBRAK
      X = X + XINC
      IF (X .GT. Q)  GOTO 26
      CON = C1 + C*X
      GOTO 27
   26 CON = C2
   27 EXPCON = EXPCON + XMASS(I)*CON
   29 CONTINUE
```

The following points are worth attention:

  1. XINC is the width of one bracket.
  2. The "initial" value of X is below XMIN by an amount equal to half the width of one bracket, but on each iteration of the DO loop the value of X is incremented by an amount equal to the width of one bracket before it is used in calculating the contribution. Accordingly the first value of X actually used in the computation is the midpoint of the first bracket, the next value is the midpoint of the second bracket, and so forth.

Instead of actually computing the function value CON in the main program as was done above, the programmer can define the function separately and then obtain its value CON for use in the main program by a simple function call. See Section 5.3.2 above.

6.4. Distribution of a Function of a Single UQ

6.4.1. *Partially Constant Functions*

In what follows we shall discuss methods for computing distributions of functions of uq's with EW distributions, but our discussion will be restricted to functions whose distributions can also be represented by EW distributions, and for the reason set forth in Section 5.4.1 above this means that we must in principle exclude functions which are "partially constant" in the sense there defined.

The exclusion need not be so rigorous in the case of EW distributions as it is in the case of EP distributions, however. If we disregard the fact that a function is partially constant and compute an EW distribution of the function by any of the methods described below, the probability that should be concentrated on a single, discrete value of the uq will be concentrated in a single bracket; and if this bracket is narrow enough, no serious error will result.

6.4.2. *Computation by Evaluation of Cumulative Probabilities*

In many situations, the most accurate and also the easiest way to compute the distribution of a function $\tilde{w}$ of a uq $\tilde{x}$ which has an EW distribution is to exploit the fact that the probability that $\tilde{w}$ will be less than or equal to any given value w is the probability of all values of $\tilde{x}$ that give rise to values of $\tilde{w}$ less than or equal to w .

1. Increasing Functions. As a first example, suppose that a programmer wishes to derive a 50-bracket EW distribution of the function $\tilde{w} = \tilde{x}^3$. Because any increase in $\tilde{x}$ produces an increase in $\tilde{w}$, the probability that $\tilde{w}$ is less than or equal to any specified value w is the probability that $\tilde{x}$ is less than or equal to the corresponding value $x = \sqrt[3]{w} = w^{\frac{1}{3}}$; and therefore the programmer can derive the <u>cumulative</u> distribution of $\tilde{w}$ from the <u>cumulative</u> distribution of $\tilde{x}$ by proceeding as follows:

```
DIMENSION WCUM(50)
 . . . . .
 . . . . .
ROOT = 1./3.
WMIN = XMIN**3
WMAX = XMAX**3
NWBRAK = 50
WINC = (WMAX - WMIN)/FLOAT(NWBRAK)

W = WMIN
DO 49 I = 1, NWBRAK
W = W + WINC
X = W**ROOT
WCUM(I) = EWCUM(X, XMIN, XMAX, XCUM, NXBRAK)
49 CONTINUE
```

If what the programmer actually wants is individual rather than cumulative bracket probabilities, he can now obtain them by calling the Manecon subroutine <u>Decum</u> described in Section 6.1.3 above.

The reader should observe that the successive W's which are generated in the DO loop in the program above are the values of $\tilde{w}$ at the <u>right edges</u> of the successive brackets of $\tilde{w}$, not the values at the bracket midpoints as in the program in Section 6.3 above. Because each bracket in an EW distribution is assigned a probability equal to the total probability of all the values of the uq in the bracket, the cumulative probability of i'th bracket is equal to the total probability of all values of the uq that are less than or equal to the value at the right edge of the i'th bracket. In the problem of Section 6.3, we were interested in the midpoint rather than the right edge of each bracket because we wanted to compute the value of a function at some value of the uq which would "represent" the bracket fairly and the midpoint was an obvious choice for this purpose (ADU 7.4.1–7.4.2).

2. Decreasing Functions. Suppose next that a programmer wishes to derive a 50-bracket EW distribution of the function $\tilde{w} = 1/\tilde{x}^2$; and suppose that all possible values of $\tilde{x}$ are strictly positive, so that over the range of $\tilde{x}$ any increase in $\tilde{x}$ produces a decrease in $\tilde{w}$. Then the probability that $\tilde{w}$ is less than or equal to any specified value $\tilde{w}$ is the probability that $\tilde{x}$ is greater than or equal to the corresponding value $x = 1/\sqrt{w}$, and the programmer can derive the cumulative distribution of $\tilde{w}$ from the cumulative distribution of $\tilde{x}$ by proceeding as follows:

```
WMIN = 1./XMAX**2
WMAX = 1./XMIN**2
NWBRAK = 50
WINC = (WMAX - WMIN)/FLOAT(NWBRAK)

W = WMIN
DO 59 I = 1, NWBRAK
W = W + WINC
X = 1./SQRT(W)
WCUM(I) = 1. - EWCUM(X, XMIN, XMAX, XCUM, NXBRAK)
59 CONTINUE
```

3. Nonmonotone Functions. Even though a function is nonmonotone in the sense that it sometimes increases and sometimes decreases when its argument increases, its distribution can in some cases be conveniently derived by a procedure very similar to the procedure used above to derive distributions of monotone functions.

Whether or not the function is monotone, the essential feature of this procedure is a loop which takes the brackets of the distribution of the function in order and for each one computes (1) the value of the function at the right edge of the bracket, and then (2) the total probability of all values of the underlying uq that make the value of the function less than or equal to its value at the given right edge. It is only the last step which is trickier in the case of a nonmonotone function, because the required total probability cannot be found by a single use of the function Ewcum.

For example, suppose that a programmer wishes to derive a 50-bracket EW distribution of the function $\tilde{w} = (\tilde{x} - c)^2$, where c is some constant whose value has previously been stored, and suppose that he knows that the least and greatest possible values of $\tilde{x}$ are respectively less and greater than c . After observing that $\tilde{w}$ will be less than or equal to any given value w if $\tilde{x}$ is anywhere between $c - \sqrt{w}$ and $c + \sqrt{w}$, he can compute the cumulative distribution of $\tilde{w}$ from the cumulative distribution of $\tilde{x}$ by the following statements:

```
      WMIN = 0.
      WMAX = AMAX1(XMAX-C, C-XMIN)
      WMAX = WMAX**2
      NWBRAK = 50
      WINC = (WMAX - WMIN)/FLOAT(NWBRAK)

      W = WMIN
      DO 69 I = 1, NWBRAK
      W = W + WINC
      SQRTW = SQRT(W)
      X1 = C - SQRTW
      X2 = C + SQRTW
      WCUM(I) = EWCUM(X2, XMIN, XMAX, XCUM, NXBRAK)
    $           - EWCUM(X1, XMIN, XMAX, XCUM, NXBRAK)
   69 CONTINUE
```

6.4.3. *Computation by Assignment of Individual Probabilities*

When the nature of a nonmonotone function $\tilde{w}$ of a uq $\tilde{x}$ is such that it is awkward if not impossible to derive its distribution by computing cumulative probabilities in the way just described, the distribution can always be obtained by computing <u>individual</u> bracket probabilities in the following way:

1. Compute the least and greatest possible values of the function and divide the interval between them into the desired number of brackets of equal width.
2. Taking each bracket of the <u>argument $\tilde{x}$</u> in turn, compute the value of the function $\tilde{z}$ at the <u>midpoint</u> of the $\tilde{x}$ bracket, determine the $\tilde{w}$ bracket to which this computed value of $\tilde{w}$ belongs, and assign the individual probability of the given $\tilde{x}$ bracket to that bracket of $\tilde{w}$.

For example, the following program could be used instead of the last program above to derive the distribution of $\tilde{w} = (\tilde{x} - c)^2$, assuming again that the programmer wants a 50-bracket distribution of $\tilde{w}$ and knows that c is between the least and greatest possible values of $\tilde{x}$.

```
      DIMENSION WMASS(50)
      ○ • ○ • •
      • • ○ • •
      NWBRAK = 50
      DO 71 K = 1, NWBRAK
      WMASS(K) = 0.
   71 CONTINUE

      WMIN = 0.
      WMAX = AMAX1(XMAX-C, C-XMIN)
      WMAX = WMAX**2
```

```
WINC = (WMAX - WMIN)/FLOAT(NWBRAK)
XINC = (XMAX - XMIN)/FLOAT(NXBRAK)

X = XMIN - .5*XINC
DO 79 I = 1, NXBRAK
X = X + XINC
W = (X - C)**2
DIST = (W - WMIN)/WINC
K = IFIX(DIST) + 1
K = MINO(NWBRAK, K)
WMASS(K) = WMASS(K) + XMASS(I)
79 CONTINUE
```

Because WINC is the width of a bracket of $\tilde{w}$, DIST is the distance from WMIN to W measured in multiples of the width of a bracket, from which it follows that the integer K will have the value 1 if W falls in the first bracket of $\tilde{w}$, and so forth.

In general, this method of computation will be less accurate than the one previously described because it assigns the entire probability of each bracket of $\tilde{x}$ to a single bracket of $\tilde{w}$ even when the w which corresponds to the midpoint of the $\tilde{x}$ bracket in question falls near to or even on the edge of the $\tilde{w}$ bracket to which the probability is assigned.

6.4.4. Description and Filing of A Distribution

If a programmer has available the individual probabilities of the brackets of an EW distribution, he can call subroutine Ewprin to allow the user of his program to obtain printed description of the distribution, or he can call subroutine Ewfile to write the distribution on a file in a form acceptable as input to any Manecon program or subroutine.[2]   The subroutines are called by statements of the form

```
CALL EWPRIN(WMIN, WMAX, WMASS, NWBRAK)
CALL EWFILE(WMIN, WMAX, WMASS, NWBRAK)
```

Concerning the way in which Ewfile will obtain the name to be given to the file, see the discussion of Epfile in Section 5.4.4 above.

6.5.   Expectation of a Function of Two or More UQ's

6.5.1.   Computation by Evaluation of All End Positions

The expectation of a function of two or more uq's with EW distributions can in principle always be obtained by multiplying the value of the function at each end

---

[2] To satisfy the requirements of certain Manecon programs, subroutine Ewfile not only files the distribution itself but also computes and files the mean and variance of the distribution.

position of the joint probability diagram by the probability of that end position and adding the products. In carrying out this procedure, it must be remembered that each branch on the diagram represents the <u>midpoint</u> of an EW bracket, that the probability of any branch is the <u>individual</u> probability of the corresponding bracket, and that the probability of any end position is the product of all the individual bracket probabilities on the path leading to that end position.

1. Two Independent UQ's. When there are only two jointly distributed uq's, the method of computation described above is not only correct in principle but almost always feasible in practice.   For example, suppose that a programmer wishes to obtain the expectation of the function $\tilde{w} = \max\{\tilde{x}, \tilde{y}\}$ where $\tilde{x}$ and $\tilde{y}$ are independent. He can obtain this expectation and store it under the name EXPW by writing:

```
     XINC = (XMAX - XMIN)/FLOAT(NXBRAK)
     YINC = (YMAX - YMIN)/FLOAT(NYBRAK)
     EXPW = 0.

     X = XMIN - .5*XINC
     DO 39 I = 1, NXBRAK
     X = X + XINC
 30  XPROB = XMASS(I)

     Y = YMIN - .5*YINC
     DO 38 J = 1, NYBRAK
     Y = Y + YINC
 35  YPROB = YMASS(J)

     W = AMAX1(X, Y)
     WPROB = XPROB*YPROB
     EXPW = EXPW + WPROB*W
 38  CONTINUE
 39  CONTINUE
```

2. Two Interdependent UQ's. Everything that was said in Section 5.5.1 above about the assessment problems that arise when two uq's are interdependent applies just as well when the distributions of the uq's are grouped into EW brackets as it does when they are grouped into EP brackets. As we saw there, one possible solution of the assessment problem is to assess and file only two or three conditional distributions and to obtain the others by interpolation.

As an example of the use of interpolation between EW distributions, suppose now that the uq's $\tilde{x}$ and $\tilde{y}$ of the last example above are interdependent rather than independent; suppose that the user files his unconditional distribution of $\tilde{x}$ and just two conditional distributions of $\tilde{y}$, one of which applies if $\tilde{x}$ has its smallest possible value while the other applies if $\tilde{x}$ has its greatest possible value; and suppose that he says that the conditional cumulative probability of any value of $\tilde{y}$ given any x between these two extremes can be found by linear interpolation between the cumulative probabilities of that value of $\tilde{y}$ under the two conditional distributions he has assessed and filed. If the programmer stores these two distributions under names beginning with Y1 and Y2, he can compute the expectation of $\tilde{w} = \max \{\tilde{x}, \tilde{y}\}$ by a program identical to the last one above except that (1) the statement

FACTOR = (X – XMIN)/(XMAX – XMIN)

is inserted immediately after statement 30, and (2) statement 35 is replaced by

YPROB = FACTOR*Y2MASS(J) + (1.–FACTOR)*Y1MASS(J)

We leave it to the reader to convince himself that this interpolation between the two conditional mass functions of $\tilde{y}$ agrees with the user's statement concerning interpolation between the two conditional cumulative functions of $\tilde{y}$.

3. More than Two UQ's. As we have already said, the expectation of a function of more than two uq's with EW distributions can in principle be computed in exactly the same way that the expectation of a function of just two uq's is computed, by multiplying the value of the function at each end position of the joint probability diagram by the probability of that end position and adding the products.

For example, suppose that $\tilde{x}$, $\tilde{y}$, and $\tilde{z}$ are mutually independent. The expectation of $\tilde{w} = \max \{\tilde{x}, \tilde{y}, \tilde{z}\}$ can in principle be found by writing:

```
    XINC = (XMAX – XMIN)/FLOAT(NXBRAK)
    YINC = (YMAX – YMIN)/FLOAT(NYBRAK)
    ZINC = (ZMAX – ZMIN)/FLOAT(NZBRAK)
    EXPW = 0.

    X = XMIN – .5*XINC
    DO 39 I = 1, NXBRAK
    X = X + XINC

    Y = YMIN –.5*YINC
    DO 38 J = 1, NYBRAK
    Y = Y + YINC

    Z = ZMIN – .5*ZINC
    DO 37 K = 1, NZBRAK
    Z = Z + ZINC

    W = AMAX1(X, Y, Z)
    WPROB = XMASS(I)*YMASS(J)*ZMASS(K)
    EXPW = EXPW + WPROB*W
 37 CONTINUE
 38 CONTINUE
 39 CONTINUE
```

Before writing such a program, however, the programmer must make sure that the cost of computation will not be excessively expensive because of the number of end positions at which the function and the probability have to be evaluated.

6.5.2. *Shortcut Evaluation of Expectations*

As we saw in Section 5.5.2, expectations of functions of a number of jointly distributed uq's can often be very easily evaluated by exploiting the fact that (1) the expectation of the sum or any other <u>linear</u> function of a number of uq's can be found by substituting the (unconditional) expectation of each individual uq in the definition of the function, and (2) the expectation of the <u>product</u> of a number of <u>mutually independent</u> uq's is equal to the product of their (unconditional) expectations. In Section 5.5.2 we gave a number of examples of the exploitation of one or both of these rules, either directly or via "intermediate functions", and all these examples remain valid when the basic uq's have EW rather than EP distributions.

We further saw in Section 5.5.3 that when the expectation of a function of three or more mutually independent uq's cannot be computed by computing the expectations of individual uq's or of "intermediate" functions of one or two uq's, it can sometimes be conveniently computed by first computing the complete distribution of some intermediate function of some or all of the uq's. The same thing is true in the present context when the distribution of the intermediate function can be computed in the way discussed in Section 6.6.4 below.

6.5.3. *Reduction of the Number of End Positions*

When the expectation of a function of three or more jointly distributed uq's cannot be evaluated by any of the shortcuts suggested just above, either because of the nature of the function or because the uq's are not mutually independent, it may be possible to reduce the problem to manageable size without risking any serious error in the computed expectation by simply reducing the numbers of brackets into which the distributions of the individual uq's are grouped. The reduction can be accomplished by first putting the original distribution into <u>cumulative</u> form and then using the Manecon function <u>Epcum</u>.

For example, suppose that a programmer wishes to work with a 10-bracket EW distribution of $\tilde{x}$ but believes that the user may group the distribution into a much larger number of brackets. If he first makes provision for reading the user's individual bracket probabilities into a vector called USERP and for storing the number of such probabilities as NUSERP, he can accomplish his purpose by writing:

```
CALL ACCUM(USERP, NUSERP, USERP)
NXBRAK = 10
XINC = (XMAX - XMIN)/FLOAT(NXBRAK)
```

```
      X = XMIN
      DO 19 I = 1, NXBRAK
      X = X + XINC
      XCUM(I) = EWCUM(X, XMIN, XMAX, USERP, NUSERP)
   19 CONTINUE
```

The following points are worth attention:

1. Because the call to subroutine <u>Accum</u> has the same argument USERP in the third or output position as it has in the first position, the subroutine stores the cumulative probabilities which it computes in the same locations that originally contained the individual probabilities supplied to the subroutine as input; cf. Section 6.1.4 above.

2. The vector XCUM as computed in the next to the last statement contains the <u>cumulative</u> probabilities of 10 brackets of $\tilde{x}$. If the programmer wants individual bracket probabilities, he can obtain them by use of subroutine <u>Decum</u>; cf. Section 6.1.3 above.

3. The vector USERP is free for another use as soon as the 10-bracket probabilities wanted by the programmer have been computed and stored in the vector XCUM. In particular, the programmer could now read into USERP the bracket probabilities of the user's distribution of some other uq; there is no need to reserve space in core for simultaneous storage of the bracket probabilities of the user's distributions of all the uq's involved in the problem.

<u>Random Sampling of End Positions</u>. In many problems there are so many jointly distributed uq's that the number of end positions on the joint probability diagram would be excessive even if the distributions of the individual uq's were grouped into very small numbers of brackets. In such situations, the expectation of a function of the uq's is usually best evaluated by taking a random sample of the end positions of the joint probability diagram, but if this is to be done it is much easier to work with a diagram in which the distributions of the individual uq's have been grouped into brackets of equal probability than with one in which they have been grouped into brackets of equal width. For this reason we shall not discuss random sampling of end positions under EW grouping; computations based on random sampling under EP grouping were discussed in Section 5.7 above.

6.6. Distribution of a Function of Two or More UQ's

6.6.1. *General Functions of Two UQ's*

Provided that a function of two uq's is not partially constant in the sense that it has exactly the same value at a substantial fraction of the end positions of the joint probability diagram, its distribution can be found by a procedure very like the procedure for deriving the distribution of a function of a single uq that was described in Section 6.4.3; and this same procedure will give good results even for partially constant functions if the distribution of the function is grouped into sufficiently narrow brackets. To find the distribution of a function $\tilde{w}$ of uq's $\tilde{x}$ and $\tilde{y}$:

1. Compute the least and greatest possible values of the function and divide the interval between them into the desired number of brackets of equal width.

2. Taking each endpoint of the joint probability diagram of $\tilde{x}$ and $\tilde{y}$ in turn, compute the value of the function $\tilde{w}$ at that endpoint, determine the $\tilde{w}$ bracket to which that value of $\tilde{w}$ belongs, and assign the probability of the given endpoint to that bracket of $\tilde{w}$.

Independent UQ's. For example, suppose that a programmer wishes to compute a 50-bracket EW distribution of $\tilde{w} = \tilde{x}\tilde{y}$. If $\tilde{x}$ and $\tilde{y}$ are independent and necessarily positive, he can accomplish his objective as follows:

```
      DIMENSION WMASS(50)
      .....
      NWBRAK = 50
      DO 19 K = 1, NWBRAK
      WMASS(K) = 0.
   19 CONTINUE

      WMIN = XMIN*YMIN
      WMAX = XMAX*YMAX
      WINC = (WMAX - WMIN)/FLOAT(NWBRAK)
      XINC = (XMAX - XMIN)/FLOAT(NXBRAK)
      YINC = (YMAX - YMIN)/FLOAT(NYBRAK)

      X = XMIN - .5*XINC
      DO 49 I = 1, NXBRAK
      X = X + XINC
   30 XPROB = XMASS(I)

      Y = YMIN - .5*YINC
      DO 48 J = 1, NYBRAK
      Y = Y + YINC
   35 YPROB = YMASS(J)

      W = X*Y
      DIST = (W - WMIN)/WINC
      K = IFIX(DIST) + 1
      K = MINO(NWBRAK, K)
      WPROB = XPROB*YPROB
      WMASS(K) = WMASS(K) + WPROB
   48 CONTINUE
   49 CONTINUE
```

Interdependent UQ's. If the uq's $\tilde{x}$ and $\tilde{y}$ were interdependent rather than independent as assumed above, computation of the distribution of the function $\tilde{w}$ would require use of the appropriate conditional distribution of one of the two uq's $\tilde{x}$ and $\tilde{y}$ in connection with each bracket-midpoint value of the other. The problem of supplying all of these conditional distributions has already been referred to in paragraph 2 of Section 6.5.1, and if the assessment problem is solved in the manner there suggested, the distribution of the function could be obtained by a program identical to the last one above except that the computation of YPROB would have to be altered in the same way that this same computation was altered in paragraph 2 of Section 6.5.1.

Choice of the Number of Brackets for the Distribution of a Function. When a programmer wishes to compute an EW distribution of a function $\tilde{w}$ of uq's $\tilde{x}$ and $\tilde{y}$, he often faces a rather serious dilemma in deciding on the number of brackets into which he will divide the interval between the least and greatest possible values of $\tilde{w}$. In the case of a great many functions of two uq's, there is only a tiny probability that the function $\tilde{w}$ will have a value anywhere near the least or greatest of its possible values, and this means that:

1. If the programmer allows only a reasonable number of brackets for the distribution of $\tilde{w}$, most of the probability may be concentrated in a very few brackets with the result that the main part of the distribution of $\tilde{w}$ is very coarsely described.
2. If, on the contrary, the programmer allows a very large number of brackets for the distribution of $\tilde{w}$, he may use a substantial amount of core to store tail probabilities which are completely negligible and may give rise to underflow when used in later computations.

In many cases, the best way around this dilemma is to start with a rather large number of brackets of $\tilde{w}$ and then to reduce the number after the distribution has been computed. Specifically, the programmer might start by dividing the range of $\tilde{w}$ into a number of brackets equal to the sum of the number of $\tilde{x}$ brackets and the number of $\tilde{y}$ brackets. Then after the distribution of $\tilde{w}$ has been computed, he can call the Manecon subroutine Normlz to examine the computed distribution and truncate it if any brackets at either end of the distribution contain completely negligible probabilities.

Truncation of a Distribution. For the purpose just described, subroutine Normlz is called by a statement of the form

CALL NORMLZ(WMIN, WMAX, WMASS, NWBRAK, WMASS)

with the name of the vector containing the individual bracket probabilities of $\tilde{w}$ appearing as both the third and the last argument in the call. If any brackets at either end of the range of $\tilde{w}$ contain really negligible probabilities,[3] the subroutine will raise the value of WMIN and/or lower the value of WMAX so as to eliminate these brackets, alter the value of NWBRAK accordingly, multiply the probabilities of the remaining brackets by a factor which makes them add to one, and finally shift these probabilities so that they appear in the first NWBRAK positions of the vector WMASS.

---

[3]A probability p is treated as negligible by subroutine Normlz if it is so small that because of finite word length 1 - p would be equal to 1 on the particular machine being used.

6.6.2.   Sums and Differences of Two Independent UQ's

Although the procedure just described can be used to compute the distribution of any function of two uq's $\tilde{x}$ and $\tilde{y}$, there is a somewhat faster and much more accurate procedure that can be used when (1) the function in question is the sum or difference of $\tilde{x}$ and $\tilde{y}$, (2) $\tilde{x}$ and $\tilde{y}$ are independent, and (3) the width of each bracket in the distribution of $\tilde{x}$ is the same as the width of each bracket in the distribution of $\tilde{y}$. When all of these conditions are met, the distribution of the function can be very easily found by calling the Manecon subroutine Convol, which computes it by a procedure known as "convolution" that is explained in Section 10.2.5 below.

For example, suppose that $\tilde{x}$ and $\tilde{y}$ are mutually independent; suppose that both uq's have EW distributions and that the width of a bracket is the same in both distributions; and suppose that the programmer wishes to derive the distribution of the sum $\tilde{w} = \tilde{x} + \tilde{y}$. If the width of a bracket in the distributions of $\tilde{x}$ and $\tilde{y}$ has been stored as BWIDTH, he can obtain the distribution of $\tilde{w}$ by writing merely:

```
ISIGNY = +1
CALL CONVOL(BWIDTH, XMIN, XMASS, NXBRAK, YMIN, YMASS, NYBRAK,
$    ISIGNY, WMIN, WMAX, WMASS, NWBRAK)
```

The following points should be noted:

1. The first eight arguments in the call list of Convol are inputs, the last four are outputs.

2. Calling Convol with ISIGNY = +1 instructs the subroutine to compute the distribution of the sum $\tilde{x} + \tilde{y}$; calling with ISIGNY = -1 would instruct it to compute the distribution of the difference $\tilde{x} - \tilde{y}$.

3. The number NWBRAK of brackets of the distribution of $\tilde{w}$ which is delivered as an output by Convol will not be greater than the sum NXBRAK + NYBRAK, this being equally true when Convol is called with ISIGNY = -1 to compute the distribution of $\tilde{x} - \tilde{y}$. The vector WMASS can be dimensioned accordingly.

4. The brackets of the distribution of $\tilde{w}$ will have the same width BWIDTH as the distributions of $\tilde{x}$ and $\tilde{y}$, this too being equally true when Convol computes the distribution of the difference $\tilde{x} - \tilde{y}$.

5. Convol automatically calls Normlz to eliminate $\tilde{w}$ brackets with negligible probabilities in the way described in Section 6.6.1 above.

Computation of Input Distributions with the Same Bracket Width. If a programmer wishes to use the procedure described above to compute the distribution of the sum or difference of uq's $\tilde{x}$ or $\tilde{y}$ whose distributions have been grouped and filed by program Disfile or any other Manecon program or subroutine, he will almost always find that the width of the EW brackets of $\tilde{x}$ is not the same as the width of the EW brackets of $\tilde{y}$. In such circumstances he will have to compute a new distribution of $\tilde{x}$ and/or $\tilde{y}$ before he can call subroutine Convol, and in most cases he will do well to proceed as follows:

1. Compute the total width XMAX - XMIN of the user's distribution of $\tilde{x}$, and similarly compute the total width of the user's distribution of $\tilde{y}$.
2. Decide on a reasonable number of brackets for the <u>wider</u> of the two distributions and compute the bracket width which this implies.
3. Use the Manecon function <u>Ewcum</u> to derive from the user's distributions of the two uq's new distributions in both of which the brackets are of the calculated width.

For example, suppose that a programmer knows that the user's distributions of $\tilde{x}$ and $\tilde{y}$ will be grouped into 100 brackets each; suppose that he knows that the width of the distribution of $\tilde{x}$ will be greater than the width of the distribution of $\tilde{y}$; and to keep the example simple, suppose that he wants to work with the user's original 100-bracket distribution of $\tilde{x}$, so that all that he has to do is derive a new distribution of $\tilde{y}$ in which the bracket width is equal to the bracket width in the user's distribution of $\tilde{x}$. After he has read in the user's distributions of $\tilde{x}$ and $\tilde{y}$ and stored them under names keyed by X and Y , he can compute his new distribution of $\tilde{y}$ and store it under names keyed by YY by proceeding as follows:

```
BWIDTH = (XMAX - XMIN)/FLOAT(NXBRAK)
NYYBRK = (YMAX - YMIN)/BWIDTH + .5
IF (NYYBRK .EQ. 0) NYYBRK = 1
YYMIN = YMIN
YYMAX = YMIN + BWIDTH*FLOAT(NYYBRK)

CALL ACCUM(YMASS, NYBRAK, YCUM)

YY = YYMIN
DO 45 I = 1, NYYBRK
YY = YYMIN + BWIDTH
YYCUM(I) = EWCUM(YY, YMIN, YMAX, YCUM, NYBRAK)
45 CONTINUE

CALL DECUM(YYCUM, NYYBRK, YYMASS)
```

The following points should be observed:

1. Because the range (YMAX - YMIN) of the user's original distribution of $\tilde{y}$ may not be evenly divisible by the new bracket width BWIDTH, the new number of brackets NYYBRK is rounded in the second statement of the program in such a way that the new maximum value YYMAX as computed in the fifth statement will be as close as possible to the old maximum value YMAX.

2. The program as written above is very wasteful of core because it requires separate storage locations for the four vectors YMASS, YCUM, YYMASS, and YYCUM. Half of this space can be saved by the device of "alternate storage" discussed in Section 6.1.4 above; still more can be saved by reusing all the space later in the program except the space required for storage of YYMASS.

6.6.3. Reduction of Other Functions to Sums or Differences

It is very frequently possible to reduce a problem of computing the distribution of a function of two independent uq's which is not a sum or difference to a problem of computing the distribution of a sum or difference. If this can be done, the problem can be solved by convolution, and because convolution is much more accurate and somewhat more rapid than the "general" method of computation described in Section 6.6.1 above, it usually pays to make the reduction when it is possible to do so.

For example, suppose that a programmer wishes to compute the distribution of the function $\tilde{w} = \tilde{x}\tilde{y}$ where $\tilde{x}$ and $\tilde{y}$ are independent and all possible values of $\tilde{x}$ and $\tilde{y}$ are positive. Taking logarithms we have

$$\log \tilde{w} = \log \tilde{x} + \log \tilde{y} ,$$

so that if we define

$$\tilde{p} = \log \tilde{x} , \qquad q = \log \tilde{y} , \qquad \tilde{s} = \tilde{p} + \tilde{q} ,$$

we have

$$\tilde{s} = \log \tilde{w} \qquad \text{and hence} \qquad \tilde{w} = e^{\tilde{s}} .$$

The distribution of $\tilde{w}$ can now be computed as follows:

1. Compute the distributions of the increasing functions $\tilde{p} = \log \tilde{x}$ and $\tilde{q} = \log \cdot \tilde{y}$ by the method described in paragraph 1 of Section 6.4.2, taking care that the bracket width is the same in both distributions.

2. Compute the distribution of $\tilde{s} = \tilde{p} + \tilde{q}$ by convolution in the way described in Section 6.6.2. The method is applicable because the fact that $\tilde{x}$ and $\tilde{y}$ are independent implies that $\tilde{p}$ and $\tilde{q}$ are independent.

3. Compute the distribution of the increasing function $\tilde{w} = e^{\tilde{s}}$ by the method described in paragraph 1 of Section 6.4.2.

6.6.4. Functions of More than Two UQ's; Computation by Repeated Reduction

The distribution of a function of more than two uq's can in principle be derived by a procedure essentially identical to the procedure for deriving the distribution of a function of two uq's which was described in Section 6.6.1 above. After computing the least and greatest possible values of the function and dividing the interval between them into brackets, the programmer can assign the probability of each endpoint on the joint probability diagram to the bracket to which the value of the function at that endpoint belongs. In practice, however, the probability diagram is likely to have so many end positions that it is economically impossible to evaluate the probability and function value at every one.

There is no universally applicable, convenient way out of this difficulty, but if the jointly distributed uq's are mutually independent, then as we saw in Section 5.6.2 it is frequently possible to compute the distribution of a function of n uq's by successively computing the distributions of n − 1 functions of just two uq's;

and when this can in fact be done, the computational burden increases only linearly rather than geometrically with the number of uq's. The examples and all the remarks in Section 5.6.2 apply just as well when the uq's have EW distributions as when they have EP distributions. The one additional point to observe when working with EW distributions is that each of the successive problems of computing the distribution of a function of two independent uq's should when possible be reduced to a problem of computing the distribution of a sum or difference; cf. Section 6.6.3 above.

When the method just described cannot be used to compute the distribution of a function of many uq's, either because the uq's are not mutually independent or because of the nature of the function (cf. Section 5.6.2 above), it will usually be necessary to resort to random sampling of end positions. We have already pointed out, however, that random sampling is much easier when the distributions of the uq's are grouped into brackets of equal probability rather than equal width, and therefore we merely refer the reader back to the discussion of random sampling in Section 5.7.

CHAPTER 7

Computations Involving Piecex or Sumex Functions; Evaluation and Description of Continuous Probability Distributions

In the first section of the present chapter we show how a programmer can use various Manecon subprograms to evaluate gambles under sumex preference functions and piecex preference and bounding functions after the parameters of the functions have been filed by programs <u>Piecexfit</u> and <u>Sumexfit.</u> In the remainder of the chapter we discuss the Manecon subprograms for evaluation and description of continuous probability distributions.

Contents of Chapter 7

1. Piecex and Sumex Functions   131
   1. Sumex Preference Functions; 2. Piecex Preference and Bounding Functions.
2. Evaluation of Strictly Continuous Probability Distributions   134
   1. Top-Level Subprograms; 2. General Comments on the Supporting Subprograms; 3. Standard Beta Distribution; 4. Standard Gamma Distribution; 5. Unit Normal Distribution.
3. Printed Description of Continuous Distributions: Subroutine <u>Prbpri</u>   137
   1. Required Functions; 2. Use of Subroutine <u>Prbpri</u>; 3. Translator Functions.

7.1. Piecex and Sumex Functions

7.1.1. *Sumex Preference Functions*

1. <u>Input and Storage of the Parameters</u>. If a programmer wishes to use a sumex preference function in his program, he must dimension a 7-position vector in which to store the parameters of the function, and on some systems he must also declare this vector to be double precision. He can then call the Manecon subroutine <u>Sxread</u> to obtain from the user at the terminal the name of the file on which the parameters have been written by <u>Sumexfit</u> and to read the parameters from this file into core.[1] These preliminary steps might take the following form.

      DIMENSION SMXPAR(7)
      . . . . .
      . . . . .
      WRITE(n, 21)
   21 FORMAT (49H SPECIFY NAME OF FILE CONTAINING SUMEX PARAMETERS)
      CALL SXREAD(SMXPAR, IERROR)

The following points should be observed.

1. As already stated, it is necessary on some systems to follow the dimension statement by the statement

      DOUBLE PRECISION SMXPAR

2. When <u>Sxread</u> is called, it prints a ready signal at the terminal and waits for the user to supply the name of the file it is supposed to read. Any explanatory message like the one in statement 21 above must be supplied by the main program.

3. If <u>Sxread</u> finds a file containing sumex parameters under the name specified by the user, it will store the seven sumex parameters in the vector SMXPAR and assign the value 0 to the trouble indicator IERROR. If it does not find such a file, it will print out an appropriate message and assign a value greater than 0 to IERROR.

Following his call to <u>Sxread</u>, the programmer should include provision for handling cases where <u>Sxread</u> fails to read parameters and so indicates by returning a value of IERROR greater than 0. If he wishes to give the user a second chance to specify the file name, he can do so by arranging to call <u>Sxread</u> a second time.

2. <u>Evaluation of Gambles</u>. Once the parameters of a sumex function have been stored in core, the programmer can (1) obtain preference for any criterion value by calling the Manecon function <u>Sxpr</u>, and (2) obtain the criterion value

---

[1]Only five parameters are actually read from the file. The other two parameters which are stored by <u>Sxread</u> are auxiliary parameters computed from the first five by <u>Sxread</u> itself.

or certainty equivalent corresponding to any preference by calling the Manecon function Sxce.

For example, suppose that after obtaining the parameters of the user's sumex function and storing them in the way described above, the programmer wishes to compute the user's certainty equivalent for a gamble whose payoff $\tilde{x}$ has an EP distribution which is stored in core in the way described in Section 5.1.1. He can do as follows.

```
     SUM = 0.
     DO 45 I = 1, NXBRAK
     X = XBRMD(I)
     PREF = SXPR(X, SMXPAR)
     SUM = SUM + PREF
 45 CONTINUE

     EXPREF = SUM/FLOAT(NXBRAK)
     CERTEQ = SXCE(EXPREF, SMXPAR)
```

Observe that the name of the vector containing the sumex parameters follows the argument (criterion value or preference) in the call lists of both Sxpr and Sxce.

3. Extrapolation of the Sumex Functions. As usual, denote by V_0 and V_1 the least and greatest of the criterion values supplied as inputs when a sumex preference function is fitted. As we saw in Section 3.4.1 above, preferences under the fitted function are mathematically well defined for all criterion values in $(-\infty, \infty)$, not just for values in $[V_0, V_1]$; and correspondingly the inverse function is mathematically well defined for all preferences in $(-\infty, \infty)$, not just for preferences in $[0, 1]$. It follows, of course, that Sxpr and Sxce can be used to compute a certainty equivalent for a gamble with payoffs below V_0 and/or payoffs above V_1; but we remind the reader that we saw in Section 3.4.1 the computed certainty equivalent is of dubious meaning if any substantial probability is attached to payoffs above V_1 and is essentially worthless if any probability at all is attached to payoffs below V_0.

7.1.2. *Piecex Preference and Bounding Functions*

1. Input and Storage of the Parameters. A single set of 18 parameters is required to define a piecex-average preference function and the two piecex bounding functions described in Section 3.2.1 above. Like sumex parameters, these piecex parameters must be stored in a vector and the vector must be typed as double precision on some systems. If the vector is called PCXPAR, the statement

CALL PXREAD(PCXPAR, IERROR)

will cause the Manecon subroutine Pxread to read in the parameters from a file on which they have been written by program Piecexfit.[2] The comments on subroutine Sxread in the previous section all apply equally to Pxread.

2. The Available Functions. If piecex parameters have been stored in a vector called PCXPAR, various Manecon piecex functions will return values as follows:

PXAVPR (V, PXCPAR) :	piecex-average preference for V
PXLBPR (V, PCXPAR) :	lower bound on preference for V
PXUBPR (V, PCXPAR) :	upper bound on preference for V
PXAVCE (Q, PCXPAR) :	value for which piecex-average preference is Q
PXLBCE (Q, PCXPAR) :	lower bound on value for which preference is Q
PXUBCE (Q, PCXPAR) :	upper bound on value for which preference is Q

3. Evaluation of Gambles. The user's preference and certainty equivalent for a gamble under a piecex-average preference function can be computed by using the functions Pxavpr and Pxavce in exactly the same way that Sxpr and Sxce are used to compute his preference and certainty equivalent under a sumex preference function.

Lower and upper bounds on the user's preference for a gamble are computed by using the bounding functions Pxlbpr and Pxubpr in exactly the same way that a proper preference function is used to compute the user's preference for the gamble.

The easiest way of obtaining bounds on the user's certainty equivalent for a gamble is by use of the Manecon subroutine Pxgam, which also computes the certainty equivalent under a piecex-average preference function. To use the subroutine, the programmer must first store the possible payoffs in a vector and store the associated probabilities in another vector. If these two vectors are called respectively PAYOFF and PROB, and if the number of payoffs is stored as NPAY, the programmer can call Pxgam by a statement of the form

CALL PXGAM(PAYOFF, PROB, NPAY, PCXPAR, VLBND, VUBND, VPXAV)

where the first four arguments contain the input and the last three will contain the output (the two bounds and the piecex-average certainty equivalent). Observe that the vector of piecex parameters is a required input.

4. Extrapolation of the Piecex Functions. The functions Pxavpr, Pxlbpr, and Pxubpr may be called with arguments outside the interval $[V_0, V_1]$ spanned by the user's inputs to program Piecexfit, but when the argument is less than V_0 Pxavpr returns the function value -1.5E33 as a code for "value undefined" and Pxlbpr returns the value -3.0E33 as a code for $-\infty$.

Similarly the functions Pxavce, Pxlbce, and Pxubce may be called with arguments outside the interval $[0, 1]$, but when the argument is greater than a certain limit which is greater than 1 the function Pxubce returns the value 3.0E33 as a code for $+\infty$.

---

[2] Three of the parameters read in by Pxread are dummies which are replaced by auxiliary parameters computed by Pxread itself.

When any of the payoffs supplied as input to the subroutine <u>Pxgam</u> is less than V_0 , the subroutine returns VPXAV with the value –1.5E33 as a code for undefined; the value of VLBND in such cases is always equal to the algebraically least of the input payoffs.

On the meaningfulness of results based on extrapolation of the piecex functions, see Section 3.4.1 above.

7.2   Evaluation of Strictly Continuous Probability Distributions

The Manecon collection contains a large number of subprograms for evaluation of densities, cumulative probabilities, and fractiles under various strictly continuous probability distributions. It also contains a few subprograms for evaluation of the mean and variance of distributions under which these quantities cannot be evaluated via simple formulas. The subprograms in the collection are divided into two quite distinct groups:

1. "Top-level" subprograms for direct use in evaluation of the distributions that appear in applied problems;
2. "Supporting" subprograms which perform the more difficult computations required by the top-level subprograms.

7.2.1.   Top-Level Subprograms

Section 8.3 below shows how the "top-level" subprograms can be used to evaluate densities, cumulative probabilities, fractiles, means, and variances under a variety of continuous probability distributions.

Densities returned by any Manecon subprogram are accurate to nearly full machine word length. The precision of the fractiles returned by any top-level subprogram depends on the value assigned to the variable TOLRNC within the subprogram in question, and the same thing is true of the cumulative probabilities returned by many of the subprograms. Cumulative probabilities whose precision is not controlled in this way are accurate to 7 decimal places. The programmer may freely reduce precision and with it the cost of calculation by increasing the value assigned to TOLRNC in any top-level subprogram, but if he wishes to increase the precision he must observe the limits inherent in the supporting subprogram which actually performs the computations.

With these remarks, the summary in Section 8.3 is a sufficient guide to the use of the top-level subprograms, and the remainder of the present section will be devoted to a discussion of the supporting subprograms. It will be of no interest to a person programming an applied problem unless he wants either (1) to increase the precision of the cumulative probabilities or fractiles returned by some top-level subprogram, or (2) to avoid the slight increase in execution time that results from calling the supporting subprograms through top-level subprograms instead of calling them directly.

7.2.2.   *General Comments on the Supporting Subprograms*

The supporting subprograms in the Manecon collection take the form of subprograms for evaluating densities, cumulative probabilities, and fractiles under three "standard" distributions which ordinarily do not appear as such in applied problems. The distributions in question are the standard beta distribution, the standard gamma distribution, and the standard or unit Normal distribution. In what follows, we shall discuss the capabilities of the subprograms which compute densities, cumulative probabilities, and fractiles under these three distributions; the computational methodology is discussed in Chapter 13 below.

No matter which of the three standard distributions is being discussed, we shall denote the density function by f , the (left-tail) cumulative function by F , and the fractile function by F^{-1} . The parameters will follow the argument in any list. Thus for a distribution with argument p and parameters a and b we shall write

$$f(p,\ a,\ b) = \text{density at } p \qquad ,$$
$$F(p,\ a,\ b) = \text{probability of } p \text{ or less} \qquad ,$$
$$F^{-1}(z,\ a,\ b) = p \text{ such that } F(p,\ a,\ b) = z \ .$$

7.2.3.   *Standard Beta Distribution*

The uq $\tilde{p}$ is said to have a standard beta distribution with parameters a and b if

$$f(p,\ a,\ b) \propto p^{a-1} (1-p)^{b-1} \ .$$

Densities and cumulative probabilities under the standard beta distribution are computed by the subroutine

DBETCU(IPRB, TOL, P, A, B, DENS, CPRB)

where the first five arguments are input and the last two are output. If called with IPRB = 1, Dbetcu computes both

DENS = f(p, a, b)   and   CPRB = F(p, a, b) ;

if called with IPRB = 0, Dbetcu computes only DENS and returns a spurious value for CPRB. Densities are always accurate to nearly full machine word length; the precision of a cumulative probability is controlled by the input variable TOL. Dbetcu is capable of computing cumulative probabilities accurate to about one decimal digit less than machine word length; subject to this limitation, the absolute error in the cumulative probabilities actually computed will not exceed TOL unless the number of terms required to achieve this precision exceeds the value assigned to the control variable NTERMS in a data statement near the beginning of Dbetcu. If the required number of terms exceeds NTERMS, Dbetcu issues the message "Dbetcu did not converge".

Fractiles under the standard beta distribution are computed by search by the function

$$\text{BETFRQ(TOL, ITOL, Z, A, B)} = F^{-1}(z, a, b).$$

If Betfrq is called with ITOL = 1 , the search continues until the absolute error in the fractile is less than TOL; if called with ITOL = 2 , the search continues until the relative errors in both the fractile and its complement are less than TOL.

On machines with a short word length like the IBM 360, Dbetcu and Betfrq work in double precision and the arguments with which they are called must be typed as double-precision in the calling program.

7.2.4. *Standard Gamma Distribution*

The uq $\tilde{x}$ is said to have a standard gamma distribution with parameter r if

$$f(x, r) \propto e^{-x} x^{r-1}.$$

Densities and cumulative probabilities under the standard gamma distribution are computed by the subroutine

$$\text{DGASCU (IPRB, TOL, X, R, DENS, CPRB)}$$

where the first four arguments are input and the last two are output. If called with IPRB = 1 , Dgascu computes both

$$\text{DENS} = f(x, r) \quad \text{and} \quad \text{CPRB} = F(x, r) \; ;$$

if called with IPRB = 0 , Dgascu computes only DENS and returns a spurious value for CPRB. Everything said in Section 7.2.3 above about the precision of values returned by Dbetcu and the role of the input variable TOL in controlling the precision of cumulative probabilities applies unchanged to Dgascu.

Fractiles under the standard gamma distribution are computed by search by the function

$$\text{GASFRC(TOL, Z, R)} = F^{-1}(z, r) \; .$$

The search continues until the relative error in the fractile is less than the value of the input variable TOL.

On machines with a short word length like the IBM 360, Dgascu and Gasfrc work in double precision and the arguments with which they are called must be typed as double-precision in the calling program.

7.2.5. *Unit Normal Distribution*

The uq $\tilde{u}$ is said to have a unit Normal distribution if

$$f(u) \propto e^{-u^2/2}$$

Densities and cumulative probabilities under the unit Normal distribution are computed by either of the subroutines

UNRCUQ(IPRB, U, DENS, CPRB)
DUNRCU(IPRB, TOL, U, DENS, CPRB)

where DENS and CPRB are output and the preceding arguments are input. When called with IPRB = 1 , either subroutine computes and returns both

DENS = f(u) and CPRB = F(u) .

When called with IPRB = 0 , either subroutine computes and returns a correct value for DENS only; a spurious value is returned for CPRB. When called with IPRB = 2 , either subroutine computes and returns a correct value for CPRB; the value returned for DENS is correct on some systems, spurious on others.

Both subroutines return densities accurate to virtually the full machine word length, but they differ as regards the precision with which they can compute cumulative probabilities. Subroutine Unrcuq returns values with absolute errors not exceeding 10^{-7} on any machine. Subroutine Dunrcu is capable of computing values accurate to about 2 decimal digits less than full machine word length; subject to this limitation, the relative error will not exceed the value of the input variable TOL.

Fractiles under the unit Normal distribution are computed by the function

UNRFRC(TOL, Z) = F^{-1} (z) ,

which computes the fractile by search and returns a value with absolute error less than TOL.

On machines with a short word length like the IBM 360, Dunrcu and Unrfrc work in double precision and the arguments with which they are called must be typed as double-precision in the calling program.

7.3. Printed Description of Continuous Distributions: Subroutine Prbpri

By use of the Manecon subroutine Prbpri, a programmer can offer the user at the terminal the same forms of printed description of any continuous distribution that are offered by program Cdispri and have been described in Section 1.2.1 above.

7.3.1. *Required Functions*

In order to use subroutine <u>Prbpri</u>, the programmer must have available three subprogram functions (not subroutines or arithmetic-statement functions) which return densities, cumulative probabilities, and fractiles under the distribution to be described.

Formally, the call list of each of the three functions must contain the name of the argument followed by the names of exactly four parameters. The last parameter must be a scalar; the first three may be either vector or scalar; all four may be either integer or real.

These formal requirements do not, however, impose any real restrictions whatever on the nature of the functions that describe the distribution. After we have shown how to use <u>Prbpri</u> in the rare cases where the "natural" density, cumulative, and fractile functions happen to satisfy the formal requirements, we shall go on to show how in all other cases the requirements can be satisfied by defining auxiliary "translator" functions.

7.3.2. *Use of Subroutine Prbpri*

Suppose that the density, cumulative, and fractile functions are called respectively <u>Xdenf</u>, <u>Xcumf</u>, and <u>Xfrcf</u>; and suppose that the call list of each of these functions is (X, A, B, C, D) where X is the argument, A ... D are parameters, and D is scalar. In order to use subroutine <u>Prbpri</u>, the programmer must proceed as follows.

1. Somewhere before the first executable statement in his program he must include the type declaration

EXTERNAL XDENF, XCUMF, XFRCF

which informs the compiler that these three names represent subprograms rather than variables.

2. He must include provision for obtaining and storing the values of the four parameters A ... D and also the mean and variance of the distribution. We shall assume that the two latter quantities are stored under the names XM and XV respectively.

3. He can then call <u>Prbpri</u> by a statement of the form

CALL PRBRPI(0, XDENF, XCUMF, XFRCF, A, B, C, D, XM, XV)

The integer 0 which appears as the first argument in the call list of <u>Prbpri</u> informs the subroutine that the distribution to be described is continuous (rather than grouped).

7.3.3. Translator Functions

As we have already said, it is easy to find a way around the difficulty which arises when the call lists of the "natural" density, cumulative, and fractile functions of a particular distribution do not satisfy the requirements of Prbpri as stated in Section 7.3.1 above.

As a first example, suppose that the call lists of Xdenf, etc., are of the form (A, B, X) where X is the argument and A and B are parameters. The programmer can define translator functions Tdenf, Tcumf, and Tfrcf which satisfy the requirements of Prbpri by writing

```
FUNCTION TDENF(X, A, B, DUMMY1, DUMMY2)
TDENF = XDENF(A, B, X)
RETURN
END
```

and similarly for Tcumf and Tfrcf.[3] He can then declare these translator functions as "external" in his main program and call Prbpri by a statement of the form

```
CALL PRBPRI(0, TDENF, TCUMF, TFRCF, A, B, D1, D2, XM, XV)
```

where the meaningless variables D1 and D2 can have any values whatever.

As a second example, suppose that the call lists of the natural functions Xdenf, etc., are of the form (X, A, B, C, D, E, F) where X is the argument and A ... F are scalar parameters. In this case, a solution can be found by consolidating the parameters A , B , and C into a vector V . The main program can accomplish this by the statements

```
DIMENSION V(3)
EQUIVALENCE (V(1), A),  (V(2), B),  (V(3), C)
```

It can then call Prbpri by a statement of the form

```
CALL PRBPRI(0, TDENF, TCUMF, TFRCF, V, D, E, F, XM, XV)
```

provided that the programmer has defined translator functions Tdenf, Tcumf,

---

[3] On some systems the compiler will issue a diagnostic if the call list of a subprogram includes arguments like DUMMY1 and DUMMY2 in the example which are not actually used in the subprogram. The diagnostics can be eliminated by including meaningless statements such as

```
DUMMY1 = DUMMY1
```

and Tfrcf along the lines of

```
FUNCTION TDENF(X, V, D, E, F)
DIMENSION V(3)
A = V(1)
B = V(2)
C = V(3)
TDENF = XDENF(X, A, B, C, D, E, F)
RETURN
END
```

CHAPTER 8

Summary Description of the General-Purpose Subprograms

The present chapter contains brief descriptions of all of the Manecon subprograms that are likely to be of use to a person programming the analysis of an applied problem. The last section of the chapter provides an alphabetical index of these subprograms and names the file in which each of them is stored.

Contents of Chapter 8

1. Grouped Probability Distributions   142
   1. Mnemonics; 2. Subprograms for EP Distributions; 3. Subprograms for EW Distributions; 4. Subprogram for both EP and EW Grouping.

2. Piecex and Sumex Functions   145
   1. Mnemonics; 2. Piecex Subprograms; 3. Sumex Subprograms.

3. Continuous Probability Distributions   146
   1. Introduction; 2. Beta Distributions; 3. Gamma Distributions; 4. Student and Logstudent Distributions; 5. Normal and Related Distributions; 6. Piecewise Quadratic Distribution; 7. Chi-Square and F Distributions; 8. Printed Description of Continuous Distributions.

4. Miscellaneous Functions   152
   1. Complete Gamma Function; 2. Exponential and Logarithmic Functions; 3. Other Functions.

5. Sorter   152

6. Subprograms for Input from Terminal and Opening and Closing of Files   153

7. Index of the General-Purpose Subprograms   153

8.1. Grouped Probability Distributions

8.1.1. Mnemonics

In describing the call lists of the Manecon subprograms for dealing with grouped probability distributions, we shall use argument names of which the following are typical:

XMIN $\}$ XMAX $\}$	$\{$ least and greatest possible values of the uq $\tilde{x}$, or two $\{$ values which are to be treated as such;
NXBRAK	number of brackets into which distribution of $\tilde{x}$ is grouped;
XMEAN $\}$ XVAR $\}$	mean and variance of the grouped distribution of $\tilde{x}$;
XBRMD	vector containing the bracket medians of brackets of equal probability;
XMASS $\}$ XCUM $\}$	$\{$ vectors containing respectively the individual and cumula-$\{$ tive probabilities of brackets of equal width.

8.1.2. Subprograms for EP Distributions

Functions

EPCUM(X, XMIN, XMAX, XBRMD, NXBRAK)

Returns the probability that the uq is less than or equal to X .

EPDEN(X, XMIN, XMAX, XBRMD, NXBRAK)

Returns the value of the density function at X .

EPFRC(Z, XMIN, XMAX, XBRMD, NXBRAK)

Returns the Z fractile of the uq—i.e., the value of the uq whose cumulative probability is Z .

EPMEAN(XBRMD, NXBRAK)

Returns the mean of the distribution (the expectation of the uq).

Subroutines

EPMOMT(XBRMD, NXBRAK, XMEAN, XVAR)

Accepts XBRMD and NXBRAK as inputs; returns XMEAN and XVAR.

EPFDIS(FMIN, FMAX, FVAL, NVAL, NBRMD, FBRMD)

First 5 arguments are inputs; last is output. Accepts the least and greatest possible values of a function and a vector FVAL containing in its first NVAL locations the values of the function at the NVAL end positions of the probability diagram; returns NBRMD equiprobable bracket medians of the function in the first NBRMD locations of the vector FBRMD. The dimension of FVAL in the calling program must be at least equal to 2 times NVAL.

EPFILE(XMIN, XMAX, XBRMD, NXBRAK)

Files the distribution described by XMIN ... NXBRAK after calling on user at terminal to supply the file name; also computes and files the mean and variance of the distribution.

EPPRIN(XMIN, XMAX, XBRMD, NXBRAK)

Offers printed description of the distribution to the user at the terminal.

EQUALZ(XMIN, XMAX, PRBRMD, NXBRAK, POPROB, POBRMD, POMEAN, POVAR)

First 5 arguments are input, last 3 are output. Accepts prior bracket medians in PRBRMD and their unequal posterior probabilities in POPROB; returns equiprobable posterior bracket medians in POBRMD and also their mean and variance.

8.1.3. Subprograms for EW Distributions

Functions

EWCUM(X, XMIN, XMAX, XCUM, NXBRAK)

Returns the probability that the uq is less than or equal to X .

EWDEN(X, XMIN, XMAX, XCUM, NXBRAK)

Returns the value of the density function at X .

EWFRC(Z, XMIN, XMAX, XCUM, NXBRAK)

Returns the Z fractile of the uq—i.e., the value of the uq whose cumulative probability is Z .

EWMEAN(XMIN, XMAX, XMASS, NXBRAK)

Returns the mean of the distribution (the expectation of the uq).

Subroutines

ACCUM(XMASS, NXBRAK, XCUM)

Accepts NXBRAK individual bracket probabilities in XMASS; returns cumulative probabilities in XCUM. If called with XMASS as both first and third arguments, replaces individual probabilities by cumulative probabilities.

DECUM(XCUM, NXBRAK, XMASS)

Accepts NXBRAK cumulative probabilities in XCUM; returns individual probabilities in XMASS. If called with XCUM as both first and third arguments, replaces cumulative probabilities by individual probabilities.

CONVOL(BWIDTH, XMIN, XMASS, NXBRAK, YMIN, YMASS, NYBRAK, ISIGNY,
         ZMIN, ZMAX, ZMASS, NZBRAK)

Accepts individual bracket probabilities of $\tilde{x}$ and $\tilde{y}$ and returns individual
bracket probabilities of either (1) $\tilde{z} = \tilde{x} + \tilde{y}$, if called with ISIGNY = +1 , or
(2) $\tilde{z} = \tilde{x} - \tilde{y}$, if called with ISIGNY = -1 . First eight arguments are inputs,
last four are outputs. BWIDTH is the bracket width, which must be the same
in both input distributions and will be the same in the output distribution.
ZMASS must be dimensioned at least equal to NXBRAK + NYBRAK, since
NZBRAK will not exceed but may equal this sum.

EWMOMT(XMIN, XMAX, XMASS, NXBRAK, XMEAN, XVAR)

Accepts XMIN ... NXBRAK as inputs; returns XMEAN and XVAR as output.

EWFILE(XMIN, XMAX, XMASS, NXBRAK)

Files the distribution described by XMIN ... NXBRAK after calling on user
at terminal to supply the file name; also computes and files the mean and variance
of the distribution.

EWPRIN(XMIN, XMAX, XMASS, NXBRAK)

Offers printed description of the distribution to the user at the terminal.

NORMLZ(XMIN, XMAX, XMASS, NXBRAK, XCUM)

First four arguments are inputs, all five are outputs. Accepts normalized
or nonnormalized individual probabilities in XMASS, alters XMIN and XMAX
so as to eliminate brackets with negligible probabilities at either end of the
distribution, alters NXBRAK accordingly, and returns normalized individual
and cumulative probabilities in the first NXBRAK positions of XMASS and
XCUM respectively. If called with XMASS as both third and fifth argument,
returns only the individual probabilities. Treats individual probabilities as
negligible if when normalized they are less than b^{-n} where b is the machine
number base and n is the number of digits to this base in the mantissa of a
real number.

8.1.4.   *Subprogram for both EP and EW Grouping*

GDREAD(IGROUP, NXBRMX, XMIN, XMAX, XVECTR, NXBRAK, IERROR)

Reads a distribution from a file after calling on user at terminal to supply
the file name. First two arguments contain input; remainder will contain
output. If distribution is EP, call with IGROUP = 1 and XBRMD in place of
XVECTR; if distribution is EW, call with IGROUP = 2 and XMASS in place of
XVECTR. NXBRMX is dimension of XVECTR in calling program. Normally
returns IERROR = 0 ; returns value greater than 0 if file does not exist or
distribution is of wrong type or too large for space allowed.

8.2. Piecex and Sumex Functions

8.2.1. Mnemonics

In describing the call lists of the Manecon subprograms for dealing with piecex and sumex functions, we shall use the following names for the arguments:

PCXPAR   18-position vector in which piecex parameters are stored;
SMXPAR   7-position vector in which sumex parameters are stored;
V   criterion value
Q   preference

On machines with a short word length like the IBM 360, the vectors PCXPAR and SMXPAR must be typed as double-precision in the calling program. The arguments V and Q are single-precision on all machines.

8.2.2. Piecex Subprograms

Subroutines

PXREAD(PCXPAR, IERROR)

Reads piecex parameters from a file and stores them in PCXPAR after calling on user at terminal to supply file name. Normally returns IERROR = 0 ; returns value greater than 0 if file does not exist or does not contain piecex parameters.

PXGAM(V, P, N, PCXPAR, VLBND, VUBND, VPXAV)

First four arguments are input; last five are output. Accepts N payoffs of a gamble in vector V and the associated probabilities in vector P ; returns lower and upper bounds on certainty equivalent and piecex-average certainty equivalent.

Functions

PXAVPR(V, PCXPAR)

Returns piecex-average preference for V .

PXLBPR(V, PCXPAR)

Returns lower bound on preference for V .

PXUBPR(V, PCXPAR)

Returns upper bound on preference for V .

PXAVCE(Q, PCXPAR)

Returns value for which piecex-average preference is Q .

145

PXLBCE(Q, PCXPAR)

Returns lower bound on value for which preference is Q .

PXUBCE(Q, PCXPAR)

Returns upper bound on value for which preference is Q .

8.2.3. *Sumex Subprograms*

Subroutine

SXREAD(SMXPAR, IERROR)

Reads sumex parameters from a file and stores them in SMXPAR after calling on user at terminal to supply file name. Normally returns IERROR = 0 ; returns value greater than 0 if file does not exist or does not contain sumex parameters.

Functions

SXPR(V, SMXPAR)

Returns sumex preference for V .

SXCE(Q, SMXPAR)

Returns value for which sumex preference is Q .

8.3. Continuous Probability Distributions

8.3.1. *Introduction*

In showing how various continuous distributions can be evaluated by use of appropriate Manecon subroutines, we shall denote the density function of any distribution by f , the (left-tail) cumulative function by F , and the fractile function by F^{-1} . The parameters will follow the argument in any list. Thus if the uq $\tilde{x}$ has a distribution with parameters a and b we shall write

$$f(x, a, b) \quad = \text{mass or density at } x \quad ,$$
$$F(x, a, b) \quad = \text{probability of } x \text{ or less} \quad ,$$
$$F^{-1}(z, a, b) \quad = x \text{ such that } F(x, a, b) = z \quad .$$

The mean of $\tilde{x}$ will be denoted by XMEAN, the variance by XVAR. The left- and right-hand linear-loss integrals defined in ASDT will be denoted by XL and XR respectively. If a variable or parameter has the algebraic name m , it will be given the Fortran name XM to indicate that its value must be stored as a floating-point number, and similarly for any other algebraic name beginning with one of the letters i-n.

8.3.2.   Beta Distributions

1.   Beta Distribution of ADU and ASDT. The uq $\tilde{p}$ is said to have the beta distribution of ADU or ASDT with parameters b and c if

$$f(p, b, c) \propto p^{b-1} (1 - p)^{c-b-1} , \qquad 0 \le p \le 1 , \ b > 0 , \ c > b .$$

The distribution can be evaluated via:

```
f(p, b, c)   = BETDEN(P, B, C)
F(p, b, c)   = BETCUM(P, B, C)
F⁻¹(z, b, c) = BETFRC(Z, B, C)
PMEAN = B/C
PVAR  = PMEAN*(1. - PMEAN)/(C + 1.)
```

The subroutine BETCUQ(P, B, C, DENS, CPRB) returns both the density and the cumulative probability. The linear-loss integrals are most efficiently computed as follows:

```
CALL BETCUQ(P, B, C + 1., DENS, CPRB)
V = P*(1.-P)/C
PL = V*DENS - (PMEAN-P)*CPRB
PR = V*DENS - (P-PMEAN)*(1.-CPRB)
```

2. Standard Beta Distribution. The uq $\tilde{x}$ is said to have a standard beta distribution with Pearson parameters p and q if

$$f(x, p, q) \propto x^{p-1} (1 - x)^{q-1} , \qquad 0 \le x \le 1 , \ p > 0 , \ q > 0 .$$

The distribution can be evaluated via

```
f(x, p, q)   = BETDEN(X, P, P+Q)
F(x, p, q)   = BETCUM(X, P, P+Q)
F⁻¹(z, p, q) = BETFRC(Z, P, P+Q)
XMEAN = P/(P + Q)
XVAR = XMEAN*(1.-XMEAN)/(P + Q + 1.)
```

8.3.3.   Gamma Distributions

1. Standard Gamma Distribution. The uq $\tilde{x}$ is said to have a standard gamma distribution with parameter r if

$$f(x, r) \propto e^{-x} x^{r-1} , \qquad x \ge 0 , \ r > 0 .$$

The distribution can be evaluated via:

```
f(x, r)   = GAMDEN(X, 1., R, 1.)
F(x, r)   = GAMCUM(X, 1., R, 1.)
F⁻¹(z, r) = GAMFRC(Z, 1., R, 1.)
XMEAN = R
XVAR = R
```

The subroutine GASCUQ(X, R, DENS, CPRB) returns both the density and the cumulative probability.

  2. Gamma-q Distribution. The uq $\tilde{x}$ is said to have a gamma-q distribution with parameters q , r , s if $\tilde{y} = (\tilde{x}/s)^q$ has a standard gamma distribution with parameter r ; the argument and parameters are restricted to

$$x \geq 0 , \quad q \neq 0 , \quad r > 0 , \quad s > 0 .$$

The distribution can be evaluated via:

```
f(x, q, r, s)    = GAMDEN(X, Q, R, S)
F(x, q, r, s)    = GAMCUM(X, Q, R, S)
F-1(z, q, r, s)  = GAMFRC(Z, Q, R, S)
CALL GAMMOM(Q, R, S, XMEAN, XVAR)
```

  3. Gamma-1 Distribution of ASDT. The uq $\tilde{x}$ is said to have the gamma-1 distribution of ASDT with parameters r and t if $\tilde{y} = t\tilde{x}$ has a standard gamma distribution with parameter r ; the argument and parameters are restricted to

$$x \geq 0 , \quad r > 0 , \quad t > 0 .$$

The distribution can be evaluated via:

```
f(x, r, t)    = GAMDEN(X, 1., R, 1./T)
F(x, r, t)    = GAMCUM(X, 1., R, 1./T)
F-1(z, r, t)  = GAMFRC(Z, 1., R, 1./T)
XMEAN = R/T
XVAR = XMEAN/T
```

The linear-loss integrals are most efficiently computed as follows:

```
CALL GASCUQ(T*X, R, DENS, CPRB)
XL = XMEAN*DENS - (XMEAN-X)*CPRB
XR = XMEAN*DENS - (X-XMEAN)*(1.-CPRB)
```

8.3.4. *Student and Logstudent Distributions*

  1. Student Distributions. The uq $\tilde{t}$ is said to have a standard or unit Student distribution (or "t distribution") with ν (nu) degrees of freedom if

$$f(t, \ \nu) \propto (\nu + t^2)^{-(\nu+1)/2} , \qquad -\infty < t < \infty , \quad \nu > 0 .$$

The uq $\tilde{x}$ is said to have a (general) Student distribution with parameters μ , σ , and ν if $\tilde{t} = (\tilde{x} - \mu)/\sigma$ has a unit Student distribution with parameter ν ; the argument and parameters are restricted to

$$-\infty < x < \infty , \quad -\infty < \mu < \infty , \quad \sigma > 0 , \quad \nu > 0 .$$

The general Student distribution can be evaluated via:

$$f(x, \ \mu, \ \sigma, \ \nu) \qquad = STUDEN(X, \ XMU, \ SIGMA, \ XNU)$$
$$F(x, \ \mu, \ \sigma, \ \nu) \qquad = STUCUM(X, \ XMU, \ SIGMA, \ XNU)$$
$$F^{-1}(z, \ \mu, \ \sigma, \ \nu) = STUFRC(Z, \ XMU, \ SIGMA, \ XNU)$$
$$XMEAN = XMU \qquad\qquad\qquad\qquad \text{if } \nu > 1 \ ,$$
$$XVAR \quad = SIGMA*SIGMA/(XNU - 2.) \qquad \text{if } \nu > 2 \ .$$

The mean is not defined if $\nu \leq 1$; the variance is infinite if $\nu \leq 2$.

The unit-Student distribution can be evaluated from these same formulas with $\mu = 0$, $\sigma = 1$.

2. Logstudent Distribution. The uq $\tilde{x}$ is said to have a logstudent distribution with parameters μ, σ, ν if $y = \log x$ has a Student distribution with parameters μ, σ, ν . The argument and parameters are restricted to

$$x \geq 0 \ , \quad - \infty < \mu < \infty \ , \quad \sigma > 0, \ \nu > 0 \ .$$

The distribution can be evaluated via:

$$f(x, \ \mu, \ \sigma, \ \nu) \qquad = ALSDEN(X, \ XMU, \ SIGMA, \ XNU)$$
$$F(x, \ \mu, \ \sigma, \ \nu) \qquad = ALSCUM(X, \ XMU, \ SIGMA, \ XNU)$$
$$F^{-1}(z, \ \mu, \ \sigma, \ \nu) = ALSFRC(Z, \ XMU, \ SIGMA, \ XNU)$$

The mean and variance of the logstudent distribution are infinite.

8.3.5. *Normal and Related Distributions*

1. Gaussian or Normal Distribution. The uq $\tilde{u}$ is said to have a unit Normal distribution if

$$f(u) \propto e^{-u^2/2} \ , \qquad - \infty < u < \infty \ .$$

The uq $\tilde{x}$ is said to have a (general) Gaussian or Normal distribution with parameters m and s if $\tilde{u} = (\tilde{x} - m)/s$ has a unit Normal distribution; the argument and parameters are restricted to

$$- \infty < x < \infty \ , \quad - \infty < m < \infty \ , \quad s > 0 \ .$$

The general Gaussian distribution can be evaluated via:

$$f(x, \ m, \ s) \qquad = GAUDEN(X, \ XM, \ S)$$
$$F(x, \ m, \ s) \qquad = GAUCUM(X, \ XM, \ S)$$
$$F^{-1}(z, \ m, \ s) = GAUFRC(Z, \ XM, \ S)$$
$$XMEAN = XM$$
$$XVAR = S*S$$

The linear-loss integrals are most efficiently computed as follows:

```
CALL UNRCUQ(1, (X-XM)/S, DENS, CPRB)
XL = S*DENS - (XM-X)*CPRB
XR = S*DENS - (X-XM)*(1.-CPRB)
```

149

The unit Normal distribution can be evaluated by these same formulas with $m = 0$, $s = 1$. Unit Normal fractiles accurate to at least 3 decimal places can be obtained more inexpensively by calling the function ANORDV(Z) than by calling GAUFRC(Z, 0., 1.).

2. Lognormal Distribution. The uq $\tilde{x}$ is said to have a lognormal distribution with parameters μ and σ if $\tilde{y} = \log \tilde{x}$ has a Normal distribution with parameters μ and σ; the argument and parameters are restricted to

$$x \geq 0, \quad -\infty < \mu < \infty, \quad \sigma > 0.$$

The distribution can be evaluated via:

    f(x, μ, σ)   = ALNDEN(X, XMU, SIGMA)
    F(x, μ, σ)   = ALNCUM(X, XMU, SIGMA)
    F⁻¹(z, μ, σ) = ALNFRC(Z, XMU, SIGMA)
    XMEAN = EXP(XMU + .5*SIGMA**2)
    XVAR = EXP(2.*(XMU + SIGMA**2)) - XMEAN**2

3. Bounded Lognormal Distribution. The uq $\tilde{p}$ is said to have a bounded lognormal distribution with parameters μ and σ if $\tilde{x} = \log[\tilde{p}/(1 - \tilde{p})]$ has a Normal distribution with parameters μ and σ; the argument and parameters are restricted to

$$0 \leq p \leq 1, \quad -\infty < \mu < \infty, \quad \sigma > 0.$$

The distribution can be evaluated via:

    f(p, μ, σ)   = BLNDEN(P, XMU, SIGMA)
    F(p, μ, σ)   = BLNCUM(P, XMU, SIGMA)
    F⁻¹(z, μ, σ) = BLNFRC(Z, XMU, SIGMA)
    CALL BLNMOM(XMU, SIGMA, PMEAN, PVAR)

4. Arcsinh-Normal Distribution. The uq $\tilde{x}$ is said to have an arcsinh-normal distribution with parameters μ, σ, m, s if $\tilde{y} = \text{arcsinh}[(\tilde{x} - m)/s]$ has a Normal distribution with parameters μ and σ; the argument and parameters are restricted to

$$-\infty < x < \infty, \quad -\infty < \mu < \infty, \quad \sigma > 0, \quad -\infty < m < \infty, \quad s > 0.$$

The distribution can be evaluated via:

    f(x, μ, σ, m, s)   = ASNDEN(X, XMU, SIGMA, XM, S)
    F(x, μ, σ, m, s)   = ASNCUM(X, XMU, SIGMA, XM, S)
    F⁻¹(z, μ, σ, m, s) = ASNFRC(Z, XMU, SIGMA, XM, S)

The mean and variance can be computed as follows:

    W = EXP(SIGMA**2)
    B = EXP(XMU)
    BSQ = B**2
    XMEAN = XM + S*SQRT(W)*(B - 1./B)/2.
    XVAR = S*S*.5*(W-1.)*(1. + W*(BSQ + 1./BSQ)/2.)

8.3.6. *Piecewise Quadratic Distribution*

A uq is said to have a piecewise quadratic distribution if its cumulative function consists of a sequence of convex quadratics, a linear segment, and a sequence of concave quadratics. The parameters of such a distribution as returned by subroutine Pcqfit consist of a vector V containing the abscissas of the junction points, a vector D containing the ordinates of the density function at the junction points, a vector P containing the ordinates of the cumulative function at the junction points, and an integer N which is the number of junction points. The distribution can be evaluated via:

    f(x, V, D, P, N)   = PCQDEN(X, V, D, N)
    F(x, V, D, P, N)   = PCQCUM(X, V, D, P, N)
    F^{-1}(z, V, D, P, N) = PCQFRC(Z, V, D, P, N)
    CALL PCQMOM(V, D, N, XMEAN, XVAR)

8.3.7. *Chi-Square and F Distributions*

1. Chi-Square Distribution. Let G denote the right-tail cumulative function of the chi-square distribution with d degrees of freedom, so that $G(\chi^2, d)$ is the "P-level" of the observed χ^2 and G^{-1}(p, d) is the χ^2 whose P-level is p .

    G(χ^2, d)   = 1. - GAMCUM(CHISQR, 1., .5*D, .5)
    G^{-1}(p, d)   = GAMFRC(1.-P, 1., .5*D, .5)

2. F Distribution. Let G denote the right-tail cumulative function of the F distribution with d_1 and d_2 degrees of freedom, so that $G(F, d_1, d_2)$ is the P-level of the observed F and G^{-1}(p, d_1, d_2) is the F whose P-level is p . Then $G(F, d_1, d_2)$ can be evaluated by computing

    R = D2/D1
    S = R/(R + F)
    G(F, d_1, d_2) = BETCUM(S, .5*D2, .5*(D1+D2))

and G^{-1}(p, d_1, d_2) can be evaluated by computing

    S = BETFRC(P, .5*D2, .5*(D1+D2))
    R = D2/D1
    G^{-1}(p, d_1, d_2) = R*(1.-S)/S

8.3.8. *Printed Description of Continuous Distributions*

PRBPRI(IGROUP, DENFCN, CUMFCN, FRCFCN, P1, P2, P3, P4, E, V)

Subroutine providing various forms of tabular and graphic printed description of any continuous distribution. See Section 7.3 above.

8.4. Miscellaneous Functions

8.4.1. *Complete Gamma Function*

ALGAMA(X)

Returns log $\Gamma(x)$.[1]

ALGAMD(X, D)

Returns log $[\Gamma(x+d)/\Gamma(x)]$. Avoids the loss of significance that occurs in computing ALGAMA(X+D) - ALGAMA(X) when D is small.

8.4.2. *Exponential and Logarithmic Functions*

BLOG(X)

Returns $\log(1 + x)$. More precise than ALOG(1. + X) for x near 0; equally precise for large positive x ; loses significance as x approaches –1.

PHI(X)

Returns $e^x - 1$. More precise than EXP(X) - 1. for x near 0; equally precise for large positive x ; loses significance as x approaches $-\infty$.

GXROOT(X, Y, Z, P)

Returns r such that $e^{-ry} = pe^{-rz} + (1 - p)e^{-rx}$.

8.4.3. *Other Functions*

IOFXF(X, XVECTR, NX)

Accepts scalar X and vector XVECTR containing NX real numbers in increasing order and returns integer I such that XVECTR(I) $\leq$ X and XVECTR(I + 1) > X . Returns 0 if XVECTR(1) > X ; returns NX if XVECTR(NX) $\leq$ X .

IPART(X)

Returns largest integer less than or equal to X .

NRANDF(N)

Returns a random integer between 1 and N .

8.5. Sorter

MSORT(NDIM, NDATA, JDATA, DATA)

Subroutine. All arguments are inputs; last two are outputs. Accepts NDATA real numbers and sorts them into ascending order. When Msort is called,

---

[1] This function is available in the system library on the IBM 360/CP67 but the Manecon collection on that system contains an alternate version in Fortran which can be translated for use on systems whose libraries do not contain the function.

numbers must be in first NDATA positions of one column of the NDIM × 2 matrix DATA and JDATA must be equal to the index of this column. When Msort returns, the sorted numbers will be in the first NDATA positions of one column of DATA and JDATA will be equal to the index of this column.

8.6. Subprograms for Input from Terminal and Opening and Closing of Files

The Manecon function IANSWR(N) prints a ready signal at the terminal and waits for the user to type his answer to a question asked by the calling program. If the user types YES or 1, the function returns the integer value 1; if he types NO or 0, it returns 0; if he types anything else, it asks him to retype his answer. The argument N is meaningless and may be replaced by any number when the function is called.

The Manecon collection as implemented on any particular system may include various subroutines which provide free-format numerical input from the terminal. For descriptions of these subroutines, whose names all begin with INPUT, see the listing of the file Utilib for the particular system being used.

The Manecon collection as implemented on any particular system also includes one or more of the following subroutines for opening and closing disk files:

Fread   :   opens a file for reading.
Cread   :   closes a file after reading.
Fwrite :   opens a file for writing.
Cwrite :   closes a file after writing.

A file which is opened and closed by Fwrite and Cwrite is identified by a file name which is obtained from the user at the terminal and a file type which is obtained from the calling program. When the file is later opened for reading by Fread, the name is again obtained from the user at the terminal while the type is obtained from the calling program; Fread issues an error message if no file with the specified name and type exists and reports the error to the calling program via an indicator variable in its call list. For descriptions of these four subroutines, see the listing of the file Utilib for the particular system being used.

8.7. Index of the General-Purpose Subprograms

The following list shows for each general-purpose subprogram the file in which it is stored and the section of the present chapter in which it is described.

Name	File	Description
Accum	Ewdlib	8.1.3
Algama	Utilib*	8.4.1
Algamd	Explib	8.4.1
Aln...	Lnrlib	8.3.5
Als...	Stulib	8.3.4

*In file Non360 on IBM 360/CP67.

Name	File	Description
Anordv	Utilib	8.3.5
Asn...	Asnlib	8.3.5
Bet...	Betlib	8.3.2
Bln...	Blnlib	8.3.5
Blog	Explib	8.4.2
Convol	Ewflib	8.1.3
Cread	Utilib	8.6
Cwrite	Utilib	8.6
Decum	Ewdlib	8.1.3
Epfdis	Epflib	8.1.2
Epprin	Epplib	8.1.2
Ep...	Epdlib	8.1.2
Equalz	See Note**	8.1.2
Ewfdis	Ewflib	8.1.3
Ewprin	Ewplib	8.1.3
Ew...	Ewdlib	8.1.3
Fread	Utilib	8.6
Fwrite	Utilib	8.6
Gam...	Gamlib	8.3.3
Gau...	Gaulib	8.3.5
Gdread	Gdrlib	8.1.4
Gxroot	Explib	8.4.2
Ianswr	Utilib	8.6
Input...	Utilib	8.6
Iofxf	Utilib	8.4.3
Ipart	Utilib	8.4.3
Msort	Epflib	8.5
Nrandf	Utilib	8.4.3
Pcq...	Pcqlib	8.3.6
Phi	Utilib	8.4.2
Prbpri	Prilib	8.3.8
Px...	Pcxlib	8.2.2
Stu...	Stulib	8.3.4
Sx...	Smxlib	8.2.3
Unr...	Unrlib	8.3.5

On systems which provide automatic search of user-created libraries of precompiled subprograms, all files with names ending in <u>lib</u> may be placed in one or more such libraries.

**In file containing program <u>Postdis</u>.

CHAPTER 9

Mathematics of Preference Functions

Contents of Chapter 9

1. Local Risk Aversion   156

2. Preference Functions with Constant Absolute or Proportional Risk Aversion   156
    1. Constant Absolute Risk Aversion; 2. Constant Proportional Risk Aversion.

3. Piecex Preference and Bounding Functions   158
    1. Introduction; 2. Test for Existence of a Solution; 3. Basis Functions;
    4. Bounding Functions; 5. Piecex-average Preference Functions; 6. Inverse
    Functions.

4. Sumex Preference Functions   162

9.1. Local Risk Aversion

Let u be a preference function. The function r defined by

$$r(x) = -u''(x)/u'(x)$$

is said to measure the local (absolute) risk aversion of u ; the function r*
defined by

$$r*(x) = x\ r(x)$$

is said to measure the local proportional risk aversion of u .

The function r is of interest because increasing every payoff of a gamble
by a fixed amount will increase the certainty equivalent by that same amount if
r is everywhere constant, by a greater amount if r is everywhere decreasing,
by a smaller amount if r is everywhere increasing. The function r* is of
interest because if all payoffs of a gamble are nonnegative, multiplication of
every payoff of the gamble by a fixed factor will multiply the certainty equivalent
by that same factor if r* is everywhere constant, by a greater factor if r* is
everywhere decreasing, by a smaller factor if r* is everywhere increasing. [1]

9.2. Preference Functions with Constant Absolute or Proportional Risk Aversion

9.2.1. *Constant Absolute Risk Aversion*

It can be proved that any preference function with constant absolute risk
aversion is equivalent[2] to the function u defined by

$$u(x,\ r) = -\frac{1}{r}\ \phi\ (-rx)\ ,\qquad -\infty < x < \infty\ ,\qquad -\infty < r < \infty\ , \qquad (9\text{–}1a)$$

where ϕ is defined by

$$\phi(z) \equiv e^z - 1 \qquad\qquad\qquad (9\text{–}1b)$$

and u(x, 0) is to be taken as the limit of u(x, r) as r approaches 0:

$$u(x,\ 0) = x\ . \qquad\qquad\qquad (9\text{–}1c)$$

The local risk aversion of u is

$$-u''(x)/u'(x) = r\ . \qquad\qquad\qquad (9\text{–}2)$$

---

[1] For a full discussion of "local" and "global" risk aversion, see John W. Pratt,
"Risk Aversion in the Small and in the Large," Econometrica, Vol. 32 (1964),
pp. 122-136.
[2] Two preference functions are said to be (behaviorally) equivalent if one is a
positive linear transformation of the other, since two such functions imply
exactly the same certainty equivalent for any gamble.

The function u defined by (9-1) is used by program <u>Conaverse</u> only in evaluating continuous gambles. To avoid loss of significance due to finite word length, finite gambles are evaluated by use of the equivalent function

$$u^*(x, \ r, \ x^*) = \begin{cases} x & \text{if} \quad r = 0 \ , \\ -\phi(-r[x - x^*]) \ \text{sgn} \ r & \text{if} \quad r \neq 0 \ , \end{cases} \qquad (9\text{-}3)$$

where x^* is the greater of the two payoffs of the gamble to which the preference function was fitted. The inverse of u^* is

$$f(q, \ r, \ x^*) = \begin{cases} q & \text{if} \quad r = 0 \ , \\ -\frac{1}{r} \ \psi(-q \ \text{sgn} \ r) + x^* & \text{if} \quad r \neq 0 \ , \end{cases} \qquad (9\text{-}4a)$$

where ψ is defined by

$$\psi(z) = \log(1 + z) \ . \qquad (9\text{-}4b)$$

9.2.2.   *Constant Proportional Risk Aversion*

It can be proved that any preference function implying constant proportional risk aversion is equivalent to the function

$$w(x, \ r) = u(\log x, \ r) \ , \qquad 0 \leq x < \infty \ , \qquad -\infty < r < \infty \ , \qquad (9\text{-}5)$$

where u is defined by (9-1). The local absolute risk aversion of w is

$$-w''(x)/w'(x) = (r + 1)/x \ ; \qquad (9\text{-}6)$$

the local proportional risk aversion is therefore simply $r + 1$.

The function w defined by (9-5) is used by program <u>Conaverse</u> in the evaluation of continuous gambles, but finite gambles are evaluated by use of the equivalent function

$$w^*(x, \ r, \ x^*) = \begin{cases} u^*(\log x, \ r, \ \log x^*) & \text{if} \quad x > 0 \ , \\ -1 & \text{if} \quad x = 0 \ , \ r < 0 \ , \\ -\infty & \text{if} \quad x = 0 \ , \ r \geq 0 \ . \end{cases} \qquad (9\text{-}7)$$

where x^* is again the greater of the two payoffs of the gamble to which the preference function is fitted. The inverse of this function is

$$g(q, \ r, \ x^*) = \begin{cases} 0 & \text{if} \ r < 0 \ , \ q = -1 \ \text{or} \ r \geq 0 \ , \ q = -\infty \ , \\ \exp[f(q, \ r, \ \log x^*)] & \text{otherwise,} \end{cases} \qquad (9\text{-}8)$$

where f is defined by (9-4).

9.3. Piecex Preference and Bounding Functions [3]

9.3.1. Introduction

Let five <u>input points</u> be defined by the criterion values V_0, $V_{.25}$, $V_{.5}$, $V_{.75}$, V_1 for which preference is 0, .25, ..., 1. It can be proved that if it is possible to construct any preference function which passes through these five points and has risk aversion which is positive but decreasing everywhere in $[V_0, V_1]$, then it is possible to fit the five points with:

1. An unlimited number of preference functions whose risk aversion is positive but decreasing everywhere in $[V_0, V_1]$;
2. Two bounding functions between which all such preference functions must lie.

In the present section we shall first describe the test which shows whether or not it is possible to construct these functions and then show how to construct them if it is possible to do so. The notation in the present section will be that of Meyer and Pratt, in which the five input values are called x_1, x_2, ..., x_5 rather than V_0, $V_{.25}$, ..., V_1.

9.3.2. Test for Existence of a Solution

Let "initial" functions f_i be defined for i = 2, 3, 4, 5 by [4]

$$f_i(x) \equiv \begin{cases} a_i - b_i(e^{-r_i x} - 1) & i = 2, 3, 4 , \\ a_i + b_i x & i = 5 , \end{cases} \tag{9-9a}$$

where the a's, b's, and r's have values such that

for i = 2, 3, 4: f_i passes through input points i-1, i, i+1,
for i = 5   : f_i passes through input points i-1, i.   (9-9b)

Then it can be proved that a preference function whose risk aversion is decreasing but positive everywhere in $[x_1, x_5]$ can be put through the five input points if and only if both the following conditions hold:

---

[3] The results outlined herein without proofs are a special case of more general results developed with proofs by Richard F. Meyer and John W. Pratt, "The Consistent Assessment and Fairing of Preference Functions," <u>IEEE Transactions on Systems Science and Cybernetics</u>, September 1968, pp. 270-278. Our special case is the "5-Point Case" discussed by Meyer and Pratt on page 277 of this article.

[4] The subtraction of 1 from $e^{-r_i x}$ in the definition of the f_i for i = 2, 3, 4 serves no purpose as far as theory is concerned, but numerical evaluation of $(e^{-r_i x} - 1)$ by use of the function <u>Phi</u> described in Section 11.5.2 below avoids the loss of significance that would occur in evaluation of $e^{-r_i x}$ for r very close to 0.

$$r_2 > r_3 > r_4 > 0 \qquad\qquad (9\text{-}10a)$$
$$f_2(x) < f_5(x) \text{ for all } x \text{ in } [x_3, x_4] . \qquad\qquad (9\text{-}10b)$$

The quantities called r_2, r_3, and r_4 in (9-9a) and (9-10a) are called respectively R_1, R_2, and R_3 in Section 3.1.2 above and in the output of program <u>Piecexfit</u>.

9.3.3. Basis Functions

When the five input points satisfy conditions (9-10), it is always possible to construct "revised" f functions and find "junction points" y_3 and y_4 such that the two <u>basis functions</u> u_1 and u_2 defined by

$$u_1(x) = \begin{cases} f_2(x) = a_2 - b_2(e^{-r_2x} - 1) & \text{if } x \le y_3 \quad , \\[2ex] f_4(x) = a_4 - b_4(e^{-r_4x} - 1) & \text{if } x \ge y_3 \quad , \end{cases} \qquad (9\text{-}11a)$$

$$u_2(x) = \begin{cases} -\infty & \text{if } x < x_1 \quad , \\[1ex] 0 & \text{if } x = x_1 \quad , \\[1ex] f_3(x) = a_3 - b_3(e^{-r_3x} - 1) & \text{if } x_1 < x \le y_4 , \\[1ex] f_5(x) = a_5 + b_5x & \text{if } x \ge y_4 \quad , \end{cases} \qquad (9\text{-}11b)$$

pass through the 5 input points and are continuous and continuously differentiable except for the upward jumps in u_2 just to the left and just to the right of x_1. The junction points y_3 and y_4 obey the inequalities $x_2 < y_3 < x_4$, $x_3 < y_4 < x_5$, and $y_3 < y_4$.

The basis function u_1 is constructed as follows. If $f_2'(x_3) > f_4'(x_3)$, the "initial" f_2 is combined with a "revised" f_4 which passes through input points 5 and 4 and is tangent to f_2 at some point between input points 4 and 3. If on the contrary $f_2'(x_3) < f_4'(x_3)$, the initial f_4 is combined with a revised f_2 which passes through input points 1 and 2 and is tangent to f_4 at some point between input points 2 and 3. In either case, the abscissa of the point of tangency is the parameter y_3.

The basis function u_2 is constructed as follows. If $f_3'(x_4) > f_5'(x_4)$, the initial f_3 is combined with a revised f_5 which passes through input point 5 and is tangent to f_3 at some point between input points 5 and 4. If on the contrary $f_3'(x_4) < f_5'(x_4)$, the initial f_5 is combined with a revised f_3 which passes through input points 2 and 3 and is tangent to f_5 at some point between input points 3 and 4. In either case, the abscissa of the point of tangency is the parameter y_4.

It is perhaps worth remarking that the basis functions u_1 and u_2 do not themselves imply risk aversion which is everywhere decreasing. Their risk aversions are nonnegative and nonincreasing, but they are piecewise constant, decreasing in steps. More specifically, the risk aversion of u_1 is equal to r_2 to the left of y_3, undefined at y_3, and equal to r_4 to the right of y_3. The risk aversion of u_2 is undefined to the left of x_1, infinite at x_1, equal to r_3 between x_1 and y_4, undefined at y_4, and equal to 0 to the right of y_4.

9.3.4. Bounding Functions

Concerning the basis function u_1 and u_2 defined by (9-11) it can be proved that:

1. The functions intersect at each input point and

$$
\begin{array}{llll}
u_1(x) < u_2(x) & \text{if} & x \in \{(x_1, x_2) \cup (x_3, x_4) \cup (x_5, \infty)\} , & \\
u_2(x) < u_1(x) & \text{if} & x \in \{(-\infty, x_1) \cup (x_2, x_3) \cup (x_4, x_5)\} . & (9\text{-}12)
\end{array}
$$

2. If u is any preference function which passes through the five input points and has risk aversion which is everywhere positive and decreasing, then

$$
\min\{u_1(x), u_2(x)\} < u(x) < \max\{u_1(x), u_2(x)\} . \qquad (9\text{-}13)
$$

It follows that we may give the name <u>bounding function</u> to the functions b_1 and b_2 defined by

$$
b_1(x) = \min\{u_1(x), u_2(x)\} , \qquad (9\text{-}14)
$$

$$
b_2(x) = \max\{u_1(x), u_2(x)\} ,
$$

and write

$$
b_1(x) < u(x) < b_2(x) . \qquad (9\text{-}15)
$$

These bounds will be shown to be "tight" in the sense that a preference function with decreasing positive risk aversion can be constructed through the five input points and one other point $(x, u(x))$ if and only if $u(x)$ satisfies (9-15).

9.3.5. Piecex-average Preference Functions

A <u>piecex-average preference function</u> with parameter k is defined in terms of the basis functions by

$$
p_k(x) = ku_1(x) + (1 - k)u_2(x) , \qquad 0 < k < 1 , \qquad x_1 \le x < \infty . \quad (9\text{-}16)
$$

Because (1) both u_1 and u_2 have nonnegative, nonincreasing risk aversion, and (2) at least u_1 has strictly positive risk aversion, the risk aversion of their weighted average p_k is everywhere strictly positive and everywhere strictly decreasing.[5] More specifically, the risk aversion of p_k is infinite at x_1, while to the right of this point it is finite and decreases continuously except for downward jumps at y_3 and y_4. The Manecon subprograms which evaluate piecex functions automatically set the parameter k of (9-16) above equal to 1/2, but they could easily be modified to allow the user to specify any k between 0 and 1.

Given any x and any q such that $b_1(x) < q < b_2(x)$, where b_1 and b_2 are the bounding functions defined in (9-14) above, we can obviously choose k such that $p_k(x) = q$. This is the proof that the bounds given by b_1 and b_2 are tight in the sense defined at the end of Section 9.3.4.

---

[5] Pratt, <u>Econometrica</u>, Vol. 32 (1964), page 132, theorem 5. A piecex-average preference function can also be thought of as a sequence of three different sumex functions (cf. Section 9.4 below) joined together at $x = y_3$ and $x = y_4$ in such a way that the resulting function and its first derivative are continuous even though there is a discontinuity in the second derivative and hence in the risk aversion at these two points.

9.3.6. *Inverse Functions*

The inverses of the basis functions u_1 and u_2 defined in (9-11) can be expressed by closed formulas. If we first define

$$w_0 = f_3(x_1), \qquad w_3 = u_1(y_3), \qquad w_4 = u_2(y_4) \qquad , \qquad (9\text{-}17)$$

we can write

$$
u_1^{-1}(q) = \begin{cases}
\dfrac{1}{r_2} \log\left(\dfrac{b_2}{a_2 + b_2 - q}\right) & \text{if} \quad -\infty < q \le w_3 \quad , \\[3ex]
\dfrac{1}{r_4} \log\left(\dfrac{b_4}{a_4 + b_4 - q}\right) & \text{if} \quad w_3 \le q < a_4 + b_4 \ ,
\end{cases}
\qquad (9\text{-}18a)
$$

$$
u_2^{-1}(q) = \begin{cases}
x_1 & \text{if} \quad -\infty < q \le w_0 \quad , \\[2ex]
\dfrac{1}{r_3} \log\left(\dfrac{b_3}{a_3 + b_3 - q}\right) & \text{if} \quad w_0 \le q \le y_4 \quad , \\[3ex]
\dfrac{q - a_5}{b_5} & \text{if} \quad y_4 \le q < \infty \quad .
\end{cases}
\qquad (9\text{-}18b)
$$

The definition of u_2^{-1} for $0 < q < w_0$ derives from the fact that u_2 should be considered as the limit of a function which is continuous to the right of 0.

The inverses of the bounding functions b_1 and b_2 defined in (9-14) follow straightforwardly from (9-18) and the convention

$$b_1^{-1}(q) = \infty \qquad \text{if} \quad a_4 + b_4 \le q < \infty, \qquad (9\text{-}19)$$

which is required because $b_1^{-1}(q)$ is $u_1^{-1}(q)$ for $q > w_3$ and $u_1^{-1}(q)$ is undefined for $q \ge a_4 + b_4$. Notice that the inverse of the lower bounding function b_1 supplies an upper bound on the criterion value corresponding to any given preference while b_2^{-1} supplies a lower bound.

The inverse of the preference function p_k defined in (9-16) is defined on $[0, \infty)$ but cannot be expressed in closed form except for arguments between 0 and $(1 - k)w_0$. For these arguments we define

$$p_k^{-1}(q) = x_1 \qquad \text{if} \quad 0 \le q < (1 - k)w_0 \qquad (9\text{-}20)$$

for the same reason that we define $u_2^{-1}(q) = x_1$ for q between 0 and w_0 .

9.4. Sumex Preference Functions

The basic, nonnormalized sumex preference function t is defined by

$$t(x) = -\phi(-ax) - c\phi(-bx), \qquad a > 0, \qquad bc > 0, \tag{9-21a}$$

where ϕ is defined by

$$\phi(z) = e^z - 1. \tag{9-21b}$$

Its local risk aversion is

$$-t''(x)/t'(x) = \frac{a^2 e^{-ax} + cb^2 e^{-bx}}{ae^{-ax} + cbe^{-bx}} \ . \tag{9-22}$$

The conditions a > 0 and bc > 0 guarantee that the risk aversion is decreasing over $(-\infty, \infty)$. If b and c are positive, the risk aversion will be everywhere positive; if b and c are negative, the risk aversion will be positive to the left of

$$x^* = \frac{1}{a - b} \log(-a^2/[b^2 c]) \ , \tag{9-23}$$

negative to the right of x^* .

Program Prefeval and the top-level Manecon function Sxpr print out or return values of the normalized sumex function

$$u(x) = \frac{t(x) - t(x_1)}{t(x_5) - t(x_1)} \tag{9-24}$$

where x_1 and x_5 are respectively the least and greatest of the criterion values supplied as input to program Sumexfit. The Manecon function Sxce accepts normalized preferences as input.

CHAPTER 10

Mathematics of Grouped Approximations

Contents of Chapter 10

1. Grouped Approximations with Brackets of Equal Probability   164

     1. Discrete and Continuous Approximations to a Continuous Distribution;
     2. Probabilities, Fractiles, and Densities; 3. Mean and Variance; 4. Distribution of a Function; 5. Subroutine Msort.

2. Grouped Approximations with Brackets of Equal Width   170

     1. Truncation of the Range of the Distribution; 2. Discrete and Continuous
     Approximations to a Continuous Distribution; 3. Probabilities, Fractiles,
     and Densities; 4. Mean and Variance; 5. Convolution.

10.1.   Grouped Approximations with Brackets of Equal Probability

10.1.1   Discrete and Continuous Approximations to a Continuous Distribution

Consider the continuous cumulative function represented by a smooth curve in Figure 10.1A, and suppose that the distribution it defines is to be grouped into 5 equiprobable brackets each represented by its bracket median.

Figure 10.1A
Continuous Probability Distribution with
Discrete and Continuous Approximations

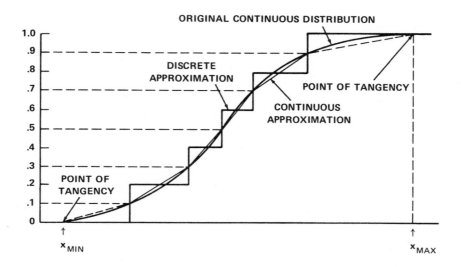

1. It follows from the definition of a bracket median (ADU 7.4.5) that the step function in Figure 10.1A represents the cumulative function of the discrete distribution that results from assigning to each bracket median the entire probability of its bracket. Observe that the original cumulative function passes through the midpoint of each "riser" in the step function. The distribution defined by this step function will be called the discrete approximation to the original continuous distribution.

2. The continuous cumulative function represented by the solid linear segments joining the midpoints of the risers of the step function in Figure 10.1A defines an improved approximation to that part of the original cumulative function which lies between the first and last bracket medians; and this improved approxi-

mation can be completed by the two dashed linear segments, which terminate at values of the uq which either are in fact, or will be treated as if they were, the least and greatest possible values of the uq. The distribution defined by this improved, piecewise linear approximation to the original cumulative function will be called the continuous approximation to the original continuous distribution.

When program Disfile is called to file an EP approximation to a continuous distribution, the program computes and files the bracket medians and the values to be treated as the least and greatest possible values of the uq. If the user's original continuous distribution was assessed graphically and processed by Disfile with the aid of subroutine Pcqfit, the values filed as the least and greatest possible values are the "0 fractile" and "1 fractile" which were supplied by the user as inputs to Disfile. In all other cases, the values filed as the least and greatest values are actually values chosen to make the continuous approximation reasonably good reasonably far into the tails. Specifically, they are the $.05/n$ and $(1 - .05/n)$ fractiles of the continuous distribution, where n is the number of brackets into which the distribution is grouped.[1]

10.1.2.   *Probabilities, Fractiles, and Densities*

The Manecon functions Epcum, Epfrc, and Epden compute cumulative probabilities, fractiles, and densities according to the piecewise-linear continuous approximation illustrated in Figure 10.1A, which implies that the density function has a jump at each bracket median but is constant between bracket medians.

When the argument of Epden is exactly equal to a bracket median, the function returns the density to the right of that bracket median.

When called with argument $p = 0$ or 1, Epfrc returns the "smallest possible" or "largest possible" value of the uq. The function issues an error message when called with argument $p < -\epsilon$ or $p > 1 + \epsilon$, where ϵ is an allowance to cover errors due to finite word length in computations which should yield $p = 0$ or 1 exactly.

If we denote by x the argument of Epcum or Epden and by x_i the i'th bracket median of the distribution of $\tilde{X}$, the calculations carried out by either function require previous determination of i such that

$$x_i \leq x < x_{i+1}$$

whenever such an i exists. Both functions obtain the required i by calling the Manecon function Iofxf, which finds i by binary search.

---

[1] The choice of these particular fractiles is made in the subroutine Grpsub in the file Epdgrp.

The corresponding preliminary step when <u>Epfrc</u> is called with argument p is to find i such that

$$\frac{i - .5}{n} = P(\tilde{x} \le x_i) \le p < P(\tilde{x} \le x_{i+1}) = \frac{i - .5}{n} \ .$$

This i is found from the formula

$$i = [pn + .5]$$

where [a] is the largest integer in a .

10.1.3.   Mean and Variance

The function <u>Epmean</u> and the subroutine <u>Epmomt</u> compute the mean and variance by use of the discrete approximation which assigns the entire probability of each bracket to the bracket median. This method of computation substantially understates the variance when the number of brackets is small.

10.1.4.   Distribution of a Function

Consider a joint probability diagram in which each fork represents a <u>discrete</u> EP approximation to the distribution actually assessed by the decision maker, and assume that all conditional distributions of any one uq have been grouped into the same number of brackets. Because the end positions of such a diagram are equiprobable, the discrete distribution of any function of the uq's that is implied by the discrete distributions in the diagram can be found by simply computing the value of the function at each end position and sorting the computed values into increasing order. The probability that the function is less than or equal to any particular value v is simply n_v/N, where N is the total number of end positions and n_v is the number of end positions at which the function value is less than or equal to v .

The step function in Figure 10.1B represents a discrete distribution of a function $\tilde{z}$ that might result from calculations of the sort just described. It is assumed in the figure that the probability diagram had 5 end positions and that the function had the value 3 at two of these end positions and the values 0, 2, and 5 at one end position each.[2]

Now suppose that (1) the true distribution of the function $\tilde{z}$ is continuous, and (2) the least and greatest possible values of the function are $z_{min} = 0$ and $z_{max} = 7$. Then (1) virtually all of the probability assigned by the discrete approximation to the value $\tilde{z} = 0$ really belongs to higher values of $\tilde{z}$, and (2) roughly half of the probability assigned to any other value of $\tilde{z}$ really belongs to lower values, half to higher values. It follows that we can obtain an improved

---

[2] Five equiprobable end positions are of course possible only if the diagram represents the distribution of a single uq, but everything we say here applies to functions of any number of uq's.

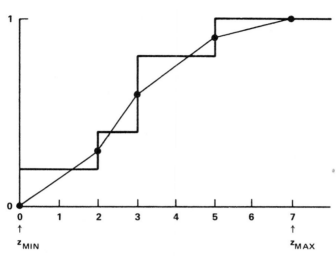

Figure 10.1B
Discrete and Continuous Approximations
To the Distribution of a Function

approximation to the distribution of the function by proceeding as follows to construct a continuous, piecewise-linear cumulative function like the one in Figure 10.1B:

1. Locate points at $(z_{min}, 0)$ and $(z_{max}, 1)$.

2. Locate a point at the midpoint of each riser in the step function unless the riser coincides with z_{min} or z_{max}.

3. Join all these points by linear segments.

Discrete and continuous approximations like those in Figure 10.1B could in principle be used directly in computations involving the distribution they describe, but in practice such direct use would give rise to serious difficulties. Storage of the function values which define the distribution requires as many core locations as there are end positions in the joint probability diagram, and it would be necessary to check for the existence of ties between the stored values every time that a density, cumulative probability, or fractile was computed. It is much better to compute once and for all a reasonably large number of equiprobable bracket medians under the distribution defined by a continuous approximation of the sort illustrated in Figure 10.1B and then to base all subsequent computations on the EP approximation defined by these bracket medians, leaving the space originally used to store the sorted end-position values free for other use.

This is the procedure which is followed by subroutine Epfdis when supplied with the least and greatest possible values of a function, the values of the function at a number of equiprobable end positions, and the desired number of bracket medians of the function. After calling subroutine <u>Msort</u> to sort the end–position values into increasing order, <u>Epfdis</u> calls subroutine <u>Epbrmd</u> to construct a piecewise-linear, continuous cumulative function like the one in Figure 10.1B and to compute the desired number of bracket medians of the distribution defined by this cumulative function.

10.1.5.   *Subroutine Msort*

The operation of subroutine <u>Msort</u> can best be understood by thinking of the input numbers as being stored in Column 1 of a two–column matrix and as being divided as shown in Figure 10.1C into numbered blocks within each of which the numbers are nondecreasing when the blocks are read alternately downward and upward. Block 1 starts at the top of the column and is to be read downward; block 2 starts at the bottom of the column and is to be read upward; block 3 starts at the end of block 1 and is to be read downward; block 4 starts at the end of block 2 and is to be read upward; and so forth. Each block ends when the next candidate for inclusion in the block is smaller than the last number included.

Figure 10.1C		Figure 10.1D		Figure 10.1E	
Start		End of First Pass		End of Second Pass	
Contents of Column 1	Block Number	Contents of Column 2	Block Number	Contents of Column 1	Block Number
1		1		1	
4	1	4		2	
10		5	1	4	
2	3	10		5	1
11		12		9	
8	5	3		10	
6	6	6	3	11	
3		8		12	
9	4	11		8	
12	2	9	2	6	2
5		2		3	

In the first pass of the sort, the results of which are shown in Figure 10.1D, <u>Msort</u> first merges blocks 1 and 2 of Column 1 (Figure 10.1C) into a single block of nondecreasing numbers which it writes downward from the top of Column 2; it then merges blocks 3 and 4 of Column 1 into a single block which it writes upward from the bottom of Column 2; it then merges blocks 5 and 6 of Column 1 into a single block which it writes downward from the end of the first combined block in Column 2; and so forth until all the numbers in Column 1 have been

written into Column 2. If the number of blocks in Column 1 is odd, the last block
is simply copied into Column 2 without merging.

In the next pass of the sort, the results of which are shown in Figure 10.1E,
the rôles of the two columns are reversed, pairs of blocks from the two ends of
Column 2 being merged into single blocks of nondecreasing numbers which are
written alternately downward and upward in Column 1. The third pass again reverses the rôles, and so forth, until the numbers are merged into a single nondecreasing block written downward from the top of one or the other of the two
columns.

The rule by which two blocks are merged is simple: look at the first and last
of the numbers in the "read" column which have not yet been written into the
"write" column and then: (1) if the smaller of the two numbers is at least as
large as the last number written out, write out this smaller number; otherwise
(2) if the larger of the two numbers is at least as large as the last number written
out, write out this larger number. When neither of the two candidates for writing
out is as large as the last number written out, it is because both the blocks being
merged have been exhausted. The two candidates are the first numbers from two
new blocks, and the smaller is written out as the first number in a new combined
block starting from the first free position at the opposite end of the write column.

If the number of blocks in the read column at the start of any pass is even,
the pairwise merging will produce just half as many blocks in the write column.
It follows that even if the numbers to be sorted are originally arranged in the
most unfavorable way possible, with each number constituting a separate block,
it will take only k passes to sort anywhere between $2^{k-1} + 1$ and 2^k numbers.
In other words, the number of passes required to sort N numbers cannot exceed
the smallest integer which is at least equal to $\log_2 N \doteq (\log_{10} N)/.3$. If there
are N = 10,000 numbers to be sorted, $\log_2 N = 4/.3 \doteq 13.3$ and the number of
passes required to sort them cannot exceed 14.

When the numbers to be sorted are generated by computing function values
at the end positions of a two-level probability diagram, the number of passes required will ordinarily be substantially below this upper bound. If all distributions
are grouped into n brackets, the n^2 function values will ordinarily be generated
in n "batches" of n numbers each and it will often be true either that the numbers are nondecreasing within every batch or else that the numbers are nonincreasing within every batch. In either of these two cases, the number of "blocks"
in the sense in which we have used that word previously will not be greater than
2n-1 and the number of passes required will not be greater than the integer k
which satisfies

$$2^{k-1} < 2n-1 \le 2^k .$$

If n = 50, it will require only 7 passes to sort the 2500 function values; if n = 100,
8 passes will suffice to sort the 10,000 function values; and so forth.

The number of comparisons required to transfer one number from the read
to the write column is:

2   if neither of the two blocks being merged has been exhausted,

3   if one of the two blocks has been exhausted,

5   when the second block is exhausted and merging of two new blocks begins.

It follows that the average number of comparisons per number transferred will be exactly 2 on the last pass of any sort but can be as high as $(3 + 5)/2 = 4$ on the first pass in the worst possible case, where every number constitutes a separate block.[3]

10.2.   Grouped Approximations with Brackets of Equal Width

10.2.1.   *Truncation of the Range of the Distribution*

If a continuous distribution is to be grouped into a finite number of brackets of equal finite width, then either the range of the distribution must in fact be finite or it must be truncated and treated as finite. And even when the range is in fact finite, truncation is usually desirable in order to avoid having virtually 0 probability in an unduly large fraction of the brackets. For this reason program <u>Disfile</u> truncates the range of any continuous distribution that it is asked to group into brackets of equal width unless the distribution is piecewise quadratic; piecewise quadratic distributions are excepted because their tails are always very short.

Choice of the truncation points is a problem of tradeoff between accuracy of description of the tails and accuracy of description of the central part of the distribution. The points chosen by <u>Disfile</u>[4] are the $.01/n$ and $1 - .01/n$ fractiles, where n is the number of brackets into which the distribution is to be grouped.

10.2.2.   *Discrete and Continuous Approximations to a Continuous Distribution*

Suppose that a uq $\widetilde{x}$ has the continuous cumulative function represented by a smooth curve in Figure 10.2A; denote by x_{min} and x_{max} the end points of the finite or truncated range of $\widetilde{x}$; suppose that the values of $\widetilde{x}$ between x_{min} and x_{max} are grouped into five brackets of equal width with edges at x_0 , x_1 , $\ldots$, x_5 , where x_0 = x_{min} and x_5 = x_{max}; and define

$$F_i = P(\widetilde{x} \leq x_i) \qquad ,$$

$$P_i = P(x_{i-1} \leq \widetilde{x} < x_i) \, ,$$

$$x_i^* = (x_{i-1} + x_i)/2 \qquad .$$

F_i is the cumulative probability of the i'th bracket, P_i is the individual probability of the i'th bracket, and x_i^* is the i'th bracket midpoint.

The distribution defined by assigning the entire probability P_i of each bracket to the bracket midpoint x_i^* will be called the <u>discrete approximation</u> to the distribution of $\widetilde{x}$. The piecewise-linear cumulative function consisting of linear segments joining successive points $(x_i$, F_i) will be said to define the <u>continuous approximation</u> to the distribution of $\widetilde{x}$.

---

[3] These figures do not include the one comparison per number transferred that is required to test the DO index which will indicate the end of the pass.

[4] The choice is actually made by the subroutine <u>Grpsub</u> in the file <u>Ewdgrp</u> which <u>Disfile</u> calls to carry out the grouping.

Figure 10.2A
Continuous Probability Distribution
and Continuous Approximation

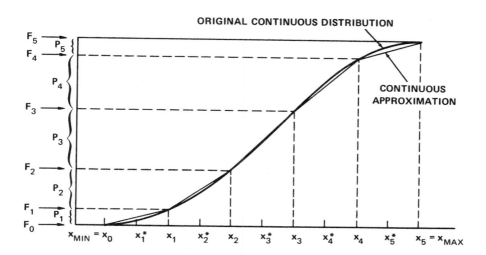

10.2.3.   *Probabilities, Fractiles, and Densities*

The functions <u>Ewcum</u>, <u>Ewfrc</u>, and <u>Ewden</u> compute cumulative probabilities, fractiles, and densities according to the piecewise-linear continuous approximation illustrated in Figure 10.2A, which implies that the density function has a jump at the edge of each bracket but is constant across any one bracket.

When the argument of <u>Ewden</u> is exactly equal to a bracket edge, the function returns the density to the right of that edge.

When called with argument $p = 0$ or 1, <u>Ewfrc</u> returns x_{min} or x_{max} respectively. The function issues an error message when called with argument $p < -\epsilon$ or $p > 1+\epsilon$, where ϵ is an allowance to cover errors due to finite word length in computations which should yield $p = 0$ or 1 exactly.

If we denote by x the argument of <u>Ewcum</u> or <u>Ewden</u>, the first step in the calculations carried out by either function is determination of i such that

$$x_{i-1} \leq x < x_i$$

where x_i is the right edge of the i'th bracket of $\tilde{x}$. This i is found from the formula

$$i = \left[(x - x_{min})/w \right] + 1$$

where $[a]$ is the largest integer in a and

$$w = (x_{max} - x_{min})/n$$

is the width of any one of the n brackets of $\tilde{x}$.

The corresponding first step when <u>Ewfrc</u> is called with argument p is to find i such that

$$P(\tilde{x} \leq x_{i-1}) \leq p < P(\tilde{x} \leq x_i)$$

whenever such an i exists. <u>Ewfrc</u> calls the function <u>Iofxf</u> to find this i by binary search.

10.2.4.   *Mean and Variance*

The function <u>Ewmean</u> and the subroutine <u>Ewmomt</u> compute the mean and variance of $\tilde{x}$ by use of the discrete approximation which assigns the entire probability of each bracket to the bracket midpoint.

10.2.5.   *Convolution*

Subroutine <u>Convol</u> computes the distribution of a sum or difference of two uq's by first calling subroutine <u>Icnvol</u> to compute a discrete approximation to the required distribution and then making the adjustments required to convert this result into a piecewise-linear continuous approximation. The entire operation can be explained by considering an example where $x_{min} = y_{min} = 0$, $x_{max} = 5$, $y_{max} = 3$, and the width of a bracket in the distribution of either $\tilde{x}$ or $\tilde{y}$ is 1, so that the bracket midpoints are .5, 1.5, 2.5, ...

The discrete approximation to the joint distribution of $\tilde{x}$ and $\tilde{y}$ in this example can be represented in the way shown in Figure 10.2B, where the entire probability is concentrated on the points designated by heavy dots. Since the sum z = x + y is constant along any one of the slanting lines in the figure, the probability that $\tilde{z}$ has any particular value z can be found by simply computing the probability of each heavy dot on the corresponding slanting line and summing these probabilities. The calculation is particularly easy when $\tilde{x}$ and $\tilde{y}$ are independent with the result that the probability of any point (x, y) is simply the product of the unconditional probabilities of x and y ; and this is the only case that can be handled by subroutine <u>Icnvol</u>.

Now suppose that the discrete approximation delivered by <u>Icnvol</u> in our example is the one defined by the step function in Figure 10.2C. If $\tilde{x}$ and $\tilde{y}$ are in reality continuous, then $\tilde{z}$ too is in reality continuous; and arguing that the probability assigned by <u>Icnvol</u> to any discrete value of $\tilde{z}$ really belongs roughly half-and-half to lower and higher values of $\tilde{z}$, we conclude that we can obtain an improved approximation to the distribution of $\tilde{z}$ by proceeding as follows to construct a continuous, piecewise-linear cumulative function of the sort shown in Figure 10.2C.

1. Locate points at $(z_{min}, 0)$ and $(z_{max}, 1)$.

2. Locate a point at the midpoint of each riser in the step function.

3. Join successive points by linear segments.

172

After calling subroutine <u>Icnvol</u> to compute a discrete approximation to the distribution of a sum, subroutine <u>Convol</u> proceeds to compute from it the probabilities of individual brackets that are implied by a piecewise-linear cumulative function constructed in the way just described. The computational method actually used to accomplish this objective consists in taking the probability assigned to each discrete value z and reassigning half of it to the bracket whose left edge is at z, half of it to the bracket whose right edge is at z.

<u>Figure 10.2B</u>
<u>Calculation of the Distribution of a Sum</u>

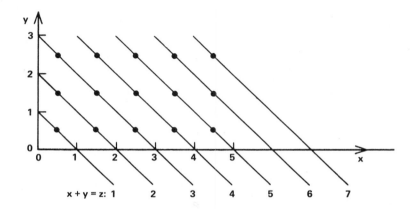

<u>Figure 10.2C</u>
<u>Discrete and Continuous Approximations</u>
<u>to the Distribution of the Sum of Two UQ's</u>

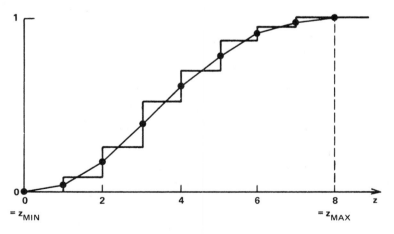

CHAPTER 11

Fitting and Evaluation of Preference Functions

Contents of Chapter 11

1. Program <u>Piecexfit</u>   175

2. Evaluation of Piecex Functions   175
   1. Basis Functions; 2. Piecex-average Functions; 3. Subroutine <u>Dpxgam</u>.

3. Program <u>Sumexfit</u>   178
   1. Definition of the Problem; 2. Reduction of the Problem to a Two-
   Dimensional Search; 3. Outline Description of the Main Program; 4. Denotation
   and Evaluation of the g , f , and u Functions; 5. Subroutine <u>Newrap</u>;
   6. Direct Search for Improved Bounds: Subroutine <u>Impvbd</u>.

4. Evaluation of Sumex Functions   186
   1. Transformation of Criterion Values; 2. Search Procedure in Function
   <u>Sxtin</u>.

5. Auxiliary Functions   188
   1. Function <u>Algamd</u>; 2. Function <u>Blog</u>; 3. Function <u>Phi</u>; 4. Function <u>Gxroot</u>.

11.1. Program Piecexfit

The following notes on program <u>Piecexfit</u> should be read in conjunction with the discussion in Section 9.3 above of the way in which piecex functions are constructed.

To avoid the loss of significance that occurs when $e^{-rx} - 1$ is evaluated for large positive x , <u>Piecexfit</u> starts by transforming the input values $x_1, \ldots, x_5$ in such a way that they are all nonnegative. The transformation consists in merely subtracting x_5 from each of the five values.

The first step in the fitting procedure is to calculate the parameters of the "initial" f_i (Section 9.3.2). Subroutine <u>Gxfit</u> is called for the parameters of the three exponential functions f_2, f_3, and f_4; the parameters of the linear f_5 are computed by <u>Piecexfit</u> itself. The only nonobvious part of these computations is the part carried out by the function <u>Gxroot</u>, which is called by <u>Gxfit</u> to return r such that

$$e^{-ry} = pe^{-rz} + (1 - p)e^{-rx} .$$

The method of computation used by <u>Gxroot</u> is described in Section 11.5.4 below.

After the parameters of the initial f_i have been computed, <u>Piecexfit</u> calls subroutine <u>Icnsis</u> to test whether the conditions (9–10) for existence of a solution are satisfied. If they are not, subroutine <u>Errmsx</u> is called to print out an appropriate message.

If the test carried out by <u>Icnsis</u> shows that a solution exists, **Piecexfit** proceeds to construct the basis functions u_1 and u_2 in the way described in Section 9.3.3. The "revised" f_i that are required for this purpose are found by binary search, in the course of which Y3 or Y4 denotes the argument for which the two f_i being joined together have equal slopes and G denotes the difference between the values of the two f_i for this argument.

The last computations performed by <u>Piecexfit</u> evaluate the accuracy of the fit. Since the functions are fitted in such a way that they necessarily go almost exactly through the five input points, the evaluation consists simply in measuring the discontinuity in each of the basis functions at the point y_3 or y_4 where the two f_i which make up the basis function are joined together.

The parameters filed by <u>Piecexfit</u> are those computed for the transformed input values. If, however, the user asks to have the parameters printed out, <u>Piecexfit</u> undoes the effect of the transformation and prints parameter values suitable for use with criterion values measured on the natural scale.

11.2. Evaluation of Piecex Functions

The methods of computation used in most of the subprograms for evaluation of piecex functions and their inverses are obvious when the program listings are read in conjunction with the general discussion of piecex functions in Section 9.3 and the remark on rescaling of criterion values in Section 11.1. The parameters read in by subroutine <u>Pxread</u> from the file written by <u>Piecexfit</u> are those calculated by <u>Piecexfit</u> for input values $x_1, \ldots, x_5$ transformed by subtraction of x_5.

11.2.1.   Basis Functions

The basis functions u_1 and u_2 are evaluated by Pxu1 and Pxu2 respectively. After subtracting the original value of x_5 from the argument for which preference is to be computed, either function simply applies the appropriate formula in Section 9.3.3. The inverse functions u_1^{-1} and u_2^{-1} are similarly evaluated by Pxu1in and Pxu2in. After using the appropriate formula in Section 9.3.6 to find the criterion value corresponding to a given preference, they add back the original value of x_5 to put the value on the natural scale.

11.2.2.   Piecex-average Functions

The piecex–average preference function defined by (9–16) with $k = 1/2$ is evaluated by the function Pxavpr by simply calling Pxu1 and Pxu2 and averaging their values.

The inverse of this function is evaluated by Pxavcd by alternating binary and secant search between running bounds, all criterion values used in the search being measured on the natural scale, not the transformed scale of Piecexfit. Initial bounds for the search are found as follows.

1. When $q \le 1$, as it normally is, the lesser of $u_1^{-1}(q)$ and $u_2^{-1}(q)$ is taken as the initial lower bound on the criterion value x; the greater is taken as the initial upper bound.

2. When $q > 1$, these bounds become very loose; the upper bound is infinite when $q \ge a_4 + b_4$. Much better bounds are found by defining functions $u*$ and $u**$ as shown in Figure 11.1A and observing that

a. For q greater than $a_4 + b_4$, the inverse of $u*$ is a better lower bound on x than the inverse of u_2.

b. For q greater than some value between 1 and $a_4 + b_4$, the inverse of $u**$ is a better upper bound on x than the inverse of u_1.

These improved bounds are first computed on the scale of Piecexfit and then transformed back to the natural scale.

11.2.3.   Subroutine Dpxgam

Subroutine Dpxgam computes lower and upper bounds on the certainty equivalent for a finite gamble in the following way.

1. Lower Bound. If none of the payoffs of a gamble is below x_1, Dpxgam computes a lower bound on the certainty equivalent by computing a lower bound on the preference, computing the criterion value which corresponds to this lower bound on preference under each of the two basis functions, and taking the lower of these two criterion values.

If one or more payoffs are below x_1, the procedure just described would yield $-\infty$ as the lower bound on preference for the gamble and therefore would yield $-\infty$ as the lower bound on the certainty equivalent. Dpxgam accordingly takes the lowest payoff of the gamble as an improved lower bound on the certainty equivalent.

Figure 11.1A
Initial Bounds for the Inverse of the
Piecex-Average Preference Function

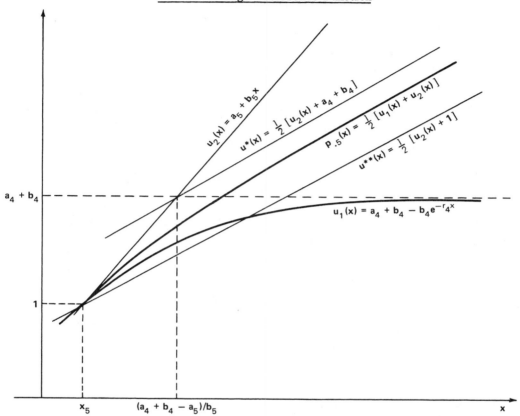

2. Upper Bound on the Certainty Equivalent. To find an upper bound on the
certainty equivalent for a gamble, Dpxgam computes an upper bound on preference
for the gamble and then proceeds as follows.

If the upper bound on preference is nonnegative, Dpxgam computes the criterion
value corresponding to the upper bound on preference under each of the two basis
functions, takes the max of these two values, and then takes the min of the selected
value and the EMV.

If the upper bound on preference is negative, the max of the values corresponding to this bound under the two basis functions would be x_1. Dpxgam takes
as the upper bound on the certainty equivalent for the gamble the min of x_1 and
an amount calculated by first calculating a lower bound on the risk premium for
the gamble and then subtracting this premium from the EMV of the gamble.

To compute the lower bound on the risk premium, <u>Dpxgam</u> first constructs a modified gamble by adding to every payoff of the original gamble an amount just sufficient to raise the lowest payoff of the gamble to x_1 . It then computes an upper bound on the certainty equivalent for the modified gamble in the way described in paragraph 1 above and subtracts this certainty equivalent from the EMV of the modified gamble to get a lower bound on the risk premium. Because risk aversion is decreasing, this lower bound on the risk premium for the modified gamble is <u>a fortiori</u> a lower bound on the risk premium for the original gamble.

11.3. Program Sumexfit

11.3.1. Definition of the Problem

Formally, the problem which program <u>Sumexfit</u> attempts to solve is that of fitting the sumex function

$$t(x) = -\phi(-ax) - c\phi(-bx) , \qquad a > 0 , \qquad bc > 0 , \qquad \text{(11-1a)}$$

where ϕ is defined by

$$\phi(v) = e^v - 1 , \qquad \text{(11-1b)}$$

to numerical specifications in the form of certainty equivalents for three 50–50 gambles.[1] More specifically, for $i = 1, 2, 3$ let x_i and z_i denote the lesser and greater payoffs of a 50–50 gamble and let y_i denote the certainty equivalent. <u>Sumexfit</u> attempts to find parameters a , b , and c such that

$$t(y_i) = \tfrac{1}{2}t(x_i) + \tfrac{1}{2}t(z_i) , \qquad i = 1, 2, 3 . \qquad \text{(11-2)}$$

If these equations have any solution other than the trivial and useless solution $a = b = 0$, they have two equivalent solutions; <u>Sumexfit</u> selects one of the two by the additional requirement

$$a > b . \qquad \text{(11-3)}$$

11.3.2. Reduction of the Problem to a Two-Dimensional Search

As they stand, the conditions (11-2) require a three-dimensional search for a , b , and c , but the search can be reduced to two dimensions as follows.[2]

---

[1] The problem of fitting a sumex function to inputs in the form of five values $V_0, V_{.25}, \dots, V_1$ for which preference is 0 , .25 , ... , 1 is reduced to the form of (11-2) by interpreting $V_{.25}, V_{.5}$, and $V_{.75}$ as certainty equivalents for 50–50 gambles between $(V_0, V_{.5})$, $(V_{.25}, V_{.75})$, and $(V_{.5}, V_1)$ respectively.

[2] This essential simplification of the problem is due to John W. Pratt.

If we define

$$u_i(t) = 2 \; \varphi(-ty_i) - \varphi(-tx_i) - \varphi(-tz_i) \; , \qquad i = 1, \, 2, \, 3, \qquad\qquad (11\text{-}4)$$

$$f_i(t) = u_i(t)/u_2(t) \qquad\qquad , \qquad i = 1, \, 3, \qquad\qquad (11\text{-}5)$$

$$g_1(a, \; b) = f_1(a) - f_1(b) \qquad\qquad , \qquad\qquad\qquad\qquad (11\text{-}6a)$$

$$g_3(a, \; b) = f_3(b) - f_3(a) \qquad\qquad , \qquad\qquad\qquad\qquad (11\text{-}6b)$$

then it can be shown that the conditions (11-2) are equivalent to

$$g_1(a, \; b) = g_3(a, \; b) = 0 \; . \qquad\qquad\qquad\qquad (11\text{-}7)$$

$$c = -u_2(a)/u_2(b) \qquad\qquad . \qquad\qquad\qquad\qquad (11\text{-}8)$$

Sumexfit first searches for a and b to satisfy (11-7); if it succeeds, it computes c from (11-8).

Assumptions concerning the Input Gambles. Each of the functions u_i defined by (11-4) can be shown to have one nonzero root which can be interpreted as average risk aversion (Section 3.1.2 above) over the interval $[x_i, \, z_i]$; denote this nonzero root by r_i . If none of the input gambles is strictly nested within another, we may without loss of generality assume that the gambles are numbered so that

$$x_1 \le x_2 \le x_3 \, , \qquad z_1 \le z_2 \le z_3 \; ; \qquad\qquad\qquad (11\text{-}9)$$

and it can then be shown that the assessed certainty equivalents y_i are not consistent with decreasing positve risk aversion unless

$$r_1 > r_2 > r_3 > 0 \; . \qquad\qquad\qquad\qquad (11\text{-}10)$$

The methodology used in Sumexfit is based on the assumption that both (11-9) and (11-10) are satisfied, and in all the discussion to follow we shall assume that this is so. It is only by accident that Sumexfit will sometimes fit a sumex function to nested gambles which satisfy (11-10) but violate (11-9). Sumexfit will always reject inputs which violate (11-10).

General Behavior of the g Functions. When (11-9) and (11-10) are satisfied, the g functions defined in (11-6) seem ordinarily if not always to behave in the way shown in Figure 11.3A, where the essential things to observe are the asymptotes, the fact that both 0 contours are strictly increasing, and the fact that the 0 contours intersect only once.

In terms of Figure 11.3A, the problem of finding a and b which satisfy (11-7) becomes one of finding the point at which the two zero contours intersect. In searching for this point, Sumexfit assumes that the contours have all three of the properties just mentioned, even though the asymptotes are the only ones that have actually been proved. The program contains traps at various points which stop the search when computational results indicate that Figure 11.3A is incorrect, but such results seem at least usually to be due merely to finite word length.

179

Figure 11.3A
Behavior of the g Functions

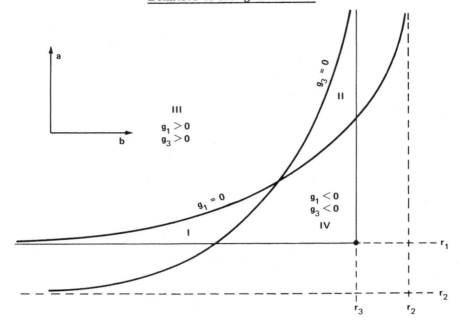

11.3.3. *Outline Description of the Main Program*

1. Rescaling of the Inputs. Let x_{max} denote the greatest of the criterion values
supplied as input to Sumexfit. Like program Piecexfit (above, Section 11.1),
program Sumexfit starts by subtracting x_{max} from each of the input values, thus
obtaining a set of transformed values all of which are negative and avoiding the
loss of significance that would otherwise occur when $\phi(-rx) = e^{-rx} - 1$ is
evaluated for large positive x .

2. Initial Computations. Sumexfit next calls the function Gxroot described
in Section 11.5.4 below to compute the nonzero root r_i of (11–4) for i = 1, 2, 3
and then tests these roots or average risk aversions for consistency with
decreasing positive risk aversion. The tests that are performed when the inputs
are descriptions of three 50–50 gambles are described in Section 3.3.2 above;
when the inputs are the values V_0, $V_{.25}$, ..., V_1 for which preference is 0, .25,
..., 1, the tests are those defined by (9–10) in Section 9.3.2 and are performed
by subroutine Icnsis.

3. Initial Bounds. If the inputs are not proved to be inconsistent with decreasing positive risk aversion, Sumexfit next establishes initial lower bounds
a_1 and b_1 and upper bounds a_2 and b_2 , thus enclosing the solution (a, b) within
the large rectangle in Figure 11.3B. The bounds $a_1 = r_1$ and $b_2 = r_3$ are already
available. The bound a_2 is found by binary search for a_2 such that $g_1(a_2, b_2) > 0$.
The bound b_1 is found by binary search for b_1 such that $g_3(a_1, b_1) > 0$.

Figure 11.3B
Bounds on the Solution

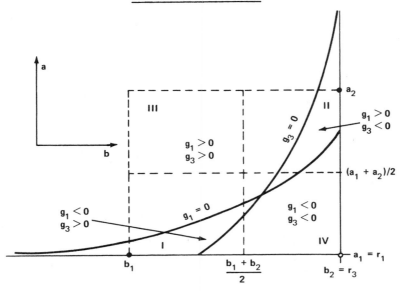

4. **Search.** The program now searches for the solution, improving the bounds as it does so by exploiting the fact that

    1. If a trial point (a, b) falls in Region I of Figure 11.3B, then a and b are improved (higher) values for the lower bounds a_1 and b_1.

    2. If a trial point (a, b) falls in Region II, then a and b are improved (lower) values for the upper bounds a_2 and b_2.

Two methods of search are used in alternation. Sumexfit first calls subroutine Newrap to conduct a Newton-Raphson search, setting new bounds each time a trial point falls in Region I or II of Figure 11.3B. If this search seems to be diverging, it is broken off and Sumexfit calls subroutine Impvbd twice to search directly for improved bounds, first by setting $a = (a_1 + a_2)/2$ and searching along the corresponding dashed line in Figure 11.3B for b such that (a, b) is in Region I or II, and then by setting $b = (b_1 + b_2)/2$ and searching along the corresponding dashed line in Figure 11.3B for a such that (a, b) is in Region I or II.

After improved bounds have been found by the method just described, a new cycle of Newton-Raphson search is begun, and the entire process continues until either subroutine Newrap finds a satisfactory solution or subroutine Impvbd reports inability to improve the bounds. Sumexfit considers a solution to be satisfactory if the preference it implies for each of the three input gambles agrees to a predetermined number of decimal places with the preference it implies for the certainty equivalent, both preferences being normalized in the sense of (9-24). A test whether the current solution is satisfactory in this sense is made by subroutine <u>Testac</u> at the end of each cycle of Newton-Raphson search.

5. **Filed vs Printed Parameters.** The parameters filed by <u>Sumexfit</u> are those computed for the transformed input values. If, however, the user asks to have the parameters printed out, <u>Sumexfit</u> undoes the effect of the transformation and prints parameter values suitable for use with criterion values measured on the natural scale.

11.3.4. *Denotation and Evaluation of the g, f, and u Functions*

1. **The g Functions.** The values at any given point (a, b) of the functions g_1 and g_3 defined by (11-6) are denoted by G1 and G3 respectively. The partial derivatives of these functions, which are required in the Newton-Raphson search, are denoted and evaluated as follows:

$$D1(1) = \frac{\partial}{\partial a} g_1(a, b) = f_1'(a) \; ,$$
$$D3(1) = \frac{\partial}{\partial a} g_3(a, b) = -f_3'(a) \; ,$$
$$D1(2) = \frac{\partial}{\partial b} g_1(a, b) = -f_1'(b) \; ,$$
$$D3(2) = \frac{\partial}{\partial b} g_3(a, b) = f_3'(b) \; . \tag{11-11}$$

2. **The f Functions.** The values at the point (a_i, b_j) of the functions f_1 and f_3 defined by (11-5) are denoted by F1(I, J) and F3(I, J) respectively. They are calculated straightforwardly from the definition except when $t = 0$ and the definition yields the meaningless value $0/0$, in which case they are calculated from the supplementary definition

$$f_i(0) = \lim_{t \to 0} f_i(t) = u_i^*/u_2^* \; , \qquad i = 1, 3, \tag{11-12a}$$

where

$$u_i^* = -2y_i + x_i + z_i \; , \qquad i = 1, 2, 3 \; . \tag{11/12b}$$

The derivatives of the f_i for arguments other than 0 are calculated from the formula

$$f_i'(t) = [u_2(t) \, u_i'(t) - u_i(t) \, u_2'(t)] / [u_2(t)]^2 \; , \qquad i = 1, 3, \tag{11-13}$$

which is derived by differentiating (11-5). For argument 0 , they are calculated from the supplementary definition

$$f_i'(0) = \lim_{t \to 0} f_i'(t) = (u_2^* \, u_i'^* - u_i^* \, u_2'^*)/u_2^{*2} \; , \qquad i = 1, 3, \tag{11-14a}$$

where u_i^* is defined by (11-12b) and

$$u_i^{\prime *} = \tfrac{1}{2}(2y_i^2 - x_i^2 - z_i^2) , \qquad i = 1, 2, 3. \qquad (11-14b)$$

3. The u Functions. The u_i defined by (11-4) are evaluated by the function Ufunc, which calls the function Phi described in Section 11.5.3 below to evaluate $\phi(v) = e^v - 1$ in such a way that the number of significant digits cannot be less than a predetermined minimum for any positive argument. When t is strictly equal to 0, Ufunc returns the spurious value u_i^* defined by (11-12b) and required by (11-12a) and (11-14a).

The derivatives of the u_i are evaluated by the function Wfunc. Except when the argument t = 0, Wfunc uses the formula

$$u_i^{\prime}(t) = -2y_i e^{-ty_i} + x_i e^{-tx_i} + z_i e^{-tz_i} , \qquad i = 1, 2, 3, \qquad (11-15)$$

which is derived from (11-4). When t = 0, Wfunc returns the value $u_i^{\prime *}$ defined by (11-14b) and required by (11-14a).

11.3.5. *Subroutine Newrap*

Each cycle of Newton-Raphson search conducted by subroutine Newrap begins from an initial trial point selected by a method to be described in a moment. Each new trial point is then selected by evaluating the g functions and their partial derivatives at the old trial point and then taking as the new trial point the point where g_1 and g_3 would both vanish if they were linear in a and b . The initial trial point is found by starting from the bounding point (a_1, b_1) and using the average slopes of the g functions between the bounds in place of the local derivatives.

After each trial point is chosen, the progress of the search is measured by evaluating the quantity

$$L(a, b) = |g_1(a, b)| + |g_2(a, b)| ,$$

called AG in the program. The search continues until either the value of L is reduced to 0, indicating that the exact solution of the problem has been found, or the search appears to be diverging for one or the other of the two following reasons:

1. A trial point falls outside the current bounds;
2. Two successive Newton-Raphson moves have yielded values of L greater than the best value previously achieved.

To prevent loss of accuracy at the end of search, not only the best value of L achieved to date but the values of a and b which yielded the best L are kept in storage under the names AGO, AO, and BO.

11.3.6. Direct Search for Improved Bounds: Subroutine Impvbd

We have already said that when subroutine Impvbd is called to improve the bounds on a and b , it is called first to set $a = (a_1 + a_2)/2$ and search for b such that (a, b) is in Region I or **II**, then to set $b = (b_1 + b_2)/2$ and search for a such that (a, b) is in Region I or **II**. The procedures used in these two searches are completely analogous; we describe only the first one.

After a is set equal to $(a_1 + a_2)/2$, Impvbd searches for a suitable b along the dashed line in Figure 11.3C below. The search is conducted by progressively

Figure 11.3C

Search for b

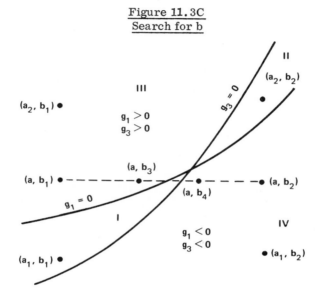

improving "temporary" lower and upper bounds on b , which are called b_3 and b_4 respectively; a trial b is known in the program as b_5. Initially, b_3 and b_4 are set equal to b_1 and b_2; thereafter, each trial b provides an improved lower bound b_3 if it lies in Region III or an improved upper bound b_4 if it lies in Region IV. The successive trial b's are selected by two different methods in alternation. The first method selects b halfway between the values b' and b'' defined by Figure 11.3D; the second one selects $b = (b_3 + b_4)/2$.

Subroutine Impvbd may be unable to improve the bounds for either of two reasons.

1. Discreteness. The search just described may fail because the initial computation $a = (a_1 + a_2)/2$ yields a value equal to a_1 or a_2 or because in the subsequent search the computation $b = (b_3 + b_4)/2$ yields a value equal to b_3 or b_4. The search

Figure 11.3D
Selection of Trial b

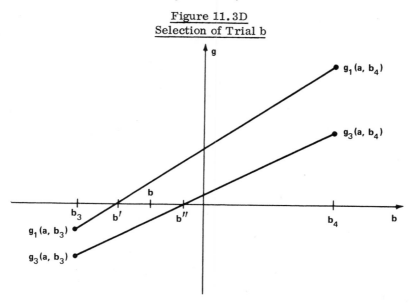

which starts by setting $b = (b_1 + b_2)/2$ may fail for the same reasons with a and b interchanged. If both searches fail because of discreteness of this kind, Impvbd reports inability to improve the bounds; it does so by setting the call-list variable IDSCRT equal to 2.

2. Zero Contours Not as Shown in Figure 11.3B. The attempt to improve the bounds may indicate that the 0 contours of the g functions are not monotone within the bounding rectangle shown in Figure 11.3B above and hence that the solution of the problem may lie outside the bounds already set. Specifically, if the 0 contours of the g functions are as shown in Figure 11.3B, then certain points defined by that figure will never fall in the "wrong regions" shown in Table 11.3A below. If Impvbd does find a point in a wrong region, it reports inability to improve the bounds; it does so by setting the call-list variable ITOPOG equal to 1.

Table 11.3A

coordinates		wrong regions
a_1	, $\frac{1}{2}(b_1 + b_2)$	II, III
a_2	, $\frac{1}{2}(b_1 + b_2)$	I, IV
$\frac{1}{2}(a_1 + a_2)$	, b_1	II, IV
$\frac{1}{2}(a_1 + a_2)$	, b_2	I, III

11.4. Evaluation of Sumex Functions

11.4.1. *Transformation of Criterion Values*

The basic sumex functions are the function t defined in (11-1) above and its inverse; they are evaluated by the Manecon functions <u>Sxt</u> and <u>Sxtin</u> respectively. For the reason explained in Section 11.3.3, the parameters that are filed by program <u>Sumexfit</u> are suitable for use with criterion values transformed by sub-traction of the constant x_{max}, the greatest of the criterion values supplied as inputs to <u>Sumexfit</u>. When called to evaluate preference for a given criterion value, <u>Sxt</u> subtracts x_{max} from the criterion value before evaluating (11-1). When called to find the criterion value corresponding to a given preference, <u>Sxtin</u> first finds the value on the transformed scale of <u>Sumexfit</u> and then adds back x_{max} to put the value on the natural scale.

11.4.2. *Search Procedure in Function Sxtin*

The function <u>Sxtin</u> finds the criterion value v for which preference is q by searching for v such that t(v) = q . The search is a Newton-Raphson search with provision for a binary move whenever a Newton-Raphson move produces only a very small reduction in the difference between t(v) and q . The initial bounds for the search are found as follows.

1. The Normal Case: Parameters b and c Positive. Let the function s be defined by

$$s(x) = t(x) - c - 1 = e^{-ax} - ce^{-bx} . \qquad (11\text{-}16)$$

When the sumex parameters b and c are positive, initial bounds for the search for $v = t^{-1}(q)$ can be found by first computing

$$r = s(v) = q - c - 1 \qquad (11\text{-}17)$$

(called QS in the program) and then exploiting the inequality

$$s(x) \geq \min\{-2e^{-ax}, -2ce^{-bx}\} \qquad (11\text{-}18)$$

and the inequalities

$$s(x) \leq \begin{cases} \max\{-2e^{-ax}, -2ce^{-bx}\} , \\ -e^{-ax} & , \\ -ce^{-bx} & , \end{cases} \qquad (11\text{-}19)$$

As can be seen from Figure 11.4A, the inequality (11-18) yields the upper bound

$$v \leq \max\{-\tfrac{1}{a}\log(-r/2), -\tfrac{1}{b}\log(-r/2c)\} \qquad (11\text{-}20)$$

while the inequalities (11-19) yield the lower bounds

Figure 11.4A
Bounds in the Normal Case (b, c > 0)

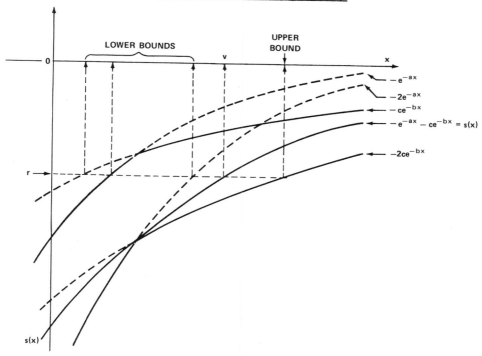

$$v \geq \begin{cases} \min \left\{ -\dfrac{1}{a} \log(-r/2), \ -\dfrac{1}{b} \log(-r/2c) \right\} , \\ \qquad -\dfrac{1}{a} \log(-r) \qquad\qquad , \\ \qquad -\dfrac{1}{b} \log(-r/c) \qquad\qquad . \end{cases} \tag{11-21}$$

2. The Abnormal Case: Parameters b and c Negative. When the parameters b and c are negative, three cases must be distinguished according to the value of r, as shown in Figure 11.4B.

1. When r = 0 , no search is required. The value satisfying s(v) = 0 is

$$v = \frac{1}{a + b} \ \log(-c). \tag{11-22}$$

2. When r < 0 , the fact that $s(x) > -e^{-ax}$ implies the upper bound

$$v < -\frac{1}{a} \log(-r) \tag{11-23}$$

and a lower bound can be found by searching to the left of the upper bound for v such that $s(v) \leq r$ or $t(v) < q$.

Figure 11.4B
Bounds in the Abnormal Case (b, c ≤ 0)

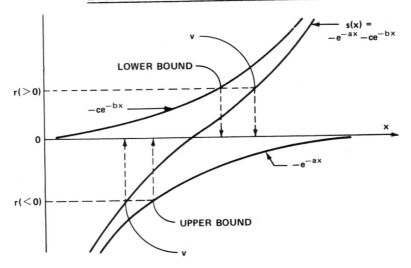

3. When $r > 0$, the fact that $s(x) < -ce^{-bx}$ implies the lower bound

$$v > -\frac{1}{b} \log(-r/c) \qquad\qquad (11\text{-}24)$$

and an upper bound can be found by searching to the right of the lower bound for v such that $s(v) > r$ or $t(v) > q$.

Much better bounds for the abnormal case exist, but the case is of such little interest that it does not seem worth the trouble of programming them.

11.5. Auxiliary Functions

11.5.1. Function Algamd

The function ALGAMD(Z, D) evaluates the quantity

$$G(z, d) = \log \Gamma(z + d) - \log \Gamma(z) . \qquad\qquad (11\text{-}25)$$

For most values of the arguments, Algamd evaluates $G(z, d)$ by calling the function Dlgama (below, Section 13.5) to evaluate each of the two terms on the right-hand side of (11-25) and then subtracting. When d is small relative to z , however, the subtraction would result in a serious loss of significance; and Algamd therefore uses the approximation

$$G(z, d) \doteq d \log z + (z+d-\tfrac{1}{2}) \log(1 + d/z) - d\left[1 - \frac{1/12}{z^2 (1 + d/z)}\right] , \qquad (11\text{-}26)$$

calling the function Blog described in Section 11.5.2 below to evaluate $\log(1 + d/z)$ in such a way as to guarantee a fixed number of significant digits no matter how small d/z may be.

To derive the approximation (11-26) we first use Stirling's approximation to each term on the right-hand side of (11-25), thus obtaining

$$G(z,\ d) = (z+d-\tfrac{1}{2})\ \log(z+d) - (z+d)\left[1 - \frac{1/12}{(z+d)^2} + \frac{1/360}{(z+d)^4} - \cdots\right]$$

$$- (z-\tfrac{1}{2})\ \log z + z\left[1 - \frac{1/12}{z^2} + \frac{1/360}{z^4} - \cdots\right] \qquad (11\text{-}27a)$$

$$= d\ \log z + (z+d-\tfrac{1}{2})\ \log(1 + d/z) - d + \frac{d/12}{z^2(1 + d/z)}$$

$$- \frac{d/120}{z^4}\ \frac{1 + d/z + (d/z)^3/3}{(1 + d/z)^3} + \cdots \qquad (11\text{-}27b)$$

Then dropping the last term on the right-hand side of (11-27b) we obtain (11-26).

Algamd uses the approximation (11-26) whenever it is sure to give results at least as accurate as (11-25) because either (a) z is so large that the last term in the series in (11-27a) adds nothing to the finite-word-length value of $\log \Gamma(z)$, or (b) d is so small relative to z that the last term in (11-27b) adds nothing to the finite-word-length value of $\log \Gamma(z)$.

11.5.2. Function Blog

The function BLOG(X) evaluates the quantity

$$\beta(x) = \log(1 + x) \qquad (11\text{-}28)$$

in such a way that as x approaches 0 the relative error will not exceed a predetermined limit. For most x, Blog simply computes $1 + x$ and calls the Fortran function Alog to deliver $\log(1 + x)$. When x is very close to 0, however, addition of 1 to x loses most if not all of the significant digits in x and hence in $\log(1 + x)$, and Blog therefore uses the first few terms of the series expansion

$$\beta(x) = x + \frac{x^2}{2} + \frac{x^3}{3} + \cdots, \qquad |x| < 1 . \qquad (11\text{-}29)$$

The number of terms that should be used in the series (11-29) and the values of x for which (11-29) should be used rather than (11-28) depend on the desired error limit and the machine word length. Let b denote the number base of the machine, let n denote the number of digits in the mantissa of a floating-point number, and let k denote the number of terms actually evaluated in the infinite series (11-29). Then:

1. The truncation of $1 + x$ involved in the use of (11-28) will reduce $1 + x$ by an amount not greater than $(1/b)^{n-1}$, and for small x the error in $\log(1 + x)$ will be roughly equal to the error in x.
2. The use of only k terms in (11-29) will result for small x in an error roughly equal to the first excluded term, viz. $x^{k+1}/(k + 1)$.

It follows that, for given n and k, the maximum relative error will be minimized if the series (11-29) is used when the magnitude of x is less than the x which satisfies

$$x_o^{k+1} / (k + 1) = (1/b)^{n-1} .$$ (11-30)

The solution of (11-30) is

$$x_o = \exp\left[\frac{1}{k+1} \{\log(k + 1) - (n - 1) \log b\}\right] ;$$ (11-31)

and if this crossover value is used, the maximum relative error in $\beta(x)$ will occur at the crossover value and will amount to approximately
$(1/b)^{n-1} / \beta(x_o) \doteq (1/b)^{n-1} / x_o$.

11.5.3. Function Phi

The function PHI(X) evaluates the quantity

$$\phi(x) = e^x - 1$$ (11-32)

in such a way that as x approaches 0 the relative error will not exceed a predetermined limit. For most x, Phi simply calls the Fortran function Exp to evaluate e^x and then subtracts 1. When x is very close to 0, however, the subtraction would result in a serious loss of significant digits and Phi therefore uses the first few terms of the series expansion

$$\phi(x) = x + \frac{x^2}{2!} + \frac{x^3}{3!} + \dots$$ (11-33)

The number of terms that should be used in the series (11-33) and the values of x for which (11-33) should be used rather than (11-32) depend on the desired error limit and on the machine word length. If we let b denote the machine number base, let n denote the number of digits in the mantissa of a floating-point number, and let k denote the number of terms taken in (11-33), then by reasoning very similar to that used in the discussion of Blog just above we can show that for given n and k, the series (11-33) should be used when the magnitude of x is less than

$$x_o = \exp\left[\frac{1}{k+1} \{\log(k + 1)! - (n - 1) \log b\}\right],$$ (11-34)

and if this crossover value is used, the maximum relative error in $\phi(x)$ will occur at the crossover value and will amount to approximately
$(1/b)^{n-1} / \phi(x_o) \doteq (1/b)^{n-1} / x_o$.

11.5.4.   Function Gxroot

The function GXROOT(X, Y, Z, P) returns r such that

$$e^{-ry} = pe^{-rz} + (1 - p)e^{-rx} . \qquad (11\text{-}35)$$

The solution is found by a Newton–Raphson search.

Multiplying both sides of (11-35) by e^{ry} we transform the problem into one of finding r such that

$$f(r) \equiv p\,\phi(-r\zeta) + q\,\phi(r\xi) = 0 \qquad (11\text{-}36a)$$

where ϕ is defined by (11-32) and

$$q = 1 - p , \quad \xi \equiv y - x , \quad \zeta = z - y . \qquad (11\text{-}36b)$$

Differentiating f wrt r we obtain

$$f'(r) = -\zeta pe^{-r\zeta} + \xi qe^{r\xi} , \qquad (11\text{-}37a)$$
$$f''(r) = \zeta^2 pe^{-r\zeta} + \xi^2 qe^{r\xi} , \qquad (11\text{-}37b)$$

from which it appears that f is a convex function which passes through the origin with slope $\xi q - \zeta p$ and goes to $+\infty$ as $r \to +\infty$ or $-\infty$. It follows that the function has a second root to the right of 0 if $\xi q < \zeta p$, to the left of 0 if $\xi q > \zeta p$, and it is this second root that is meaningful in the applications when $\xi q \neq \zeta p$.

An inner bound on the meaningful root is obtained by setting (11-37a) equal to 0 and solving to obtain

$$r^* = \frac{1}{\xi + \zeta} \log \frac{\zeta p}{\xi q} . \qquad (11\text{-}38)$$

When the meaningful root is positive, an outer (upper) bound can be obtained by observing that (11-36) implies that

$$f(r) > q\,\phi(r\xi) + p\,\phi(-\infty) = qe^{r\xi} - 1 . \qquad (11\text{-}39)$$

Setting the right–hand side of this inequality equal to 0 and solving we obtain the upper bound

$$r < -\frac{1}{\xi} \log q . \qquad (11\text{-}40)$$

When the meaningful root is negative, similar reasoning leads to the lower bound

$$r > \frac{1}{\zeta} \log p . \qquad (11\text{-}41)$$

To obtain an initial trial value of r , we expand (11-36a) in a Maclaurin series as far as the terms of second order, thus obtaining

$$f(r) \doteq (q\xi - p\zeta)r + \tfrac{1}{2}(q\xi^2 + p\zeta^2)r^2 , \tag{11-42}$$

set this approximation equal to 0, and solve to obtain

$$r = -2(q\xi - p\zeta)/(q\xi^2 + p\zeta^2). \tag{11-43}$$

CHAPTER 12

Programs for Description, Grouping, and Filing of Probability Distributions

Contents of Chapter 12

1. Programs Cdispri, Fdispri, and Disfile   194
   1. General Nature of the Programs; 2. Generic Names for Subprograms;
   3. Specification of Continuous Distributions: Subroutines Fitsub;
   4. Grouping of Continuous Distributions: Subroutines Grpsub;
   5. Standard Form for Filed Distributions.

2. Addition of New Families of Continuous Distributions to the Manecon   198
   Collection

193

12.1.   Programs Cdispri, Fdispri, and Disfile

12.1.1.   *General Nature of the Programs*

Programs Cdispri, Fdispri, and Disfile are all very brief drivers which call on subroutines to do almost all of the work.

Program Disfile calls subroutine Dscprb to input the user's description of a discrete distribution, calls subroutine Fitsub to input the user's description of a continuous distribution and compute its parameters, calls subroutine Grpsub to group the continuous distribution, and then files the output of Dscprb and Grpsub.

Programs Cdispri and Disfile are even shorter. Program Cdispri calls Fitsub for the parameters of the user's continuous distribution and then calls subroutine Prbpri to describe the distribution. Program Fdispri reads the user's distribution from the file and itself prints out the summary statistics of a discrete or mixed distribution and the listing of a discrete distribution, but it calls Prbpri to describe a grouped distribution.

12.1.2.   *Generic Names for Subprograms*

The ability of the main programs to process many different types of continuous distributions and two different types of grouped distributions derives from the fact that various subprograms required for their operation are defined, not in the files containing the main programs, but in separate files loaded selectively to support the main program. The main programs call these subprograms by "generic" names which designate, not one particular subprogram, but any subprogram which serves a certain purpose.

Subroutine Fitsub. There is a different subroutine called Fitsub for every different type of continuous distribution that can be processed by the main programs. For example, the file Betdis contains a Fitsub which will input the user's specifications concerning a beta distribution and compute the parameters of the beta distribution which meets these specifications; the file Pcqdis contains a Fitsub which will perform this same function for a piecewise quadratic distribution, and so forth.

Subroutine Grpsub. There are two different subroutines called Grpsub. The file Epdgrp contains a subroutine by this name which will group any continuous distribution into brackets of equal probability; the file Ewdgrp contains a different Grpsub which will group any continuous distribution into brackets of equal width.

Generic Function Names for Continuous Distributions. In order to describe or group a particular continuous distribution, the programs must (either directly or via an intervening subroutine such as Fitsub or Grpsub) call the functions which return densities, cumulative probabilities, and fractiles under the distribution in question. If the distribution is a beta distribution, they must call Betden, Betcum, and Betfrc; if it is piecewise quadratic, they must call Pcqden, Pcqcum, and Pcqfrc; and so forth.

In order to achieve this flexibility, the programs do not call any such function by its own name. Instead, they call the generic functions Cdenfn, Ccumfn, and

Cfrcfn, which are identified with specific functions in a supporting file. Thus the file Betdis contains definitions identifying Cdenfn with Betden, Ccumfn with Betcum, and so forth; the file Pcqdis contains definitions identifying Cdenfn with Pcqden, and so forth.

The generic functions have four generic parameters, called P1, P2, P3, P4. Since the programs which call the generic functions merely pass the addresses of the parameters, without performing any numerical operations thereon, the parameters may be either integer or real; and in order to handle piecewise quadratic distributions, three of whose four parameters are vectors, the first three parameters of the generic functions are dimensioned as vectors wherever dimensioning is needed to secure a correct return from a function call.

Generic Function Names for Grouped Distributions. Functions which return densities, cumulative probabilities, and fractiles under grouped distributions are handled in essentially the same way as the corresponding functions for continuous distributions. The main programs call the functions by the generic names Gdenfn, Gcumfn, and Gfrcfn. The file Epdgrp identifies Gdenfn with Epden, the file Ewdgrp identifies Gdenfn with Ewden, and so forth. In the same way, the generic moment-computing subroutine Gdmomt is identified with Epmomt in the file Epdgrp, with Ewmomt in Ewdgrp.

Function Names in Subroutine Prbpri. In subroutine Prbpri, which must be capable of describing either continuous or grouped distributions, the required functions are known by the still more general dummy names Denfcn, Cumfcn, and Frcfcn. When Cdispri calls Prbpri to describe a continuous distribution, it identifies these names through the call list with Cdenfn, etc; when Fdispri calls Prbpri to describe a grouped distribution it identifies them with Gdenfn, etc. The ultimate identification with specific functions is then made through the definition of Cdenfn in a supporting file like Betdis or through the definition of Gdenfn in a supporting file like Epdgrp.

12.1.3. *Specification of Continuous Distributions: Subroutines Fitsub*

As we have already said, there is a separate subroutine called Fitsub for every different family of continuous distributions that can be processed by Cdispri and Disfile. The essential function of any of these subroutines is to input from the terminal the user's numerical specification of a particular distribution of the family in question and to return to the calling program (1) the parameters of the specified distribution, and optionally (2) its mean and variance.

The Fitsub for any type or family of distributions is called by a statement of the form

CALL FITSUB(IPRINT, P1, P2, P3, P4, E, V, IFIT, IERR)

where the first variable in the call list is an input and all others are outputs. P1, P2, P3, and P4 are the parameters of the distribution specified by the user; P4 is a dummy when this distribution has less than four parameters, P3 is also a dummy when it has only two. E and V are the mean and variance of the distribution. IERR is a trouble indicator which will have the value 0 if Fitsub succeeds in fitting a distribution to the user's specification, the value 1 if Fitsub cannot fit the specification. IFIT will have the value 1 if the fitted distribution is piecewise quadratic, 2 if it is of any other type; the use of this indicator will appear in Section 12.1.4 below. When Fitsub is called by Cdispri with IPRINT = 1 , Fitsub computes and returns the mean and variance for use by Prbpri and also, except in the case of piecewise quadratic distributions, offers to print out at the terminal any parameters not directly specified by the user. When Fitsub is called by Disfile with IPRINT = 0 , these operations are suppressed.

When the user at the terminal specifies the mean and variance of a distribution, Fitsub itself computes the parameters of the distribution. When the user specifies fractiles or points on the cumulative function, Fitsub calls a subroutine with a name like Betfit or Pcqfit to compute the parameters; these latter subroutines are discussed in Chapter 14 below.

12.1.4. *Grouping of Continuous Distributions; Subroutines Grpsub*

The subroutine Grpsub for either type of grouping is called by a statement of the form

    CALL GRPSUB(IFIT, P1, P2, P3, P4, NBRAK, XVECTR, XMIN, XMAX,
    XMEAN, XVAR, IGROUP)

where the first six arguments in the call list contain input and the remainder contain output. Program Disfile obtains the first five inputs from Fitsub; it obtains the last input, NBRAK, from the user at the terminal.

1. Brackets of Equal Probability. The subroutine Grpsub in the file Epdgrp groups a distribution into n brackets of equal probability by simply calling the fractile function of the distribution being grouped to return the $(i - .5)/n$ fractile for $i = 1, 2, \ldots , n$; these fractiles are the bracket medians of the grouped distribution and are returned in the array XVECTR. The precision of the computed fractiles is controlled by the value assigned to the variable TOLRNC in the fractile function which Grpsub calls via the function Cfrcfn.

As explained in Section 10.1.1 above, Grpsub also returns either the least and greatest possible value of the uq, if the distribution is piecewise quadratic, or else the values of two extreme fractiles which will be treated as if they were the least and greatest possible values in computations involving the grouped distribution. The value of the variable IFIT which Disfile obtains from Fitsub and passes to Grpsub informs Grpsub whether the distribution that it is processing is or is not piecewise quadratic.

Finally, Grpsub computes and returns the mean and the variance of the grouped distribution and sets the call-list variable IGROUP = 1 to indicate that the call-list array XVECTR contains the bracket medians of brackets of equal probability.

2. Brackets of Equal Width. For the reasons explained in Section 10.2.1. above, the subroutine Grpsub in the file Ewdgrp truncates any continuous distribution other than a piecewise quadratic distribution at a lower and an upper cutoff fractile. After thus establishing the range of the distribution, Grpsub divides it into the number of brackets specified by the user and then computes the bracket

probabilities by first computing and storing the density at the midpoint of each bracket and then calling subroutine Normlz to normalize these densities, which are returned in the array XVECTR. Finally, Grpsub computes and returns the mean and variance of the grouped distribution and sets the call-list variable IGROUP = 2 to indicate that the call-list array XVECTR contains the probabilities of brackets of equal width.

12.1.5. *Standard Form for Filed Distributions*

The various quantitites which describe a discrete, grouped, or mixed distribution are filed in the following order by program Disfile or any other Manecon program or subroutine which files a distribution.[1]

NDVAL:	number of discrete values to which individual probabilities have been assigned.
NBRAK:	number of brackets into which a continuous distribution has been grouped (= 0 if the distribution being filed is purely discrete).
IGROUP:	type of grouping: 1 if equiprobable, 2 if equal-width, 0 if the distribution being filed is purely discrete.
TGPRB:	total unconditional probability distributed by the grouped distribution; the complement of the sum of the probabilities assigned individually to discrete values of the uq.
CMEAN } CVAR }	mean and variance of the complete distribution.
GDIS:	set of NBRAK bracket medians if IGROUP = 1, set of NBRAK unconditional bracket probabilities if IGROUP = 2.
DVAL } DPRB }	set of NDVAL discrete values of the uq each followed by its probability.

The six scalars which head this list constitute one logical record; the vector GDIS constitutes one logical record; the vectors DVAL and DPRB together constitute one logical record.

Two points about the filing of distributions grouped into brackets of equal width deserve particular attention.

1. It is the individual and not the cumulative probabilities of the brackets which are filed.

2. If the distribution is mixed, it is the unconditional probabilities of the brackets which are filed, so that these probabilities plus the discrete probabilities will add to 1. This is so even though the user of Disfile is obliged to describe his original continuous distribution conditionally, i.e., as he would assess it if he had assigned 0 probabilities to all discrete values of the uq.

About all that can be said in justification of these two choices is that their disadvantages seem no greater than the disadvantages of their opposites.

---

[1] On some systems, these quantities may be preceded in the file by the file name and the file type.

12.2.   Addition of New Families of Continuous Distributions to the Manecon Collection

If a programmer wishes to enable programs Cdispri and Disfile to process a family of continuous distributions not presently in the Manecon collection, he must create a file which contains:

1.   Subprogram functions which return densities, cumulative probabilities, and fractiles under distributions of the family in question. These functions must be called respectively Cdenfn, Ccumfn, and Cfrcfn, and their call lists must satisfy the requirements of subroutine Prbpri as described in Section 7.3.1 above. Ordinarily, they will be "translator" functions of the sort described in Section 7.3.3.

2.   A subroutine which (1) calls on the user at the terminal to supply numerical specifications sufficient to determine the parameters of a particular member of the family, and (2) computes the numerical values of the parameters and of the mean and variance of the distribution and returns them to the calling program. This subroutine must be called

FITSUB(IPRINT, P1, P2, P3, P4, XM, XV, IFIT, IERR)

The variables in the call list were explained in Section 12.1.3 above.

CHAPTER 13

Evaluation of Continuous Probability Distributions

As was explained in Section 7.2 above, the "top-level" Manecon subprograms for evaluation of continuous probability distributions call on "supporting" subprograms for the more difficult computations. For this reason the computational methods used in the top-level subprograms are self-evident from the program listings, and we shall comment on only the supporting subprograms in the present chapter. Evaluation of piecewise quadratic distributions is discussed, not in the present chapter, but in Section 14.5.3 below.

Contents of Chapter 13

1. Standard Beta Cumulative Function: Subroutine Dbetcu   200

   1. Definitions and Parametrization; 2. Series Expansions; 3. The Combined Series; 4. Termination of the Computation; 5. Computation of the Complementary Probability; 6. Special Cases.

2. Standard Gamma Cumulative Function: Subroutine Dgascu   205

   1. Definitions and Parametrization; 2. Series Expansions; 3. Accuracy Achievable with the Right-Tail Series; 4. Choice Between the Two Series; 5. Termination of the Computation; 6. Special Cases.

3. Unit Normal Cumulative Function: Subroutines Unrcuq and Dunrcu   210

   1. Computation using the Complementary Error Function; 2. Approximation by a Rational Fraction; 3. Expansion in a Continued Fraction.

4. Fractiles of Standard Distributions: Functions Betfrq, Gasfrc, and Unrfrc   211

5. Complete Gamma Function: Functions Algama and Dlgama   212

13.1.   Standard Beta Cumulative Function: Subroutine Dbetcu

13.1.1.   *Definitions and Parametrization*

The standard beta distribution is parametrized by writing its density function as

$$f_{\beta *}(p, \ a, \ b) = \frac{1}{B(a, \ b)} \ p^{a-1} \ (1 - p)^{b-1} \ . \tag{13-1}$$

The cumulative function is then defined by

$$F_{\beta *}(p, \ a, \ b) = \frac{1}{B(a, \ b)} \ \int_0^p t^{a-1} \ (1 - t)^{b-1} \ dt \ . \tag{13-2}$$

13.1.2.   *Series Expansions*

1.   <u>The Binomial Series.</u> Integrating (13-2) by parts s times we obtain

$$F_{\beta *}(p, \ a, \ b) = S_1(s) + R(s) \tag{13-3a}$$

$$S_1(s) = \Sigma_{i=0}^{s-1} u_i \ , \tag{13-3b}$$

$$u_i = \frac{1}{b \ B(a, \ b)} \ \frac{b(b - 1) \ \dots \ (b - i)}{a(a + 1) \ \dots \ (a + i)} \ p^{a+i} \ (1 - p)^{b-i-1} \ , \tag{13-3c}$$

$$R(s) = \frac{1}{B(a, \ b)} \ \frac{(b - 1) \ (b - 2) \ \dots \ (b - s)}{a(a + 1) \ \dots \ (a + s - 1)} \ \int_0^p t^{a+s-1} \ (1 - t)^{b-s-1} \ dt \tag{13-3d}$$

$$= F_{\beta *}(p, \ a+s, \ b-s) \ , \qquad \text{if } s < b \ . \tag{13-3e}$$

If we define

$$u_{-1} = \frac{p^{a-1} \ (1 - p)^b}{b \ B(a, \ b)} \ , \tag{13-4a}$$

the u_i of (13-3c) have the recursion relation

$$u_i = \frac{b - i}{a + i} \ \frac{p}{1 - p} \ u_{i-1} \ , \qquad i = 0, \ 1, \ \dots \ , \ s-1 \ . \tag{13-4b}$$

We shall refer to the series $S_1(s)$ of (13-3b) as the "binomial" series because when r is integral and s = b the remainder R(s) vanishes and the successive terms in $S_1(s)$ can be interpreted as the binomial probabilities of a, a+1, ... , a+b-1 successes in a+b-1 trials of a Bernoulli process with parameter p . In the general case of nonintegral b , the remainder does not vanish for any s . The u_i are positive for $i < b$, alternately negative and positive thereafter. The remainder $R(s)$ is positive for $s < b$, alternately negative and positive for larger s .

   2. The Power Series. Expanding the integrand of (13-2) in a power series in p and integrating term by term we get

$$F_{\beta *}(p, \ a, \ b) = S_2 = \Sigma^\infty_{j=0} \ w_j \tag{13-5a}$$

where

$$w_o = \frac{p^a}{a \ B(a, \ b)} \ , \tag{13-5b}$$

$$w_j = \frac{a + j - 1}{a + j} \ \frac{j - b}{j} \ p \ w_{j-1} \ , \qquad j = 1, \ 2, \ \ldots \ ,$$

and from this we have at once

$$F_{\beta *}(p, \ a+s, \ b-s) = \Sigma^\infty_{i=s} \ v_i \tag{13-6a}$$

where

$$v_s = \frac{p^{a+s}}{(a + s) \ B(a+s, \ b-s)} \ , \tag{13-6b}$$

$$v_i = \frac{a + i - 1}{a + i} \ \frac{i - b}{i - s} \ p \ v_{i-1} \ , \qquad i = s+1, \ s+2, \ \ldots \ . \tag{13-6c}$$

All terms in this series will be positive if $s + 1 > b$.

13.1.3.   The Combined Series

   From the results obtained in Section 13.1.2, it is apparent that if we set

$$s = \text{greatest integer in } b \tag{13-7}$$

and then substitute (13-6) for the remainder (13-3e), the result will be an infinite series with all positive terms, Direct evaluation of the complete beta function in the definition (13-6b) of v_s can be avoided by exploiting the fact that by (13-3c)

$$u_{s-1} = \frac{p^{a+s-1} \ (1 - p)^{b-s}}{(b - s) \ B(a+s, \ b-s)} \ ,$$

from which we have by (13-6b)

$$v_s = \frac{b - s}{a + s} \ \frac{p}{(1 - p)^{b-s}} \ u_{s-1} \ . \tag{13-8}$$

Summing up, the combined series can be written

$$F_{\beta*}(p,\ a,\ b) = \Sigma_{i=0}^{s-1}\ u_i + v_s + \Sigma_{i=s+1}^{\infty}\ v_i \qquad (13\text{-}9)$$

where after u_{-1} has been evaluated by (13-4a) the u_i can be evaluated recursively by (13-4b), and then after v_s has been evaluated by (13-8) the v_i can be evaluated by (13-6c).

This computational scheme was developed by Arthur Schleifer, Jr.

13.1.4. Termination of the Computation

Computation of the infinite series (13-9) is terminated as soon as a bound on the sum of the remaining terms is less than a specified tolerable error t . The termination may take place within either the binomial series (13-3) or the power series (13-6).

<u>1. Termination within the Binomial Series.</u> Because $R(s+1)$ as defined by (13-3d) is negative, the sum $S_1(s+1) = \Sigma_{i=0}^{s}\ u_i$ is an upper bound on $F_{\beta*}(p,\ a,\ b)$ and therefore

$$R_i = \Sigma_{j=i+1}^{s}\ u_i = \Sigma_{k=1}^{s-i}\ u_{i+k} \qquad (13\text{-}10)$$

is an upper bound on the error that will result from terminating after the term u_i in the binomial series. Starting from (13-4b) we have

$$u_{i+1} = \frac{b-i-1}{a+i+1}\ \frac{p}{1-p}\ u_i\ ,$$

$$u_{i+k} < r^k\ u_i \qquad \text{where} \qquad r = \frac{b-i-1}{a+i+1}\ \frac{p}{1-p}\ , \qquad (13\text{-}11a)$$

$$R_i < \Sigma_{k=1}^{s-i}\ r^k\ u_i = \frac{r}{1-r}(1-r^{s-i})\ u_i$$

$$< \frac{r}{1-r}\ u_i \qquad \text{if} \qquad r < 1\ . \qquad (13\text{-}11b)$$

It follows at once that the error due to termination after u_i in the binomial series will be less than any specified t if

$$u_i < \frac{1-r}{r}\ t \quad \cdot \ \text{and} \qquad r < 1\ . \qquad (13\text{-}12)$$

<u>Dbetcu</u> terminates computation if and when the first of these two conditions is satisfied; there is no need to verify the second condition because r as defined by (13-11a) cannot be equal to 0 and $r > 1$ implies

$$\frac{1 - r}{r} \ t < 0 < u_i \ .$$

2. Termination within the Power Series. The power series is computed only if $s < b$, and we then have by (13-6c) that for $i > s$

$$v_{i+1} < p \ v_i \ ,$$

$$\Sigma_{k=1}^{\infty} v_{i+k} < \Sigma_{k=1}^{\infty} p^k v_i = \frac{p}{1 - p} \ v_i \ . \tag{13-13}$$

It follows that the error due to termination after v_i in the power series will be less than any specified t if

$$v_i < \frac{1 - p}{p} \ t \ . \tag{13-14}$$

13.1.5. *Computatioj of the Complementary Probability*

Instead of using the procedure described above to compute $F_{\beta *}(p, \ a, \ b)$ directly, this procedure can be used to compute the complementary probability $F_{\beta *}(1\text{-}p, \ b, \ a)$, whereupon the desired probability can be computed as

$$F_{\beta *}(p, \ a, \ b) = 1 - F_{\beta *}(1\text{-}p, \ b, \ a) \ . \tag{13-15}$$

Because this indirect computation is as likely as not to require evaluation of fewer terms than are required by direct computation, subroutine Dbetcu makes rough estimates of the numbers of terms required for both computations and chooses the one which seems quicker.

Except when b is integral and the power series does not exist, Dbetcu first computes an upper bound on the index of the term at which computation of the power series will be truncated and takes this bound as the required estimate unless it is smaller than the index s of the first term in the power series, in-dicating that computation should be truncated before the power series is reached. If this happens, or if b is integral and the power series does not exist, Dbetcu uses a Normal approximation to estimate the number of terms that will have to be computed in the binomial series.

Estimation of the Truncation Point in the Power Series. Denoting by t the tolerable error in the function value, the last term computed in the power series will by (13-14) be roughly equal to $t(1 - p)/p$, and by (13-6c) the index of this term will be no greater than the i which satisfies

$$t(1 - p)/p = v_s \ p^{i-s} \quad \text{where} \quad v_s = \frac{p^{a+s}}{(a + s) \ B(a+s, \ b-s)} \ . \tag{13-16}$$

Solving we obtain

$$i = \frac{A}{\log p} - a - 1 \qquad\qquad (13\text{-}17a)$$

where

$$A = \log\left[t(1 - p)\ \frac{\Gamma(a+s+1)}{\Gamma(a+b)}\ \Gamma(b-s)\right] \quad . \qquad\qquad (13\text{-}17b)$$

Evaluation of A would be expensive if the gamma functions had to be accurately evaluated, but because $0 < b-s < 1$ it is possible to find easily computed approximations which are adequate for the purpose at hand. Treating the derivative of $\log \Gamma(x)$ as if it were constant over $(x, x+1)$ and equal to $\log \Gamma(x+1) - \log \Gamma(x)$ $= \log x$, we have

$$\begin{aligned}
\log \frac{\Gamma(a+s+1)}{\Gamma(a+b)} &= \log \Gamma(a+s+1) - \log \Gamma(a+b) \\
&\doteq [(a + s + 1) - (a + b)] \ \log(a+b) \\
&= [1 - (b-s)] \ \log (a+b) \quad . \qquad\qquad (13\text{-}18)
\end{aligned}$$

Writing $\Gamma(x) = \Gamma(x+1)/x$ and recalling that $\Gamma(x+1)$ is not far from 1 for x in [0, 1] we have

$$\log \Gamma(b-s) \doteq -\log(b-s) \quad . \qquad\qquad (13\text{-}19)$$

The formula for A which is used by Dbetcu is obtained by substituting (13-18) and (13-19) in (13-17b).

Estimation of the Truncation Point in the Binomial Series. We have already seen in Section 13.1.2 that when b is integral, the binomial series can be interpreted as the right tail of a binomial distribution with parameters p and n = $a + b - 1$, the first term in the tail being the term for a successes; and this distribution can be approximated for better or worse by a Normal distribution with mean and standard deviation $\mu = pn$ and $\sigma = \sqrt{p(1 - p)n}$. Whether or not b is integral, Dbetcu uses this approximation to estimate the number of terms that will be computed before truncation; the estimate is

$$i = \min\left\{s, \ \mu + k\sigma - a\right\} \qquad\qquad (13\text{-}20)$$

where k must be chosen to agree with the criterion for actual truncation of the series. It is easy enough to find a k which yields very good estimates when p is not too far from .5, and while there is nothing to be done about the fact that any k will give very bad estimates when p is close enough to 0 or 1, the fact that the estimate is not allowed to exceed s prevents these bad estimates from leading to seriously wrong decisions—i.e., decisions to compute F(p, a, b) directly when this computation is materially more expensive than computation of F(1-p, b, a) or vice versa.

13.1.6. Special Cases

Subroutine <u>Dbetcu</u> calls subroutine <u>Spcase</u> to handle the special cases that arise when $p = 0$ or 1, when a or $b = 0$, or when the density at p would give rise to underflow or overflow.

Because beta and binomial cumulative probabilities are related by

$$G_b(r, n, p) = F_{\beta *}(p, r, n-r+1)$$

where G_b is the right–tail binomial cumulative function, subroutine <u>Dbetcu</u> can be used to compute binomial as well as beta probabilities. The subroutine makes special provision for two combinations of arguments for which the binomial tail is well defined even though the integral (13-2) which defines the beta tail is not defined, namely

$$F_{\beta *}(p, 0, b) = G_b(0, b-1, p) = 1 \; ,$$

$$F_{\beta *}(p, a, 0) = 1 - G_b(0, a-1, 1-p) = 0 \; . \tag{13-21}$$

13.2. Standard Gamma Cumulative Function: Subroutine Dgascu

13.2.1. Definitions and Parametrization

The standard gamma distribution is parametrized by writing its density function as

$$f_{\gamma *}(z, r) = \frac{1}{\Gamma(r)} \; e^{-z} \; z^{r-1} \; . \tag{13-22}$$

The cumulative function is then defined by

$$F_{\gamma *}(z, r) = \frac{1}{\Gamma(r)} \int_0^z e^{-t} \; t^{r-1} \; dt \; . \tag{13-23}$$

13.2.2. Series Expansions

1. The Left–Tail Series. Repeated integration of (13-23) by parts yields

$$F_{\gamma *}(r, z) = \Sigma_{i=1}^{\infty} u_i \tag{13-24a}$$

where

$$u_i = \frac{z}{r - 1 + i} u_{i-1} \; , \qquad i = 1, 2, \ldots , \tag{13-24b}$$

$$u_o = \frac{1}{\Gamma(r)} \; e^{-z} \; z^{r-1} = f_{\gamma *}(z, r) \; . \tag{13-25}$$

When r is integral, the successive terms in the left-tail series (13-24) can be interpreted as the right-tail Poisson probabilities of r, r+1, ... events when the expected number of events is z .

    2. The Right-Tail Series. Instead of computing $F_{\gamma *}(z, r)$ directly we can compute the right tail

$$G_{\gamma *}(z, r) = \frac{1}{\Gamma(r)} \int_z^\infty e^{-t} t^{r-1} dt \qquad (13-26)$$

and then compute

$$F_{\gamma *}(z, r) = 1 - G_{\gamma *}(z, r) \qquad . \qquad (13-27)$$

Integrating (13-26) by parts s times we obtain

$$G_{\gamma *}(z, r) = S(s) + R(s) \qquad (13-28a)$$

where

$$S(s) = \sum_{i=0}^{s-1} u_i \qquad , \qquad (13-28b)$$

$$u_o = \frac{1}{\Gamma(r)} e^{-z} z^{r-1} = f_{\gamma *}(z, r) \qquad , \qquad (13-28c)$$

$$u_i = \frac{r - i}{z} u_{i-1} \qquad , \qquad i = 1, 2, \ldots , s-1 \quad , \qquad (13-28d)$$

$$R(s) = \frac{1}{\Gamma(r-s)} \int_0^z e^{-t} t^{r-s-1} dt \qquad (13-28e)$$

$$= G_{\gamma *}(z, r-s) \qquad \text{if } r - s > 0 \qquad . \qquad (13-28f)$$

The definition of u_o in (13-28c) is identical to (13-25).

    When r is integral and s = r , the remainder R(s) vanishes and the successive terms in the right-tail series S(s) can be interpreted as the left-tail Poisson probabilities of r-1, r-2, ..., 0 events when the expected number of events is z .

    In the general case of nonintegral r , the remainder does not vanish for any s . The u_i are positive for i < r , alternately negative and positive for i > r ; in the alternating part of the series, the u_i decrease in magnitude as long as i - r < z , increase in magnitude thereafter. The remainder R(s) is positive for s < r , alternately negative and positive for larger s .

13.2.3. *Accuracy Achievable with the Right-Tail Series*

    From the behavior of the u_i and of R(s) as described just above, it follows that when r is not integral, (1) the magnitude of the error in the sum will be less than the magnitude of the last included term if the series is truncated after the last term in the all-positive part or after any term in the alternating part. Hence (2) the smallest possible bound on the error will be obtained by truncating the series after the last term in the all-positive part or the smallest term in the alternating part, whichever is smaller; but (3) this bound may or may not be less than a predetermined tolerable error t . Accordingly Dgascu does not compute the right-tail series unless an upper bound on the magnitude of either the last term in the all-positive part or the smallest term in the alternating part has been computed and found to be less than the tolerable error.

1. Bound on the Last Term in the All-Positive Part. A rather loose bound on the magnitude of the last term in the all-positive part of the right-tail series can be found very easily. If we denote by [r] the greatest integer in r , we have by (13-28c) and (13-28d) that the last term in the all-positive part is

$$u_{[r]} = \frac{1}{\Gamma(r - [r])} \; e^{-z} \, z^{r - [r] - 1} \tag{13-29}$$

Since $\Gamma(r-[r]) > 1$ and $r-[r]-1 < 0$, we have the bound

$$u_{[r]} < e^{-z} \qquad \text{if } z \geq 1 \; ; \tag{13-30}$$

and from this it follows at once that the error in the series will be less than any specified t if

$$e^{-z} < t \qquad \text{and} \qquad z \geq 1$$

or equivalently if

$$z > \log(-t) \qquad \text{and} \qquad z \geq 1 \; . \tag{13-31}$$

The second condition can be disregarded in practice because the first condition implies $z \geq 1$ if $t < 1/e$, as it always is.

2. Bound on the Smallest Term in the Alternating Part. If the test (13-31) fails, Dgascu goes on to test a rather close bound on the magnitude of the smallest term in the alternating part of the series, which by (13-28d) is the term with index

$$i^* = \text{greatest integer in } [r + z] \; . \tag{13-32}$$

By (13-28d) the magnitude of this term is

$$|u_{i^*}| = a \, b \, u_o / z^{i^*} \tag{13-33a}$$

where u_o is defined by (13-28c) and

$$a = (r - 1) \ (r - 2) \ \ldots \ (r - [r]) \ , \tag{13-33b}$$

$$b = ([r] + 1 - r) \ ([r] + 2 - r) \ \ldots \ (i^* - r) \ .$$

In order to bound a and b economically, we first observe that

$$x(x + 1) \ (x + 2) \ \ldots \ (x + k - 1) = \Gamma(x+k)/\Gamma(x) \tag{13-34}$$

and we then substitute herein the bound

$$\Gamma(x) = \Gamma(x+1)/x > .885/x \ , \qquad\qquad 0 < x < 1 \ , \tag{13-35}$$

to obtain the bound

$$x(x + 1) \ (x + 2) \ \ldots \ (x + k) < x \ \Gamma(x+k+1)/.885 \ , \quad 0 < x < 1 \ . \tag{13-36}$$

Using this result in (13-33b) we obtain

$$
a \ \le \ \begin{cases} 1 & \text{if } 0 < r < 1 & , \\ r - [r] & \text{if } 1 < r < 2 & , \\ (r - [r]) \ \Gamma(r)/.885 & \text{if } 2 < r & , \end{cases}
$$
$$\tag{13-37}$$
$$
b \ \le \ \begin{cases} 1 & \text{if } 0 < i^* - r + 1 < 1 & , \\ [r] + 1 - r & \text{if } 1 < i^* - r + 1 < 2 & , \\ ([r] + 1 - r) \ \Gamma(i^* - r - 1)/.885 & \text{if } 2 < i^* - r + 1 & , \end{cases}
$$

and the bound on the error in the right–tail series that is used by <u>Dgascu</u> is obtained by substituting (13-37) in (13-33a).

13.2.4.   Choice between the two Series

    1. <u>Integral</u> r . We have already seen that when r is integral, the left- and right-tail series defined in Section 13.2.2 correspond respectively to the right and left tails of a Poisson distribution with argument r and mean z . For large z , where economy of computation really counts, the Poisson distribution will be nearly symmetric and it will be most economical to use series (13-28) to compute the left Poisson tail when $r < z$ and to use series (13-24) to compute the right Poisson tail when $r > z$. Because an accurate criterion for small z is hard to come by, <u>Dgascu</u> uses the rule just stated for all values of z .

    2. <u>Nonintegral</u> r . When r is nonintegral, subroutine <u>Dgascu</u> uses the same criterion for choice between the two series that it uses when r is integral, except that when this criterion indicates choice of the divergent series (13-28) <u>Dgascu</u> starts by computing one or both of the error bounds described in Section 13.2.3. If these bounds fail to show that the error in series (13-28) will be less than the specified tolerable error, <u>Dgascu</u> computes the convergent series (13-24) instead.

13.2.5. *Termination of the Computation*

Computation of either series is terminated as soon as a bound on the sum of the remaining terms is less than the specified tolerable error t.

1. Left-Tail Series. A bound on the remainder R_i after the i'th term in the left-tail series (13-24) can be obtained by starting from (13-24b) and arguing that

$$u_{i+1} = \frac{z}{r+1} u_i \qquad ,$$

$$u_{i+k} < p^k u_i \qquad \text{where} \qquad p = \frac{z}{r+1} \qquad , \qquad (13\text{-}38a)$$

$$R_i \equiv \Sigma_{k=1}^{\infty} u_{i+k} < u_i \Sigma_{k=1}^{\infty} p^k \qquad ,$$

so that

$$R_i < \frac{p}{1-p} u_i \qquad \text{if} \qquad p < 1 . \qquad (13\text{-}38b)$$

It follows at once that the remainder will be less than any specified tolerable t if

$$u_i > \frac{1-p}{p} t \qquad \text{and} \qquad p < 1 , \qquad (13\text{-}39)$$

and there is no need to check the second of these conditions in practice because p as defined by (13-38a) cannot be 0 and p > 1 implies

$$\frac{1-p}{p} t < 0 < u_i .$$

2. Right-Tail Series, All-Positive Part. Because R([r] + 1) as defined by (13-28) is negative, the sum S([r] + 1) as defined by (13-28b) is an upper bound on $G_{\gamma *}$ (r, z) and therefore

$$R_i = \Sigma_{j=i+1}^{[r]} u_i = \Sigma_{k=1}^{[r]-i} u_{i+k}$$

is an upper bound on the error that will result from terminating after the term u_i in the all-positive part of series (13-28). Starting from (13-28d) we have

$$u_{i+1} = \frac{r-i-1}{z} u_i$$

$$u_{i+k} < p^k u_i \qquad \text{where} \qquad p = \frac{r-i-1}{z} \qquad ,$$

$$R_i < \sum_{k=1}^{[r]-i} p^k u_i = \frac{p}{1-p} (1 - p^{[r]-i}) u_i \qquad (13\text{-}40)$$

$$< \frac{p}{1-p} u_i \quad \text{if} \quad p < 1 \ .$$

It follows that termination after u_i in the all-positive part will entail an error less than any specified t if

$$u_i < \frac{1-p}{p} t \quad \text{and} \quad p < 1 \ , \qquad (13\text{-}41)$$

and as in the case of (13-39) only the first condition has to be checked in practice.

3. Right-Tail Series, Alternating Part. We have already seen in Section 13.2.3 that the error due to termination anywhere in the alternating part of series (13-28) will be less than the last included term.

13.2.6. *Special Cases*

Subroutine Dgascu calls subroutine Spcase to handle the special cases that arise when $z = 0$ or $r = 0$ or when the density at r would give rise to underflow or overflow.

Because gamma and Poisson cumulative probabilities are related by

$$G_p(r, z) = F_{\gamma*}(z, r)$$

where G_p is the right-tail Poisson cumulative function, subroutine Dgascu can be used to compute Poisson as well as gamma probabilities. The subroutine makes special provision for one combination of arguments for which the Poisson tail is well defined even though the integral (13-23) which defines the gamma tail is not, namely

$$F_{\gamma*}(z, 0) = G_p(0, z) = 1 \ . \qquad (13\text{-}42)$$

13.3. Unit Normal Cumulative Function: Subroutines Unrcuq and Dunrcu

13.3.1. *Computation using the Complementary Error Function*

The Fortran library on the IBM-360/CP67 includes the single-precision and double-precision "complementary error function"

$$\left.\begin{matrix} \text{ERFC}(X) \\ \text{DERFC}(X) \end{matrix}\right\} = 2 \int_{-\infty}^{-x} \pi^{-\frac{1}{2}} e^{-t^2} dt = 2F(-x) \qquad (13\text{-}43)$$

where F is the cumulative function of the Normal distribution with mean 0 and standard deviation $1/\sqrt{2}$. The Manecon subroutine Unrcuq evaluates the standard or unit-normal cumulative function by use of the relation

$$F_{n*}(u) = .5*ERFC(-X) \qquad \text{where} \qquad X = u/\sqrt{2}. \qquad (13-44)$$

Subroutine Dunrcu uses the same formula with DERFC instead of ERFC.

13.3.2. *Approximation by a Rational Fraction*

On systems without the complementary error function (13-43), subroutine Unrcuq evaluates the unit-normal cumulative function by use of a rational-fraction approximation due to C. Hastings, Jr., which appears as no. 26.2.17 in the NBS Handbook. The error is less than 7.5×10^{-8} for any argument.

13.3.3. *Expansion in a Continued Fraction*

On systems without the complementary error function (13-43), subroutine Dunrcu makes use of two expansions in continued fractions, the Laplace expansion (NBS Handbook no. 26.2.14) when the argument is large, the Shenton expansion (NBS Handbook no. 26.2.15) when the argument is small. Successive convergents are computed as ratios, the numerators and denominators of which are computed by updating a second-order difference equation whose coefficients are determined by the terms in the continued fraction; the required formulas appear in Section 3.10 of the NBS Handbook. Because both the numerator and the denominator may increase without limit, provision is made for rescaling both when there is any danger of their exceeding the capacity of the computer.

This version of Dunrcu was developed by Arthur Schleifer, Jr.

13.4. Fractiles of Standard Distributions: Functions Betfrq, Gasfrc, and Unrfrc

Fractiles of the three "standard" distributions — the beta, gamma, and unit-normal — are computed respectively by the functions Betfrq, Gasfrc, and Unrfrc. In all three cases the fractile is found by a Newton-Raphson search, and in all three cases the search terminates when it can be shown that the error in the computed fractile does not exceed the tolerance t specified via the call-list variable TOLRNC. In the case of the unit-normal fractile, it is the absolute error in the fractile which is guaranteed less than t ; in the case of the gamma fractile, it is the relative error; in the case of the beta fractile, the absolute error will be controlled if the function is called with ITOL = 1; if it is called with ITOL = 2, the relative error in both the fractile and its complement will be less than t .

13.5. Complete Gamma Function: Functions Algama and Dlgama [1]

The Manecon function ALGAMA(X) evaluates the natural logarithm of the complete gamma function $\Gamma(x) = (x - 1)!$ by use of the asymptotic Stirling approximation

$$\log \Gamma(x) = \log \sqrt{2\pi} + (x - \tfrac{1}{2}) \log x - x[1 - \frac{1/12}{x^2} + \frac{1/360}{x^4} - \frac{1/1260}{x^6} + \dots] \qquad (13\text{-}45)$$

For any specified ϵ, there exists x_0 such that for $x \geq x_0$ the error in this approximation will not exceed ϵ. For $x < x_0$, <u>Algama</u> adds to x an integer n just large enough to make $x + n \geq x_0$, uses the Stirling approximation to compute $\log \Gamma(x + n)$, and then computes

$$\log \Gamma(x) = \log \Gamma(x + n) - \log[x(x + 1) (x + 2) \dots (x + n - 1)]. \qquad (13\text{-}46)$$

The critical value x_0 decreases as more terms in the Stirling series are used, but terms after the one in $1/x^4$ reduces x_0 very little when the permitted error is of the order of 10^{-8}.

On systems with a short word length, the computations just described are performed by the Manecon function <u>Dlgama</u>, which works in double precision. <u>Algama</u> merely calls <u>Dlgama</u> and exists only because it can be called with a single-precision argument, whereas the argument of <u>Dlgama</u> must be double-precision.

---

[1]On the IBM 360/CP67 <u>Algama</u> and <u>Dlgama</u> are system library functions. In the present section we describe the corresponding Manecon Fortran functions.

CHAPTER 14

Fitting of Continuous Probability Distributions to Points on the Cumulative Function

Contents of Chapter 14

1. Beta Distribution   214

    1. Subroutine Betfit; 2. Subroutine Betfiq.

2. Gamma-q Distribution   215

    1. Subroutine Gamfit; 2. Subroutine Gasfit.

3. Logstudent Distribution   217

    1. Subroutine Alsfit; 2. Subroutine Stufiq.

4. Arcsinh-normal Distribution   220

    1. Subroutine Asnfit; 2. Test for Existence of a Solution; Initial Bounds on σ; 3. General Method of Solution; 4. Search Procedure; 5. Distributions Skewed to the Left; 6. Notation.

5. Piecewise Quadratic Distribution   225

    1. Definition of a Piecewise Quadratic Distribution; 2. Fitting of a Distribution: Subroutine Pcqfit; 3. Evaluation of Piecewise Quadratic Distributions.

14.1. Beta Distribution

14.1.1. Subroutine Betfit

Subroutine <u>Betfit</u> requests the user at the terminal to specify the .25 and .75 fractiles of a beta distribution, checks the user's values for consistency, calls subroutine <u>Betfiq</u> to compute the parameters of the standard beta distribution having these fractiles, translates these parameters into the parameters b and c of an ADU beta distribution, and returns b and c to the calling program.

14.1.2. Subroutine Betfiq

Let k_1 and k_2 be such that $0 < k_1 < k_2 < 1$ and let p_1 and p_2 be such that $0 < p_1 < p_2 < 1$. There exists one and only one beta distribution whose k_1 and k_2 fractiles are p_1 and p_2, and subroutine <u>Betfiq</u> will find the parameters a and b of this distribution by a two-dimensional Newton-Raphson search for a and b such that

$$F(p_1, a, b) = k_1 \qquad \text{and} \qquad F(p_2, a, b) = k_2 . \qquad (14\text{-}1)$$

Initial trial values for a and b are obtained from the formulas

$$a = \left[(u_1 \sqrt{p_2} - u_2 \sqrt{p_1})/\Delta \right]^2 + \tfrac{1}{3} \qquad (14\text{-}2a)$$

$$b = \left[(u_1 \sqrt{1-p_2} - u_2 \sqrt{1-p_1})/\Delta \right]^2 + \tfrac{1}{3} \qquad (14\text{-}2b)$$

where

$$\Delta = 2 \left[\sqrt{p_1(1-p_2)} - \sqrt{p_2(1-p_1)} \right] \qquad (14\text{-}2c)$$

and u_1 and u_2 are the k_1 and k_2 fractiles of the unit-normal distribution. Thereafter, the cumulative probabilities of (14-1) are obtained by calling the subroutine <u>Dbetcu</u>, which provides the partial derivatives

$$\frac{\partial}{\partial p_i} F(p_i, a, b) = f(p_i, a, b) , \qquad i = 1, 2$$

as free byproducts. The partial derivatives

$$\frac{\partial}{\partial a} F(p_i, a, b) \qquad \text{and} \qquad \frac{\partial}{\partial b} F(p_i, a, b) , \qquad i = 1, 2$$

are approximated by average rates of change over finite intervals of a or b ; the approximations are obtained by calling the function <u>Betslp</u>, which returns

$$\frac{\partial}{\partial a} F(p, a, b) \doteq \begin{cases} [F(p, a{+}1, b) - F(p, a{-}1, b)] /2 & \text{if} \quad a > 1 , \quad (14\text{-}3a) \\[2ex] [F(p, 1.5a, b) - F(p, .5a, b)] /a & \text{if} \quad a \le 1 , \quad (14\text{-}3b) \end{cases}$$

and similarly for the partial derivative wrt b .

Formula (14-3b) is evaluated by actually computing $F(p, 1.5a, b)$ and $F(p, .5a, b)$; formula (14-3a) is evaluated by use of the recursion formula

$$F(p, a+1, b) - F(p, a-1, b) = -\tfrac{1}{2}(1 - p)\left[\frac{p}{a} + \frac{1}{a + b - 1}\right] f(p, a, b) \qquad (14\text{-}4)$$

which is derived from the formula

$$F(p, a, b) = F(p, a+1, b) + \frac{p(1 - p)}{a} f(p, a, b) \; . \qquad (14\text{-}5)$$

Use of these approximations was suggested by Arthur Schleifer, Jr., who showed that searches based on them converge quite rapidly.

The search for a and b satisfying (14-1) is terminated when a and b have been found such that $|k_1 - F(p_1, a, b)|$ and $|k_2 - F(p_2, a, b)|$ are both less than the value assigned to the variable TOLRNC in a data statement near the beginning of Betfiq.

The notation used in subroutine Betfiq is the same as that used above except that k_1 and k_2 are called AK1 and AK2.

14.2. Gamma-q Distribution

14.2.1. Subroutine Gamfit

Subroutine Gamfit accepts the value of the parameter q of a gamma-q distribution (Section 8.3.3 above) from the calling program, requests the user at the terminal to specify the .25 and .75 fractiles of the distribution, and returns to the calling program the parameters r and s of the distribution having these fractiles if such a distribution can be found. If the required distribution is found, Gamfit assigns the value 0 to the trouble indicator IERR; otherwise it assigns the value 1.

To see how the required distribution is found, let p_1 and p_2 denote any two cumulative probabilities such that $0 < p_1 < p_2 < 1$; let x_1 and x_2 be the p_1 and p_2 fractiles of a gamma-q distribution with specified parameter q ; recall that if $\tilde{x}$ has a gamma-q distribution with parameters q , r , s , then $\tilde{z} \equiv (\tilde{x}/s)^q$ has a standard gamma distribution with parameter r ; and distinguish two cases according to the specified value of the parameter q .

Case 1: $q > 0$. In this case $\tilde{z}$ is an increasing function of $\tilde{x}$ and consequently the quantities z_1 and z_2 defined by

$$z_1 = (x_1/s)^q , \qquad z_2 = (x_2/s)^q , \qquad (14\text{-}6)$$

are the p_1 and p_2 fractiles of $\tilde{z}$. Because there exists one and only one standard gamma distribution whose p_2 and p_1 fractiles have any specified ratio H , we can find the required gamma-q distribution by computing

$$H = z_2/z_1 = (x_2/x_1)^q , \qquad (14\text{-}7)$$

215

finding the parameter r of the standard gamma distribution under which $z_2/z_1 = H$, and then computing

$$s = x_1/z_1{}^c = x_2/z_2{}^c \qquad \text{where} \qquad c = 1/q \ . \qquad (14\text{-}8)$$

Case 2: $q < 0$. In this case $\tilde{z}$ is a decreasing function of q and consequently the quantities z_1 and z_2 defined by

$$z_1 = (x_2/s)^q \qquad \text{and} \qquad z_2 = (x_1/s)^q \qquad (14\text{-}9)$$

are the $(1 - p_2)$ and $(1 - p_1)$ fractiles of $\tilde{z}$. Accordingly we can find the required gamma-q distribution by computing

$$H = z_2/z_1 = (x_1/x_2)^q \ , \qquad (14\text{-}10)$$

finding the parameter r of the standard gamma distribution under which $z_2/z_1 = H$, and then computing

$$s = x_1/z_2{}^c = x_2/z_1{}^c \quad \text{where} \quad c = 1/q \ . \qquad (14\text{-}11)$$

Subroutine <u>Gamfit</u> computes H as defined by (14-7) or (14-10), calls subroutine <u>Gasfit</u> to find the parameter r by search, and then computes s from (14-8) or (14-11).

14.2.2. *Subroutine Gasfit*

Let p_1 and p_2 be such that $0 < p_1 < p_2 < 1$, and let z_1 and z_2 denote the p_1 and p_2 fractiles of a standard gamma distribution with parameter r . Then for any given p_1, p_2, and H , there exists one and only one r such that $z_2/z_1 = H$; and subroutine <u>Gasfit</u> will find this r and with it the values of z_1 and z_2 by a two-dimensional Newton-Raphson search for r and z_1 such that

$$F(z_1,\ r) = p_1 \qquad \text{and} \qquad F(Hz_1,\ r) = p_2 \ . \qquad (14\text{-}12)$$

Initial trial values for r and z_1 are obtained from the Wilson-Hilferty approximation to $F(z,\ r)$ by computing successively

$$a = 3\sqrt{H} - 1 \qquad ,$$

$$b = (u_1 \sqrt[3]{H} - u_2)/3 \qquad ,$$

$$c = (-b + \sqrt{b^2 + 4a^2/9})/(2a) \ , \qquad (14\text{-}13)$$

$$r = c^2 \qquad ,$$

$$z_1 = r \left[1 - \frac{1}{9r} + \frac{u_1}{3c} \right]^3 \qquad ,$$

216

where u_1 and u_2 are the p_1 and p_2 fractiles of the unit-normal distribution. If the initial approximation to z_1 is not positive, subroutine <u>Gasfit</u> gives up and reports inability to find r such that $z_2/z_1 = H$.

If the initial $z_1 > 0$, the cumulative probabilities (14-12) required for the search are obtained by calling subroutine <u>Dgascu</u>, which provides as free by-products the densities required to evaluate the partial derivatives

$$\frac{\partial}{\partial z_1} F(z_1, r) = f(z_1, r) \quad \text{and} \quad \frac{\partial}{\partial z_1} F(Hz_1, r) = Hf(Hz_1, r) . \qquad (14\text{-}14)$$

The partial derivatives

$$\frac{\partial}{\partial r} F^*(z_1, r) \quad \text{and} \quad \frac{\partial}{\partial r} F^*(Hz_1, r)$$

are approximated by average rates of change over finite intervals; the approximations are obtained by calling the function <u>Gamslp</u>, which returns

$$\frac{\partial}{\partial r} F^*(z, r) \doteq \begin{cases} [F^*(z, r+1) - F^*(z, r-1)] / 2 & \text{if } r > 1 , & (14\text{-}15a) \\[2mm] [F^*(z, 1.5r) - F^*(z, .5r)] / r & \text{if } r \leq 1 . & (14\text{-}15b) \end{cases}$$

Formula (14-15b) is evaluated by actually computing the two cumulative probabilities; formula (14-15a) is evaluated by use of the recursion formula

$$F^*(z, r+1) - F^*(z, r-1) = -\tfrac{1}{2} (1 + \tfrac{z}{r}) \ f^*(z, r) \qquad (14\text{-}16)$$

which in turn is derived from

$$F^*(z, r+1) = F^*(z, r) - \tfrac{z}{r} f^*(z, r) .$$

The search for r and z_1 satisfying (14-12) is terminated when r and z_1 have been found such that $|p_1 - F(z_1, r)|$ and $|p_2 - F(Hz_1, r)|$ are both less than the value assigned to the variable TOLRNC in a data statement near the beginning of <u>Gasfit.</u>

The notation used in subroutine <u>Gasfit</u> is the same as that used above except that H is called FRCRAT and p_1 and p_2 are called AK1 and AK2.

14.3. Logstudent Distribution

14.3.1. *Subroutine Alsfit*

Subroutine <u>Alsfit</u> requests the user at the terminal to specify the .25, .75, and .875 fractiles of a logstudent distribution and returns the parameters μ , σ , ν of the required distribution to the calling program if such a distribution exists. The trouble indicator IERR is returned with value 0 if a distribution meeting the specifications exists, with the value 1 otherwise.

217

The method used to test whether a suitable distribution exists, and to compute its parameters if it does, rests on the fact that if $\tilde{x}$ has a logstudent distribution with parameters μ , σ , ν then $t = (\log \tilde{x} - \mu)/\sigma$ has a unit-student distribution with parameter ν . The symmetry of the unit-student distribution implies that

$$\log x_{.75} - \mu = \mu - \log x_{.25}$$

where x_k is the specified k fractile of the logstudent distribution; and hence μ can be immediately computed as

$$\mu = (\log x_{.25} + \log x_{.75})/2 \ . \tag{14-17}$$

Having computed μ , we can compute the ratio of the .875 and .75 fractiles of the unit-student distribution of $\tilde{t}$ as

$$C = \frac{t_{.875}}{t_{.75}} = \frac{\log x_{.875} - \mu}{\log x_{.75} - \mu} \ ; \tag{14-18}$$

and we can then find the parameter ν of the required logstudent distribution by finding the parameter ν of the unit-Student distribution under which $t_{.875}/t_{.75} = C$ if such a distribution exists. Finally, having found ν we can compute $t_{.75}$ and then compute

$$\sigma = \frac{\log x_{.75} - \mu}{t_{.75}} \ . \tag{14-19}$$

Subroutine <u>Alsfit</u> computes μ and C from (14-17) and (14-18), calls subroutine <u>Stufiq</u> to check whether a solution exists and to return ν and $t_{.75}$ if it does, and then computes σ from (14-19).

14.3.2. *Subroutine Stufiq*

Subroutine <u>Stufiq</u> accepts as input a number C , tests whether there exists a unit-Student distribution under which the ratio $t_{.875}/t_{.75}$ of the .875 and .75 fractiles is equal to C , and if such a distribution does exist, returns its parameter ν and its .75 fractile $t_{.75}$ to the calling program.

The test for existence of a solution exploits the fact that as the parameter ν of a unit-Student distribution increases from 0, the fractile ratio $t_{.875}/t_{.75}$ decreases monotonically from $+\infty$ toward the ratio $C^* = u_{.875}/u_{.75}$ of the .875 and .75 fractiles of the unit-Normal distribution. It follows that there exists a unique ν such that $t_{.875}/t_{.75} = C$ if and only if $C > C^*$. Because of computational difficulties that arise with extremely high values of ν , <u>Stufiq</u> actually rejects a problem unless the specified ratio C is greater than a number slightly greater than the true value of C^*.

Provided that the specified C passes the test just described, <u>Stufiq</u> finds the required ν by a two-dimensional search for ν and t such that

$$G_{s*}(t, \nu) = .25 \qquad \text{and} \qquad G_{s*}(Ct, \nu) = .125 \; , \tag{14-20}$$

where G_{s*} denotes the right-tail cumulative function of the unit-Student distribution. The required cumulative probabilities are obtained via the relation

$$G_{s*}(t, \nu) = \tfrac{1}{2} F_{\beta *}(p, \tfrac{1}{2}\nu, \tfrac{1}{2}) \tag{14-21a}$$

where

$$p = 1/(1 + z) \; , \qquad z = t^2/\nu \; , \tag{14-21b}$$

and $F_{\beta*}(p, a, b)$ is the cumulative function of the standard beta distribution, evaluated by calling subroutine Dbetcu.

If the specified fractile ratio $C \le 2.4$, an initial trial value for ν is found by computing

$$e = (C/C^*)^2 - 1$$

$$b = e(1 + u^2_{.875}) + u^2_{.875} - u^2_{.75} \tag{14-22}$$

$$\nu = \tfrac{1}{4} e / (b - \sqrt{b^2 - e^2}) \; ,$$

an approximation derived from the approximation to $F_{s*}(t, \nu)$ which appears as no. 26.7.8 in the NBS Handbook. If $C > 2.4$, ν is initially set equal to 1; numerical tests show that the search converges from this starting value at least as rapidly as it does from any easily computed approximation. In either case, the initial value of t is the .75 fractile of the unit-Student distribution with parameter equal to the initial trial value of ν .

Thereafter, the search proceeds as a Newton-Raphson search for

$$a \equiv \tfrac{1}{2}\nu \qquad \text{and} \qquad z_1 \equiv t^2_{.75}/\nu \tag{14-23}$$

such that

$$F_{\beta *}(p_1, a, \tfrac{1}{2}) = .5 \qquad \text{and} \qquad F_{\beta *}(p_2, a, \tfrac{1}{2}) = .25 \tag{14-24a}$$

where

$$p_1 = 1/(1 + z_1) \qquad \text{and} \qquad p_2 = 1/(1 + C^2 z_1) \; , \tag{14-24b}$$

these conditions being equivalent by (14-21) to those of (14-20) above. The partial derivatives with respect to z_1 are computed from

$$\frac{\partial}{\partial z_1} F_{\beta *}(p_1, a, \tfrac{1}{2}) = \frac{-1}{(1 + z_1)^2} \, f_{\beta *}(p_1, a, \tfrac{1}{2}) \; ,$$

$$\frac{\partial}{\partial z_1} F_{\beta *}(p_2, a, \tfrac{1}{2}) = \frac{-C^2}{(1 + z_1)^2} \, f_{\beta *}(p_2, a, \tfrac{1}{2}) \; . \tag{14-25}$$

The partial derivatives with respect to a are approximated in the same way as in subroutine Betfig; cf. Section 14.1.2 above.

The search for a and z_1 satisfying (14-24) is terminated when a and z_1 have been found such that

$$|.5 - F_{\beta}*(1/[1+z_1] \ , \ a, \ \tfrac{1}{2})| \quad \text{and} \quad |.25 - F_{\beta}*(1/[1+C^2 z_1] \ , \ a, \ \tfrac{1}{2})|$$

are both less than the value assigned to the variable TOLRNC in a data statement near the beginning of Stufiq. The values of ν and $t_{.75}$ are then computed by inverting (14-23).

The ratio called   C above is called FRCRAT in the program; C^2 is called R .

14.4. Arcsinh-normal Distribution

14.4.1. Subroutine Asnfit

Subroutine Asnfit requests the user at the terminal to specify the .25, .5, and .75 fractiles of an arcsinh-normal distribution (Section 8.3.5 above) and also the last octile in the longer tail — the .875 fractile if $(x_{.75} - x_{.5})$ $\geq (x_{.5} - x_{.25})$, the .125 fractile otherwise. The subroutine then tests for the existence of an arcsinh-normal distribution with the specified fractiles, and if such a distribution does exist, computes its parameters μ , σ , n₁ , s , and returns them to the calling program. The trouble indicator IERR is returned with value 0 if the specifications can be satisfied, with value 1 if they cannot.

14.4.2. Test for Existence of a Solution; Initial Bounds on σ

If $\tilde{x}$ has an arcsinh-normal distribution with parameters μ , σ , m , s , then by definition the quantity

$$\tilde{u} = (\tilde{z} - \mu)/\sigma \qquad \text{where} \quad \tilde{z} = \text{arcsinh} \ [(\tilde{x} - m)/s] \qquad (14\text{-}26)$$

has a unit-normal distribution. It follows that to any value u of $\tilde{u}$ there corresponds the value

$$x = m + s \ \sinh(\mu + \sigma u) \ ; \qquad (14\text{-}27)$$

and because x is an increasing function of u , the p fractiles of the distributions of $\tilde{x}$ and $\tilde{u}$ are related by

$$x_p = m + s \ \sinh(\mu + \sigma u_p) \ . \qquad (14\text{-}28)$$

Now suppose that the value of x_p has been specified for p = .25, .5, .75, and .875, so that we can compute

$$k_1 = \frac{x_{.75} - x_{.5}}{x_{.5} - x_{.25}} \quad , \qquad k_2 = \frac{x_{.875} - x_{.75}}{x_{.75} - x_{.5}} \quad ; \qquad (14\text{-}29)$$

assume without loss of generality that $k_1 \geq 1$[1]; define

$$u \equiv u_{.75} = -u_{.25} \; , \qquad v \equiv u_{.875} \qquad\qquad (14\text{-}30)$$

observe that $u_{.5} = 0$; and define

$$r_1(\mu, \sigma) = \frac{\sinh(\mu + \sigma u_{.75}) - \sinh(\mu + \sigma u_{.5})}{\sinh(\mu + \sigma u_{.5}) - \sinh(\mu + \sigma u_{.25})}$$

$$= \frac{\sinh(\mu + \sigma u) - \sinh \mu}{\sinh \mu - \sinh(\mu - \sigma u)} \qquad\qquad (14\text{-}31a)$$

$$r_2(\mu, \sigma) = \frac{\sinh(\mu + \sigma u_{.875}) - \sinh(\mu + \sigma u_{.75})}{\sinh(\mu + \sigma u_{.75}) - \sinh(\mu + \sigma u_{.5})}$$

$$= \frac{\sinh(\mu + \sigma v) - \sinh(\mu + \sigma u)}{\sinh(\mu + \sigma u) - \sinh \mu} \qquad . \qquad (14\text{-}31b)$$

Then an arcsinh-normal distribution with the specified fractiles x_p exists if and only if there exist μ and $\sigma > 0$ such that

$$r_1(\mu, \sigma) = k_1 \; , \qquad r_2(\mu, \sigma) = k_2 \; . \qquad\qquad (14\text{-}32)$$

In order to determine whether a solution exists, we shall make use of the fact that both r_1 and r_2 can be shown to be increasing functions of both μ and σ , and we shall also make use of the following limiting values of r_1 and r_2:

$$r_1(0, \sigma) = 1 \quad , \qquad r_2(0, \sigma) = \frac{\sinh(\sigma v)}{\sinh(\sigma u)} - 1 \quad ,$$

$$r_1(\infty, \sigma) = e^{\sigma u} \quad , \qquad r_2(\infty, \sigma) = \frac{e^{\sigma v} - e^{\sigma u}}{e^{\sigma u} - 1} \quad ,$$

$$r_1(\mu, 0) = 1 \quad , \qquad r_2(\mu, 0) = \frac{v}{u} - 1 \quad ,$$

$$r_1(\mu, \infty) = e^{2\mu} \quad , \qquad r_2(\mu, \infty) = \infty \quad .$$

Case 1: $k_1 = 1$ (symmetric distribution).
increases with μ , we have $\mu = 0$. Then b~

---

[1] A problem with $k < 1$ is solved by solving ~
Section 14.4.5 below.

$(v - u)/u$ to ∞ as σ increases from 0 to ∞ , we conclude that a solution exists if and only if $k_2 > (v - u)/u$.

When this test shows that a solution exists, 0 is taken as an initial lower bound on σ and an initial upper bound is found by starting with $\sigma = .1$ and doubling until σ is found such that $r_2(0, \sigma) > k_2$.

Case 2: $\underline{k_1 > 1}$ (asymmetric distribution). In Figure 14.4A we show (1) the locus of the equation $r_1(\mu, \sigma) = k_1$, and (2) the locus of the equation $r_2(\mu, \sigma) = k_2$ as it appears when (a) k_2 is greater, and (b) k_2 is less, than

$$k_2^* = k_2(k_2^p - 1)/(k_2 - 1) \qquad \text{where} \qquad p = (v - u)/u . \qquad (14\text{--}34)$$

Figure 14.4A

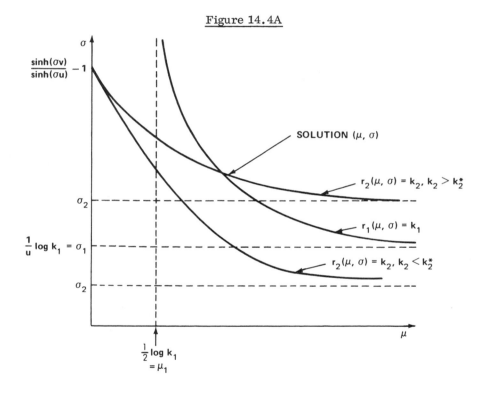

The geometry of the r_1 curve in Figure 14.4A is justified by the fact that (1) r_1 increases with both μ and σ , (2) $r_1(\infty, \sigma) = e^{\sigma u}$, and (3) $r_1(\mu, \infty) = e^{2\mu}$, implying that the r_1 curve is convex and has asymptotes $\sigma = \sigma_1 \equiv (1/u) \log k_1$ and $\mu_1 \equiv \frac{1}{2} \log k_1$. The shape of the r_2 curves is justified by the fact that (1) r_2 eases with both μ and σ , (2) $r_2(\infty, \sigma) = (e^{\sigma v} - e^{\sigma u})/(e^{\sigma u} - 1)$, and (3)
) $= \infty$, implying that the r_2 curve is convex and has the asymptote $\sigma = \sigma_2$
r_2 satisfies $(e^{\sigma 2v} - e^{\sigma 2u})/(e^{\sigma 2u} - 1) = k_2$. We assume without proof

that there exists at most one solution of (14-31), implying that the r_1 and r_2 curves intersect at most once.

From Figure 14.4A it follows that a solution exists if and only if $\sigma_2 > \sigma_1$, or equivalently if

$$r_2(\infty, \sigma_1) = \frac{e^{\sigma_1 v} - e^{\sigma_1 u}}{e^{\sigma_1 u} - 1} < k_2 . \tag{14-35}$$

It is easily shown that these conditions are equivalent to the condition $k_2 > k_2^*$ where k_2^* is defined by (14-34).

When the test (14-35) shows that a solution exists, σ_1 is taken as an initial lower bound on σ and an initial upper bound is found by doubling until σ is found such that $r_2(\mu_1, \sigma) > k_2$.

14.4.3. General Method of Solution [2]

Assume that a solution has been shown to exist; for $i = 1, \ldots, 4$ let $p_i = .25, .5, .75, .875$; let x_i and u_i denote the p_i fractiles of $\tilde{x}$ and $\tilde{u}$, so that x_1 is the .25 fractile of $\tilde{x}$, and so forth; and define

$$C_1 = \frac{x_2 - x_1}{x_4 - x_3} , \qquad\qquad C_2 = \frac{x_3 - x_2}{x_4 - x_1} . \tag{14-36}$$

By (14-28) we have

$$x_i = m + \tfrac{1}{2} se^{-\mu} (\beta \eta_i + 1/\eta_i) \tag{14-37a}$$

where

$$\beta = e^{2\mu} , \qquad \eta_i = e^{\sigma u_i} . \tag{14-37b}$$

Substituting (14-37a) in (14-36) we obtain

$$S_1/S_3 = \beta , \qquad\qquad S_2/S_4 = \beta , \tag{14-38a}$$

where

$$S_1 = -1/\eta_1 + 1/\eta_2 + C_1/\eta_3 - C_2\eta_4$$
$$S_2 = C_2\eta_1 - \eta_2 + \eta_3 - C_2\eta_4$$
$$S_3 = -\eta_1 + \eta_2 + C_1\eta_3 - C_1\eta_4 \tag{14-38b}$$
$$S_4 = C_2/\eta_1 - 1/\eta_2 + 1/\eta_3 - C_2/\eta_4 .$$

---

[2]The computational methodology described in this section and the next was devised by Robert R. Glauber and Arthur Schleifer, Jr.

Because $\eta_i = e^{\sigma u_i}$ does not involve β, we can find the parameter σ of the required distribution by equating the left-hand sides of (14-38a) and searching in one dimension for the σ which satisfies the resulting equation

$$S_1/S_3 = S_2/S_4 .\qquad (14-39)$$

Having found σ, we can compute β and hence $\mu = \frac{1}{2} \log \beta$ from either of the two equations in (14-38a). The parameters m and s can then be found by solving the two equations that result when we substitute in (14-37), first the numerical values of x_2 and u_2, then the numerical values of x_3 and u_3.

14.4.4. Search Procedure

The search for σ satisfying (14-39) takes the form of a search between running bounds for σ such that

$$f(\sigma) \equiv S_1 S_2 - S_3 S_4 = 0 .\qquad (14-40)$$

On each iteration, a tentative new trial value of σ is computed by the Newton-Raphson formula

$$\sigma_{n+1} = \sigma_n - f(\sigma)/f'(\sigma)$$

where

$$f'(\sigma) = S_1 S_2' + S_2 S_1' - S_3 S_4' - S_4 S_3' .\qquad (14-41)$$

If the first such tentative value falls outside the bounds, it is replaced by the midpoint between the bounds, and similarly on subsequent iterations so long as every Newton-Raphson value falls outside the bounds. As soon as one Newton-Raphson value falls within the bounds, the search proceeds like an ordinary Newton-Raphson search. The search terminates when next a Newton-Raphson value falls outside the bounds, because numerical investigation shows that after this happens the value of $f(\sigma)$ contains so much computational error that further improvement is impossible.

14.4.5. Distributions Skewed to the Left

All the methodology described above applies to distributions fitted to specifications where $(x_{.75} - x_{.5}) \geq (x_{.5} - x_{.25})$, implying that the distribution of $\tilde{x}$ is symmetric or skewed to the right. When the specifications from the terminal are such that $x_{.75} - x_{.5} < x_{.5} - x_{.25}$, <u>Asnfit</u> computes $x_p^* = -x_p$ for all four values of p, uses the methodology described above to find the parameters of the distribution satisfying these artificial specifications, and then reverses the signs of the parameters μ and m of this distribution.

14.4.6. *Notation*

The notation in subroutine <u>Asnfit</u> corresponds to that used above except that k_1 and k_2 are called R1 and R2, $r_1(\mu, \sigma)$ and $r_2(\mu, \sigma)$ are called R1TEST and R2TEST, and β is called BSQ.

14.5. Piecewise Quadratic Distribution

14.5.1. *Definition of a Piecewise Quadratic Distribution*

A piecewise quadratic distribution is by definition a distribution whose cumulative function is constructed by smoothly joining together (1) a series of convex quadratics, (2) a linear segment, and (3) a series of concave quadratics; the joining is smooth in the sense that the resulting function is continuous and continuously differentiable. This implies a continuous density function which consists of a number of linear segments one of which, the modal segment, has zero slope. The slope of the density function and the second derivative of the cumulative function are discontinuous at the points where the segments are joined together.

14.5.2. *Fitting of a Distribution: Subroutine Pcqfit*

Subroutine <u>Pcqfit</u> will fit a piecewise quadratic cumulative function to any set of points such that:

1. The slope of the function constructed by joining successive points by straight lines has only one local maximum.
2. The first point has ordinate 0 and the last has ordinate 1.

The procedure used by <u>Pcqfit</u> to fit a cumulative function can best be understood by thinking in terms of the corresponding density function rather than the cumulative function itself. In these terms, the procedure consists merely in (1) establishing the ordinate of the density function at each input value of the uq, and then (2) inserting an additional point on the density function between each pair of original points. The additional point is computed in each case in such a way that the area under the density function between any two successive input values of the uq is equal to the difference between the cumulative probabilities of those values as specified by the user.

An example of a density function constructed by <u>Pcqfit</u> is shown in Figure 14.5A, where V_1, V_3, ..., V_{11} are the input values of the uq, the circled points above these values are the densities established in Step 1 of the procedure sketched above, and the points denoted by crosses are the additional points established in the second step. The points are computed as follows.

<u>Establishment of the Densities at the Input Values of the UQ.</u> Let the input points specified by the user be numbered 1, 3, 5, ... as they are in Figure 14.5A;

Figure 14.5A
Density Function Constructed by Pcqfit

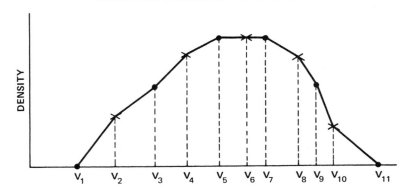

let V_i and P_i denote the value of the uq and the cumulative probability specified by the user at input point i ; and let D_i denote the ordinate at V_i of the density function constructed by Pcqfit. The D_i for i = 1, 3, 5, ... are established by Pcqfit as follows.

    1.   Let $V_{i'}$ and $V_{i''}$ denote the values of the uq which mark the ends of the modal interval (V_5 and V_7 in Figure 14.5A).[3] The density at these two V's is set equal to the true average density between them — i.e., to $(P_{i''} - P_{i'})/$ $(V_{i''} - V_{i'})$.

    2.   Except when the modal interval is the interval between the first two input points, the density at the first input point is set equal to 0; and except when the modal interval is the interval between the last two input points, the density at the last input point is set equal to 0.

    3.   At each other input V_i the density is set equal to the slope at V_i of a quadratic passing through the corresponding input point (V_i, P_i) and the input points immediately to the left and right of this point on the graph of the cumulative function.

Computation of the Intermediate Points on the Density Function.   The way in which a new point is now inserted on the density function between each pair of original points (V_i, D_i) can be explained by taking the point at V_4 in Figure 14.5A as an example.

    1.   The ordinate D_4 of the new point is set equal to the true average density between the input values V_3 and V_5 — i.e., to $(P_5 - P_3)/(V_5 - V_3)$.

    2.   The abscissa V_4 of the new point is then chosen in such a way that the area under density function between V_3 and V_5 will have the correct value $P_5 - P_3$. To do so, Pcqfit simply chooses the V_4 which satisfies

---

[3]The indices of these points are found by the subroutine Fitsub in the file Pcqdis and passed to Pcqfit through the call list.

$$(V_4 - V_3) \frac{D_3 + D_4}{2} + (V_5 - V_4) \frac{D_4 + D_5}{2} = P_5 - P_3 \ .$$

Insertion of a new point between the points at the end of the modal interval is unnecessary because the densities at these points are equal to the true average density across the segment, so that all that is needed is to join the two end points by a single linear segment. <u>Pcqfit</u> nevertheless inserts a new point at the midpoint of this segment (the point above V_6 in Figure 14.5A), simply to avoid a special case in the indexing of all the points.

14.5.3. Evaluation of Piecewise Quadratic Distributions

<u>Densities and Cumulative Probabilities.</u> Let V denote any value of the uq between the first and last input values and let i be such that $V_i \le V < V_{i+1}$. Because the density function is linear over $[V_i, V_{i+1}]$, the density at V is simply

$$D = D_i + \frac{V - V_i}{V_{i+1} - V_i} (D_{i+1} - D_i) \ , \tag{14-42}$$

and the cumulative probability at V is the probability at V_i plus the area under the linear segment of the density function between V_i and V:

$$P = P_i + (V - V_i) \frac{D_i + D}{2} \tag{14-43}$$

where D is given by (14-42).

<u>Fractiles.</u> Now let P denote a specified cumulative probability and let i be such that $P_i \le P < P_{i+1}$. The P fractile V_p is found by substituting (14-42) and the numerical value of P in (14-43) and solving the resulting quadratic equation for V .

<u>Moments.</u> The mean M and second moment about the origin S of a "smooth" distribution can be found by integration of V and V^2 with respect to the density function as given by (14-42); the variance is then equal to $S - M^2$.

CHAPTER 15

Posterior and Preposterior Analysis: Programs Postdis, Truchance, and Valinfo

Contents of Chapter 15

1. Program Postdis   229
   1. Core Allocation; 2. Computation of Equiprobable Posterior Bracket Medians.

2. Program Truchance   230
   1. Computation of the Posterior Distribution of the True/Quote Ratio;
   2. Computation of the Probability of a Still Uncertain Event.

3. Program Valinfo   231

15.1 Program Postdis

15.1.1. Core Allocation

If the details of the computation of a posterior distribution are to be printed out in the format of a worksheet like ADU Table 10.6 (page 408) or 12.5 (page 490), the following quantities must be stored for all values of the uq:

1. Possible values of the uq,
2. Prior probabilities,
3. Standardized arguments u (if likelihood function is Gaussian),
4. Likelihoods,
5. Joint probabilities,
6. Posterior probabilities,
7. Equiprobable posterior bracket medians (if grouping is equiprobable).

If the details are not to be printed, only items 1, 2, 6, and 7 need to be stored simultaneously.

After reading the prior distribution and learning how many different values of the uq are involved, Postdis determines whether or not it is possible to store all seven items. If it is, Postdis allocates separate locations in core to each item and sets the indicator IDETL = 1 to indicate that a detailed printout is possible. Otherwise, Postdis allocates core in such a way that items 4, 5, and 6 will be successively written over item 3 and sets the indicator IDETL = 0 to indicate that detailed printout is not available.

15.1.2. Computation of Equiprobable Posterior Bracket Medians

In computing a posterior distribution, program Postdis treats the bracket medians of an EP prior distribution as if they were the only possible values under a discrete distribution and computes the corresponding discrete posterior distribution, which might be represented by a step function like the one in Figure 15.1A below. This distribution will be called the "discrete approximation" to the true posterior distribution of the uq.

Figure 15.1A
Discrete and Continuous Approximations to a Posterior Distribution

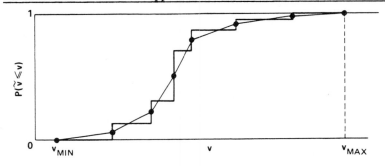

229

Since the probability assigned to any bracket median value of the uq under the prior distribution really belongs exactly half and half to lower and higher values of the uq, we now argue that the posterior probability of any such value under the discrete approximation really belongs roughly half and half to lower and higher values. It follows that we can construct an improved, continuous approximation to the true continuous posterior distribution by the following procedure, which is illustrated in Figure 15.1A:

1. Locate a heavy dot at the points $(v_{min}, 0)$ and $(v_{max}, 1)$;
2. Locate a heavy dot at the midpoint of each riser in the discrete step function;
3. Join successive pairs of heavy dots by linear segments.

When Postdis is asked to file the posterior distribution resulting from an EP prior, the program calls subroutine Equalz to construct a continuous approximation like the one in Figure 15.1A and to compute and return as many equiprobable bracket medians under this distribution as there were under the prior distribution.

15.2. Program Truchance

15.2.1. *Computation of the Posterior Distribution of the True/Quote Ratio*

Assume that the historical record shows the chance quoted by an expert for each of N events; assume that these chances have M different values ($M \leq N$); and for $i = 1, 2, \ldots, M$ define

q_i: quoted chance,
n_i: number of events for which quoted chance was q_i,
r_i: number of these events which actually occurred;

assume that all events for which the quoted chance is q_i have the same true chance

p_i: true chance of event for which quoted chance is q_i;

and assume that p_i is related to q_i by

$$R = \frac{p_i/(1 - p_i)}{q_i/(1 - q_i)} \tag{15-1}$$

where R is a fixed but unknown parameter. Then given any R the conditional probability of the data is

$$L(R) = \prod_{i=1}^{M} p_i^{r_i} (1 - p_i)^{n_i - r_i} \tag{15-2}$$

where

$$p_i = R q_i / (1 - q_i + R q_i) \ . \tag{15-3}$$

230

To compute the posterior distribution of $\tilde{R}$, program <u>Truchance</u> first computes the logarithm of L(R) for every bracket-midpoint R and then computes the maximum of these logarithms. In order to avoid the possibility of underflow it next computes, not the actual values of L(R), but the values scaled so that the greatest of them is 1. The joint probabilities are then computed as if these scaled likelihoods were the true likelihoods; the effect of the scaling cancels out when subroutine <u>Normlz</u> is called to compute the posterior probabilities by dividing the joint probabilities by their sum.

15.2.2. *Computation of the Probability of a Still Uncertain Event*

If q is the chance quoted for an as yet uncertain event, the probability that should be assigned to this event is $E\tilde{p}$, and by (15-1)

$$E\tilde{p} = E \lfloor \tilde{R}q/(1 - q + \tilde{R}q) \rfloor \quad . \tag{15-4}$$

Program <u>Truchance</u> evaluates this expectation in a perfectly straightforward manner.

15.3. **Program Valinfo**

EVPI is computed for program <u>Valinfo</u> by subroutine <u>Presam</u>, which carries out the computation by the method described in ADU 14.2.2. The subroutine first computes the EVASROPI by taking in turn each value of $\tilde{v}$ on the first fork of Figure 4.4A on page 71 above, multiplying its probability into the value of the optimal act on the following act fork, and summing these products. The values of $\tilde{v}$ to which discrete probabilities are assigned (if any) are taken first, then the bracket-median values (if IGROUP = 1) or bracket-midpoint values (if IGROUP = 2), if any. The EVPI is found by subtracting the value of the optimal immediate act from the EVASROPI.

ENGS is computed for <u>Valinfo</u> by subroutine <u>Binsam</u>, where the basic uq is called $\tilde{p}$ rather than $\tilde{v}$ because this subroutine is applicable only when the uq is a fraction of successes. The ENGS is computed by first computing expected total revenue VALN at position N in Figure 4.4B on page 72 above, and then subtracting the expected revenue VALQ at position Q . The basic logic of the computations is that of ADU 14.1, but there are some shortcuts in the execution.

To compute VALN, <u>Binsam</u> takes the values of $\tilde{r}$ on the fork at N in Figure 4.4B and for each one computes (1) its unconditional probability UPRB, (2) the expected revenue VALR at position R , and (3) the product of these two quantities, which is the contribution of the particular r in question to the value of position N . To avoid carrying out these computations for extreme values of $\tilde{r}$ which contribute nothing material to VALN, <u>Binsam</u> starts with an r close to the prior expectation of $\tilde{r}$ and then considers successively smaller r's until an r is reached whose unconditional probability is less than a specified fraction of the total probability of the r's already evaluated; it then evaluates the r next above the r first evaluated and continues with successively larger r's until a similar cutoff is reached.

The value VALR at any particular position R in Figure 4.4B is evaluated by first computing the corresponding posterior expectation of $\tilde{p}$, using this expectation to compute the values of positions R_1 and R_2, and taking the maximum of these values. The posterior expectation of $\tilde{p}$ given any r , called PBAR2, and the unconditional probability of r , called UPRB, are computed by taking the possible values of $\tilde{p}$ in turn and adding the contribution of each one to the running sums SJPRB = Σ_p P(p) P(r|p) and SPROD = Σ_p P(p) P(r|p) p . When these sums have been evaluated, UPRB is equated to SJPRB and PBAR2 is equated to SPROD/SJPRB.

If there are any discrete values of $\tilde{p}$, the computation of the running sums starts by taking all of these values in their natural order. The bracket-median or bracket-midpoint values of $\tilde{p}$ are taken next, if there are any, but in this case the values are taken in an order which makes it possible to avoid evaluating p's which contribute virtually nothing to the sums that are to be evaluated. The program starts with a p close to the maximum-likelihood value for the given r and proceeds with successively smaller p's until one is reached whose contribution to SJPRB is less than a certain fraction of the current value of this sum. The program then returns to the next p above the first one evaluated and continues with successively larger p's until a similar cutoff is reached.

CHAPTER 16

Optimal Sample Size: Program Opsama

Contents of Chapter 16

1. Beta and Hyperbinomial Distributions; Reduction of the Hypergeometric   234
   to the Binomial Case

   1. Beta and Hyperbinomial Distributions; 2. Reduction of the Hypergeometric
   to the Binomial Case.

2. Analysis When the Number of Units Subjected to the Terminal Act is Fixed   235

   1. The Standard Problem with n_t Fixed; 2. Reduction of the General Problem
   to Standard Form; 3. Analysis of the Standard Problem.

3. Analysis When the Number of Units Subjected to the Terminal Act Depends on
   the Sample Size   239

   1. The Standard Problem with n_t Dependent on Sample Size; 2. Reduction of
   the General Problem to Standard Form; 3. Analysis of the Standard Problem.

16.1.   Beta and Hyperbinomial Distributions; Reduction of the Hypergeometric to the Binomial Case

16.1.1.   *Beta and Hyperbinomial Distributions*

The beta distribution assumed in program <u>Opsama</u> when a problem is stated in terms of the chance $\tilde{p}$ that any unit will be a success is defined with parameters ρ and ν by writing its density in the form

$$f_\beta \ (p) \propto p^{\rho-1} \ (1 - p)^{\nu-\rho-1} \ . \tag{16-1}$$

A hyperbinomial distribution with parameters N, ρ, and ν has been defined[1] as a beta mixture of binomial distributions of the number $\tilde{R}$ of successes in N trials, so that the mass function is

$$f_{hb}(R) \propto \int_0^1 p^R \ (1 - p)^{N-R} \ p^{\rho-1} \ (1 - p)^{\nu-\rho-1} \ dp \ . \tag{16-2}$$

We shall, however, also refer to the corresponding distribution of the fraction $\tilde{f} = \tilde{R}/N$ of successes as hyperbinomial with parameters N, ρ, and ν.

It is assumed in program <u>Opsama</u> that the parameter N is equal to the size of the finite population from which a sample is to be taken. When N is at all large, the general shape of a hyperbinomial distribution with given values of the parameters ρ and ν will be very similar to the shape of a beta distribution with the same parameter values. There will be a noticeable difference only when the variance of the beta distribution is small relative to the variance of a binomial distribution with one parameter equal to the parameter N of the hyperbinomial distribution and its other parameter equal to the expectation of $\tilde{f}$.

When program <u>Opsama</u> calls on the user to specify the parameters of his distribution of $\tilde{p}$ or $\tilde{f}$, it uses the names B and C instead of ρ and ν in order to agree with the notation of ADU 11.2.5 - 11.2.6.

16.1.2.   *Reduction of the Hypergeometric to the Binomial Case*

Program <u>Opsama</u> handles any problem involving a finite population with a hyperbinomially distributed fraction of successes $\tilde{f}$ and hypergeometric sampling distributions by reducing it at the outset to an equivalent problem involving the output of a Bernoulli process with a beta-distributed parameter $\tilde{p}$ and binomial sampling distributions. The logic and method by which the reduction is made are as follows.

If the process average $\tilde{p}$ of a Bernoulli process has a beta prior distribution with parameters ρ and ν , then by (16-2) above the unconditional (marginal) distribution of the fraction $\tilde{f} = \tilde{R}/N$ of successes generated by the process in N trials is hyperbinomial with parameters N, ρ, and ν . Denoting the mean and variance of the beta distribution of $\tilde{p}$ by

---

[1] See ASDT 7.11, where the distribution is called "beta-binomial" rather than "hyperbinomial".

$$\bar{p} = E(\tilde{p}) \,, \qquad \overset{\vee}{p} = V(\tilde{p}) \,, \tag{16-3}$$

it is easy to show that the mean and variance of the distribution of $\tilde{f} = \tilde{R}/N$ are respectively

$$\bar{f} = E(\tilde{f}) = \bar{p} \,, \qquad \overset{\vee}{f} = V(\tilde{f}) = \frac{\bar{p}(1 - \bar{p})}{N} + \frac{N - 1}{N} \overset{\vee}{p} \,. \tag{16-4}$$

It follows at once that any decision problem involving a finite population of size N with a hyperbinomially distributed $\tilde{f}$ is equivalent to a problem involving a Bernoulli process with a beta-distributed $\tilde{p}$ whose mean and variance are determined by the mean and variance of $\tilde{f}$ through the inverses of the relations just given, viz.

$$E(\tilde{p}) \overset{\backprime}{=} \bar{f}, \qquad V(\tilde{p}) = \frac{N}{N - 1} \left[\overset{\vee}{f} - \frac{\bar{f}(1 - \bar{f})}{N} \right]. \tag{16-5}$$

Observe that by (16-4)

$$\overset{\vee}{f} \geq \frac{\bar{f}(1 - \bar{f})}{N} \,.$$

The program will reject a problem if the user's specifications of $\overset{\vee}{f}$ and $\bar{f}$ violate this condition.

16.2. Analysis When the Number of Units Subjected to the Terminal Act is Fixed

Any problem in which the number n_t of units that will be subjected to the terminal act does not depend on the sample size is analyzed by first reducing the problem as stated by the user to a standard form defined in Section 16.2.1 just below and then analyzing this reduced problem.

16.2.1. *The Standard Problem with n_t Fixed*

The standard form to which all problems with n_t fixed are reduced is defined by the following assumptions:

1. There are just two possible terminal acts, a_1 and a_2 .
2. The <u>revenue</u> of a_i depends on the parameter p of a Bernoulli process via

$$u_t(a_i, \tilde{p}) = K_i + k_i p \,, \qquad i = 1, 2. \tag{16-6}$$

3. The prior distribution of $\tilde{p}$ is beta with parameters ρ and ν defined by (16-1) above.
4. The prior expectation of the <u>cost</u> of observing n_s trials of the process is

$$\bar{c}_s(n_s) = K_s + k_s n_s \,. \tag{16-7}$$

16.2.2. *Reduction of the General Problem to Standard Form*

1. <u>Reduction of Sampling Revenue.</u> Given a problem with sampling revenue stated in the form specified in Section 4.5.3 above, viz.

$$V_s(n_s, \ r_s) = \begin{cases} 0 & \text{if } n_s = 0 \ , \\ F_s + A_s n_s + B_s r_s & \text{if } n_s > 0 \ , \end{cases} \tag{16-8}$$

program <u>Opsama</u> reduces this revenue to a cost of the form of (16-7) by computing

$$K_s = -F_s \ , \qquad k_s = -(A_s + B_s \bar{p}') \ , \tag{16-9}$$

where $\bar{p}'$ is the mean of the prior distribution of $\tilde{p}$.

To show that this reduction is correct, we first observe that the prior expectation of $\tilde{r}_s$ is $E(n_s \tilde{p}) = n_s \bar{p}'$. We then have by (16-8) and (16-9) that the expectation of sampling <u>cost</u> (the negative of revenue) is

$$\bar{c}_s(n_s) = -E(F_s + A_s n_s + B_s \tilde{r}_s) = K_s + k_s n_s \ .$$

This is the sampling cost assumed in (16-7), as was to be shown.

2. <u>Reduction of Terminal Revenue to Standard Form when Terminal Units are Distinct from Sample Units.</u> As specified in Section 4.5.3 above, the user of program <u>Opsama</u> states the terminal revenues of the two acts in the form

$$V_t(a_i, \ n_t, \ r_t) = \begin{cases} 0 & \text{if } n_t = 0 \ , \\ F_i + A_i n_t + B_i r_t & \text{if } n_t > 0 \ , \quad i = 1, \ 2 \ . \end{cases} \tag{16-10}$$

When the n_t units affected by the terminal act are distinct from the n_s units drawn in the sample (and necessarily $n_t > 0$), <u>Opsama</u> reduces this revenue to the form of (16-6) by computing

$$k_t = |k_2 - k_1| \ , \qquad p_b = \frac{K_2 - K_1}{k_1 - k_2} \ , \tag{16-11a}$$

where

$$K_i = F_i + A_i n_t \ , \qquad k_i = B_i n_t \ , \qquad i = 1, \ 2 \ . \tag{16-11b}$$

To show that this reduction is correct, we first observe that the conditional expectation of $\tilde{r}_t$ given p is $n_t p$. We then have by (16-10) that the corresponding expectation of the terminal revenue of act a_i is

$$u_t(a_i, \ p) = E(F_i + A_i n_t + B_i \tilde{r}_t \,|\, p) = K_i + k_i p \ , \qquad n_t > 0 \ , \quad i = 1, \ 2.$$

This is the terminal revenue assumed in (16-6), as was to be shown.

3. <u>Reduction of Terminal Revenue to Standard Form When Sample Units are Included Among Terminal Units.</u> When the n_t units affected by the terminal act include the n_s units drawn in the sample, Program <u>Opsama</u> reduces the terminal revenue of (16-10) to the form of (16-6) by computing

$$k_t = |k_2 - k_1| \;, \qquad p_b = \frac{K_2 - K_1}{k_1 - k_2} \;, \qquad (16\text{-}12a)$$

where in terms of the parameters ρ and ν of the beta prior distribution of $\tilde{p}$

$$K_i = F_i + A_i n_t - B_i \rho \;,$$
$$k_i = B_i(n_t + \nu) \;, \qquad\qquad i = 1,\, 2 \;. \qquad (16\text{-}12b)$$

To show that the reduction yields the correct prior expectation of terminal revenue, we shall show that it yields the correct posterior expectation of terminal revenue for either act for every value of the posterior mean $\bar{p}''$. To do so, we first define

$$n_t^* \equiv n_t - n_s \;, \qquad \tilde{r}_t^* \equiv \tilde{r}_t - r_s \;;$$

n_t^* is the number of units <u>not</u> included in the sample that will be subjected to the terminal act and $\tilde{r}_t^*$ is the number of successes among these n_t^* units. Next, we substitute $\tilde{r}_t = \tilde{r}_t^* + r_s$ in (16-10) to obtain

$$V_t(a_i,\, n_t,\, \tilde{r}_t) = F_i + A_i n_t + B_i(r_s + \tilde{r}_t^*) \;.$$

Then since the posterior expectation of $\tilde{r}_t^*$ is $n_t^* \bar{p}'' = (n_t - n_s)\bar{p}''$, the posterior expectation of the terminal revenue of act a_i is

$$\bar{V}_t''(a_i,\, n_t \mid r_s) = F_i + A_i n_t + B_i r_s + B_i(n_t - n_s)\bar{p}'' \;;$$

and since under a beta prior distribution

$$\bar{p}'' = (\rho + r_s)/(\nu + n_s) \;,$$

we can substitute

$$r_s = (\nu + n_s)\bar{p}'' - \rho$$

in this expression to obtain

$$\bar{V}_t''(a_i,\, n_t \mid r_s) = F_i + A_i n_t + B_i(\nu \bar{p}'' + n_s \bar{p}'' - \rho) + B_i(n_t - n_s)\bar{p}'' \;.$$

From this result and (16-12b) we obtain

$$\bar{V}_t''(a_i,\, n_t \mid r_s) = K_i + k_i \bar{p}'' \;;$$

and this is the posterior expectation of the terminal revenue

$$u_t(a_i,\, \tilde{p}) = K_i + k_i \tilde{p}$$

that is assumed in (16-6), as was to be shown.

16.2.3.   *Analysis of the Standard Problem*

Program <u>Opsama</u> analyzes the standard problem defined in Section 16.2.1 above by recursively computing the ENGS of sample sizes n = 1, 2, 3, ... until an n is reached which can be proved to exceed the optimal sample size.

1. <u>Recursive Computation of the ENGS.</u> A method for recursive computation of ENGS in the problem of Section 16.2.1 above is developed in Section 5.6 of ASDT. Program <u>Opsama</u> uses this method with the following minor modifications.

1. The quantity k_s has been substituted for the κ of ASDT and the initial value of ϕ as given in ASDT has been multiplied by k_t so as to compute net gain in natural rather than dimensionless units.

2. Instead of being left to be brought in at the end, fixed sampling cost is brought into the ENGS computed on each iteration.

3. The three conditions involving comparison of g(n) with κn at the bottom of page 130 of ASDT have been eliminated as both unnecessary and incorrect.

The notation of the program is related to the notation of ASDT as follows:

$$FSC = K_s , \qquad\qquad R = \rho ,$$
$$VSC = k_s , \qquad\qquad ENGS = g ,$$
$$VTR = k_t .$$

2. <u>Termination of the Computations.</u> Because the ENGS function may have any number of local optima when the sample statistic is discrete, it is not possible to identify the optimal n immediately after its ENGS has been computed, and in some cases the only way of making sure that the optimal sample size has been evaluated is actually to evaluate every possible sample size. In most cases, however, the computations can be cut short by arguments based on the behavior of an easily computed upper bound on the ENGS of a sample of any given size.

The ENGS of a sample of size n (n > 0) is

$$g(n) = -K_s - k_s n + k_t g^*(n) \tag{16-13a}$$

where

$$g^*(n) = E \max\{0, -K_t - k_t \bar{p}_r''\} \tag{16-13b}$$

is a positive and strictly increasing function of n . An upper bound on g(n) is provided by

$$B(n) = -K_s - k_s n + k_t B^* \tag{16-14a}$$

where

$$B^* = E \max\{0, -K_t - k_t \tilde{p}\} \tag{16-14b}$$

is the limit approached by g*(n) as n increases without limit, implying that the difference B(n) – g(n) is a strictly decreasing function of n which approaches 0 as limit. The bound B(n) can be easily evaluated because under a beta distribution with parameters ρ and ν

$$B^* = [p_b(1 - p_b)/\nu] \; f_\beta(p_b|\rho, \nu+1) - (\bar{p}' - p_b) \; F_\beta(p_b|\rho, \nu+1) \tag{16-15a}$$

where

$$p_b = K_t/k_t . \tag{16-15b}$$

To investigate the use of the bound B , we distinguish two cases according to the sign of the per-unit sampling cost k_s.

Case 1: $k_s \geq 0$ (the normal case of positive sampling cost). In this case we have by (16-14a) that B is a decreasing function of n , and if we define

$$g^o(n) = \max_{i=1}^{n} \{g(i)\}$$

we see at once that if $B(n+1) \leq g^o(n)$ for any n , the optimal sample size is no greater than n . Program <u>Opsama</u> applies this test after evaluating each successive n and terminates its computations as soon as the test is satisfied.

Case 2: $k_s < 0$. In this abnormal case the actual ENGS g(n) is an increasing function of n and the optimal n is either 0 or equal to the population size N (possibly infinite). To distinguish between these two possibilities, program <u>Opsama</u> proceeds as follows.

1. If $K_s + k_s N < 0$, then by (16-13) the optimal sample size is N .
2. If $K_s + k_s N$ is positive and greater than $k_t B^*$ (the EVPI), then by (16-14) the optimal sample size is 0.
3. If $0 < K_s + k_s N < k_t B^*$, <u>Opsama</u> actually evaluates g(N) and compares it with g(0).

16.3. Analysis When the Number of Units Subjected to the Terminal Act Depends on the Sample Size

Any problem in which the total number of units N is fixed and $n_t = N - n_s$ is analyzed by first reducing the problem as stated by the user to a standard form defined in Section 16.3.1 below and then analyzing this reduced problem.

16.3.1. *The Standard Problem with n_t Dependent on Sample Size*

The standard form to which all problems with N fixed and $n_t = N - n_s$ are reduced is defined by the following assumptions, where we write n for n_s and r for r_s.

1. There are just two terminal acts, a_1 and a_2 .
2. The <u>revenue</u> that will result from either of these acts depends on the output of a Bernoulli process as follows:

$$V_t(a_1, n_t, \tilde{r}_t) = 0$$

$$V_t(a_2, n_t, \tilde{r}_t) = \begin{cases} 0 & \text{if } n_t = 0 , \\ -K_t - c_t n_t + \pi_t \tilde{r}_t & \text{if } n_t > 0 , \end{cases}$$ (16-16)

where $\pi_t > 0$ and K_t and c_t are such that $K_t/N + c_t > 0$.

3. A beta prior distribution is assigned to $\tilde{p}$.
4. The <u>revenue</u> that will result from observing n sample trials of the process will be:

$$V_s(n, \tilde{r}) = \begin{cases} K^* & \text{if } n = 0 , \\ -K_s - c_s n + \pi_s \tilde{r} + K^* & \text{if } 0 < n < N , \\ -K_s - c_s n + \pi_s \tilde{r} + K^* - F^* & \text{if } n = N . \end{cases}$$ (16-17)

16.3.2. *Reduction of the General Problem to Standard Form*

When the terminal revenue coefficient B_2 in the problem as stated by the user in terms of (16-8) and (16-10) above is algebraically greater than B_1 , program Opsama computes the coefficients of the corresponding standard problem as follows:

$$\begin{array}{lll} K_s = -F_s , & c_s = -A_s + A_1 , & \pi_s = B_s - B_1 , \\ K_t = F_1 - F_2 , & c_t = A_1 - A_2 , & \pi_t = B_2 - B_1 , \\ F^* = F_1 , & K^* = F_1 + (A_1 + B_1 \bar{p}')N . \end{array}$$ (16-18)

When $B_1 > B_2$, the subscripts 1 and 2 are interchanged. If $B_1 = B_2$, one of the two terminal acts is dominated and the problem is rejected.

To show that this reduction leads to a correct value for expected total revenue with a sample of any size, we first observe that neither choice between terminal acts nor expected total revenue will be altered for any sample size or outcome if we subtract an arbitrary function of n , n_t, and $\tilde{r}_t$ from the revenues of both terminal acts and add back the unconditional expectation of this function to the revenue of sampling. We then distinguish two cases according to the value of n .

Case 1: $n < N$. Assuming by way of example that $B_2 > B_1$, we subtract

$$F_1 + A_1 n_t + B_1 \tilde{r}_t$$

from the revenues of both terminal acts as given in (16-10) and obtain (in terms of the coefficients defined in (16-18) above)

$$\begin{array}{l} V_t(a_1, n_t, \tilde{r}_t) = 0 , \\ V_t(a_2, n_t, \tilde{r}_t) = -K_t - c_t n_t + \pi_t \tilde{r}_t , \end{array}$$

in agreement with (16-16) above. Then recalling that $E(\tilde{r}_t) = \bar{p}'n_t$ and that $n_t = N - n$, we add back

$$E(F_1 + A_1 n_t + B_1 \tilde{r}_t) = F_1 + A_1 n_t + B_1 n_t \bar{p}'$$

$$= K^* - (A_1 + B_1 \bar{p}')n$$

to the revenue of sampling (16-8), thus obtaining

$$V_s(n_s, \tilde{r}_s) = \begin{cases} K^* & \text{if } n = 0 \\ -K_s - c_s n + \pi_s \tilde{r} + K^* & \text{if } 0 < n < N, \end{cases}$$

in agreement with (16-17) above.

<u>Case 2: n = N</u>. In this case $n_t = 0$ and the revenues of both terminal acts in both the real and the standard problem are 0. The only revenue is sampling revenue, and it can easily be verified that substitution of (16-18) in (16-17) leads to the correct expectation of sampling revenue, viz. $F_s + A_s N + B_s N \bar{p}'$.

16.3.3.   *Analysis of the Standard Problem* [2]

Program <u>Opsama</u> analyzes the standard problem defined in Section 16.3.1 above by recursively computing expected total revenue with sample sizes n = 1, 2, 3, ... until a point is reached where it can be proved that the optimal sample size is either less than n, or equal to the population size N.

1. <u>Total Expected Revenue</u>. From (16-16), (16-17), and the fact that $n_t = N - n$ it is apparent that the expected total revenue of sampling n and then acting optimally is

$$\bar{V}(n) = \bar{V}_s(n) + \bar{V}_t(n) \tag{16-19a}$$

where the expected sample-stage revenue

$$\bar{V}_s(n) = E(-K_s - k_s n + \pi_t \tilde{r}) \tag{16-19b}$$
$$= -K - k_s n + \pi_t n \bar{p}'$$

and the expected terminal-stage revenue

$$\bar{V}_t(n) = E\{\max 0, -K_t - k_t(N - n) + \pi_t(N - n)\bar{p}''_{\tilde{r}}\}. \tag{16-19c}$$

---

[2] The analytical procedure used in program <u>Opsama</u> is taken in large part from Chapter 2 of an unpublished dissertation by José Faus (Harvard Business School, 1964). The chief differences from the procedure described by Faus are (1) provision for negative values of the fixed cost K_t, and (2) use of an upper bound on expected total revenue as a means of proving that the optimal sample size has been found.

To evaluate $\overline{V}_t(n)$ we first define the breakeven value

$$p_n = [K_t/ (N-n) + c_t]/ \pi_t \tag{16-20}$$

and rewrite (16-19c) in the form

$$\overline{V}_t(n) = \pi_t(N - n) \, h(n) \tag{16-21a}$$

where

$$h(n) = \int_{p_n}^{1} (\overline{p}_r'' - p_n) \, dP(r)$$

$$= \overline{p}' - p_n + \int_{0}^{p_n} (p_n - \overline{p}_r'') \, dP(r) . \tag{16-21b}$$

Then because the prior distribution of $\tilde{p}$ is beta with parameters ρ and ν , the unconditional distribution of $\tilde{r}$ is hyperbinomial, and it follows from ASDT (9-22a) that if we define the "nonintegral critical number"

$$s(n) = p_n(\nu + n) - \rho , \tag{16-22}$$

the "integral critical number"

$$r_n = \begin{cases} -1 & \text{if} \quad s < 0 \quad , \\ [s(n)] & \text{if} \quad 0 \le s < n \ , \\ n & \text{if} \quad n \le s \quad , \end{cases} \tag{16-23}$$

and the functions

$$\begin{aligned} \phi_1(r_n, n) &= F_{hb}(r_n | \rho , \nu , n) \quad , \\ \phi_2(r_n, n) &= \overline{p}' \, F_{hb}(r_n | \rho+1, \nu+1, n) \quad , \end{aligned} \tag{16-24}$$

we can evaluate h(n) by the formula

$$h(n) = \overline{p}' - p_n[1 - \phi_1(r_n, n)] - \phi_2(r_n, n) \tag{16-25}$$

where p_n is defined by (16-20).

2. Behavior of s as a Function of n . The essence of the computational scheme by which Opsama evaluates the expected total revenue $\overline{V}(n)$ of successive sample sizes n = 1, 2, ... is recursive evaluation of the functions ϕ_1 and ϕ_2 defined in (16-24) above. Because a different set of recursion formulas is required in each of the three cases $s(n) < 0$, $0 \le s(n) < n$, and $n \le s(n)$, we must examine the various ways in which s can behave as a function of n before we can show how these various formulas can be used in a complete computational scheme.

Starting from the definition of s in (16-22) and using the definition of p_n in (16-20) we obtain by differentiation

$$s'(n) = [K_t(N+\nu)/(N-n)^2 + c_t]/ \pi_t ,$$

$$s''(n) = K_t(N + \nu)/[2\,\pi_t(N - n)^3] . \tag{16-26}$$

Then recalling that π_t and the quantity $K_t/N + c_t$ are both strictly positive by hypothesis, we distinguish two main cases according to the sign of K_t.

1. $K_t \geq 0$. At the origin, the value of s may be either positive or negative but its slope must be positive; the second derivative is positive for all n; and s becomes infinite at n = N. It follows that the possible forms of behavior are those shown in Figure 16.3A.

Figure 16.3A

Behavior of s(n) when $K_t \geq 0$

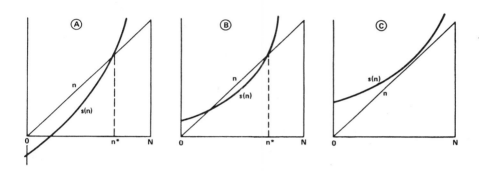

2. $K_t < 0$. Both the value and the slope of s may be either positive or negative at the origin; the second derivative is negative for all n; and s approaches $-\infty$ as n approaches N. It follows that the possible forms of behavior are those shown in Figure 16.3B.[3]

3. General Nature of the Recursive Computations. As already stated, program Opsama makes use of one of three recursive routines, according to the relation between s(n) and n. Routine 1 is an introductory routine used as long as s(n) $\geq$ n in cases B, C, and D of Figures 16.3A and B. Routine 2 is an alternate

---

[3] It might be thought that there is still another possible form of behavior viz., a case like E except that the s(n) curve actually rises above the 45° line. To show that this cannot happen, write (16-22) in the form

$$\frac{\rho + s(n)}{\nu + n} = p_n .$$

If s(0) < 0, then $\rho/\nu > p_0$; and since p_n as defined by (16-20) is a decreasing function of n, it follows that s(n)/n can never be as great as ρ/ν and hence that s(n) can never be as great as n.

Figure 16.3B
Behavior of $s(n)$ when $K_t < 0$

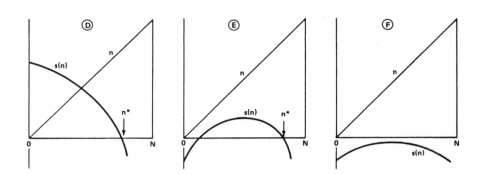

introductory routine used as long as $s(n) < 0$ in cases A, E, and F. Routine 3 is the main routine, used after $0 \le s(n) < n$ in cases A, B, D, and E. We shall describe the main routine first, then the two introductory routines.

Main Routine. The functions ϕ_1 and ϕ_2 are computed recursively together with the auxiliary function

$$\psi(r_n, n) = f_{hb}(r_n + 1 | \rho, \nu, n) . \tag{16-27}$$

The recursion formulas are all derived from the following basic formulas, which in turn can be derived from formulas in ASDT Section 7.11.

$$\psi(r, n) = \frac{(\nu + n - \rho - r - 2)\, n}{(\nu + n - 1)\,(n - r - 1)} \psi(r, n-1)$$

$$\psi(r, n) = \frac{(\rho + r)\,(n - r)}{(\nu + n - \rho - r - 1)\,(r + 1)} \psi(r-1, n)$$

$$\phi_1(r, n) = \phi_1(r, n-1) - \frac{r+1}{n} \psi(r, n) \tag{16-28}$$

$$\phi_1(r, n) = \phi_1(r-1, n) + \psi(r-1, n)$$

$$\phi_2(r, n) = \phi_2(r, n-1) - \frac{(\rho + r + 1)\,(r + 1)}{(\nu + n)\, n} \psi(r, n)$$

$$\phi_2(r, n) = \phi_2(r-1, n) + \frac{\rho + r}{\nu + n} \psi(r-1, n) .$$

After ϕ_1 and ϕ_2 have been updated by use of (16-28) or relations derived therefrom, expected total revenue is computed from formula (16-19a)

$$\overline{V}(n) = \overline{V}_s(n) + \overline{V}_t(n) \tag{16-29a}$$

where by (16-19b)

$$\overline{V}_s(n) = -K_s - k_s n + \pi_s n \, \overline{p}' \qquad (16\text{-}29\text{b})$$

and by (16-21a) and (16-25)

$$\overline{V}_t(n) = \pi_t (N - n) \, \{ \overline{p}' - p_n [1 - \phi_1 (r_n, \, n)] - \phi_2 (r_n, \, n) \} . \qquad (16\text{-}29\text{c})$$

Introductory Routine 1. When $s(n) \geq n$, both ϕ_1 and ϕ_2 as defined by (16-24) have the value 1 and formula (16-29) for the total revenue reduces to

$$\overline{V}(n) = \overline{V}_s(n) = -K_s - k_s n + \pi_s n \, \overline{p}' . \qquad (16\text{-}30)$$

The only nontrivial computation is that of the special auxiliary function

$$\chi(n) = f_{hb}(n \mid \rho, \, \nu, \, n) , \qquad (16\text{-}31)$$

the recursion formula being

$$\chi(n) = \frac{\rho + n + 1}{\nu + n + 1} \, \chi(n\text{-}1) . \qquad (16\text{-}32)$$

When $s(n)$ first becomes less than n, the transition to the main routine is based on the relation

$$\psi(n\text{-}1, \, n) = \chi(n\text{-}1) . \qquad (16\text{-}33)$$

Introductory Routine 2. When $s(n) < 0$, both ϕ_1 and ϕ_2 have the value 0 and formula (16-29) for the total revenue reduces to

$$\overline{V}(n) = -K_s - k_s n + \pi_s n \overline{p}' + \pi_t (N - n) \, (\overline{p}' - p_n) . \qquad (16\text{-}34)$$

The only recursive computation is that of the auxiliary function ψ defined in (16-27), and the appropriate recursion formula in (16-28) reduces in this case to

$$\psi(\text{-}1, \, n) = \frac{\nu + n - \rho - 1}{\nu + n - 1} \, \psi(\text{-}1, \, n\text{-}1) \qquad (16\text{-}35)$$

4. **Termination of the Computations.** Program <u>Opsama</u> employs two different methods to determine when the recursive evaluation of ENGS can be determined. One is based on the behavior of $s(n)$, the other on the use of an upper bound on the ENGS.

Termination Based on the Behavior of $s(n)$. Observe that by (16-29b) the sample-stage revenue $V_s(n)$ is a linear function of n which may be either increasing or decreasing, and consider again cases A-F in Figures 16.3A and B.

1. In case C, act a_1 will always be chosen. Total revenue for any n is therefore simply sample-stage revenue, and because sample-stage revenue is linear in n, the optimal sample size is either 0 or N. Case C can be identified by the conditions $s(n) \geq n$, $s'(n) \geq 1$; and program <u>Opsama</u> terminates

recursive computations whenever these two conditions are satisfied. By a similar argument the optimal sample size in case F is either 0 or N and computations can be terminated if $s(n) < 0$ and $s'(n) \leq 0$.

2. In cases A and B, act a_1 will be chosen regardless of the sample outcome if $n^* \leq n \leq N$. Expected total revenue in this interval will therefore be simply the sample-stage revenue; and since this is a linear function of n , the optimal sample size is either N or less than n^*. The two conditions $s(n-1) \leq n - 1$ and $s(n) \geq n$ suffice to identify case A or B and to show that $n = n^*$, and Opsama terminates computations when these two conditions are satisfied. By a similar argument, the optimal sample size is either N or less than n^* in case D or E and Opsama terminates computations when $s(n-1) \geq 0$ and $s(n) < 0$.

In all of these cases, it is necessary to determine whether the optimal sample size is N or the best of the sample sizes actually evaluated before the recursive computations were terminated. To make this determination, program Opsama computes both $\overline{V}(0)$ and $\overline{V}(N)$ before beginning the recursive evaluations and computes and stores both the maximal revenue

$$V^o(0) = \max\{\overline{V}(0), \text{ and } \overline{V}(N)\} \tag{16-36a}$$

and the optimal sample size

$$n^o(0) = \begin{cases} 0 & \text{if} & \overline{V}(0) \geq \overline{V}(N) \ , \\ N & \text{if} & \overline{V}(0) < \overline{V}(n) \ . \end{cases} \tag{16-36b}$$

Then as the recursive computation proceeds, the program at each iteration computes and stores

$$V^o(n) = \max\{V^o(n-1) \ , \ \overline{V}(n)\}$$

$$n^o(n) = \begin{cases} n^o(n - 1) & \text{if} & \overline{V}(n) \leq V^o(n - 1) \\ n & \text{if} & \overline{V}(n) > V^o(n - 1) \ . \end{cases} \tag{16-37}$$

It follows that the optimal sample size and maximal total revenue are already in storage when the recursive computations are ended for any of the reasons described above.

Termination Based on a Bound. It can be shown that the total expected revenue given by (16-19) cannot exceed the bound

$$B(n) = \overline{V}_s(n) + E \max\{0, -K_t - c_t(N - n) + \pi_t(N - n)\tilde{p}\}$$
$$= \overline{V}_s(n) + \pi_t(N - n) B^*(n) \tag{16-38}$$

where $\overline{V}_s(n)$ is the sample-stage revenue defined by (16-19b) and

$$B^*(n) = \int_{p_n}^{1} (p - p_n) \, dP(p)$$

$$= (p' - p_n) \, G_\beta(p_n | \rho, \nu+1) - [\, p_n(1 - p_n)/\nu\,] f_\beta(p_n | \rho, \nu+1) \ . \tag{16-39}$$

and p_n is defined by (16-20). It can be shown that B is a convex function of n, and since we have by (16-38) that $B(N)$ is equal to the expected revenue $\bar{V}(N) = \bar{V}_s(N)$ actually achievable with a 100% sample, it follows at once that if $B(n) \leq V^o(n)$ for any $n > 0$, then $n^o(n)$ is the optimal sample size.

Program <u>Opsama</u> applies this test at $n = 1, 2, 4, 8, 16, \ldots$. The tests are applied at intervals rather than at each successive n because evaluation of $B(n)$ involves computation of a beta cumulative probability and therefore usually requires much more computation than does the recursive evaluation of one sample size.